Acting Action

Acting Action

A Primer for Actors

Hugh O'Gorman

ROWMAN & LITTLEFIELD
Lanham • Boulder • New York • London

Published by Rowman & Littlefield
An imprint of The Rowman & Littlefield Publishing Group, Inc.
4501 Forbes Boulevard, Suite 200, Lanham, Maryland 20706
www.rowman.com

6 Tinworth Street, London, SE11 5AL, United Kingdom

British Library Cataloguing in Publication Information Available

Library of Congress Cataloging-in-Publication Data

Names: O'Gorman, Hugh, 1965– author.
Title: Acting action : a primer for actors / Hugh O'Gorman.
Description: Lanham : Rowman & Littlefield, 2021. | Includes bibliographical references and index. | Summary: "A vigorous inquiry into the art of acting focusing on playing action, this book teaches actors how to do the 'doing of acting.' Hugh O'Gorman provides special insight into the acting methods of Earle Gister and Lloyd Richards."—Provided by publisher.
Identifiers: LCCN 2020046475 (print) | LCCN 2020046476 (ebook) | ISBN 9781538139295 (paperback) | ISBN 9781538139301 (epub)
Subjects: LCSH: Acting. | Movement (Acting)
Classification: LCC PN2061 .O36 2021 (print) | LCC PN2061 (ebook) | DDC 792.02/8—dc23
LC record available at https://lccn.loc.gov/2020046475
LC ebook record available at https://lccn.loc.gov/2020046476

This book is dedicated to Hubert and Marion who showed me the path,
Lila and Marly who illuminate the path,
and Nathalie, who walks the path with me.

Your purpose in life is to find your purpose and give your whole heart
and soul to it.

—*Buddha*

Contents

Length of time depends upon our ideas.
Size of space hangs upon our sentiments.
For one whose mind is free from care,
A day will outlast the millennium.
For one whose heart is large,
A tiny room is as the space between heaven and earth.

—Translated from *Saikontan*
(*Vegetable Roots Talks*), Yuhodo, Tokyo, 1926

Foreword

One fine day in 2003, Hugh O'Gorman arrived at the Actors Center in New York City and, at least in spirit, never left. This tall, handsome man had come to study our theater training methods. Why? He already had the training methods of an actor at a very good school in Washington and was finding his way as a working professional actor, something of which he had long dreamed. When I asked him why he had come to us, he said, "I love what I am doing, but I want to know more." In that moment, one knew that this was a man on a mission. Moments later, I was urging him to take Earle Gister's class. "Yes, sir," he replied with a grin, as though to say, "I am in the right place—Earle as my teacher, Michael is my guide." The following year he returned and said that he would like to continue, which he did for another five years, finishing each level of the work. I was impressed with his thoroughness but cautioned that this work takes time—each person has to find his or her own way. Hugh just looked at me, smiled, and said, "I know, Boss." He finished the five-year program as planned but never left the Actors Center. Even though he had relocated to Los Angeles, he somehow managed to get to New York City about two times per year and continued to engage in our Teacher Development Program.

The Teacher Development Program, affectionately known as the TDP, was highly successful due to our own long-term theater practices based on Stanislavski and those grown from Russia, Italy, France, and England, as well as our own versions of life in this world. After sixteen years, our program was very successful, but I felt it was avoiding our purpose. One evening, I called

Hugh and five others to a meeting and asked them if they would like to take over running the TDP. Hugh, ever still the man on a mission, and his brilliant colleagues accepted the challenge and grew together. It has grown into a national program, the National Alliance of Acting Teachers, which is the only official society of acting teachers in the country. I could not be prouder of what they have achieved, and I have no doubt that it will serve us all for some time.

My purpose here is to give you, the reader, a glimpse of this man, Hugh O'Gorman. He fools us with his open smile and puts us all at ease when there is tension in the air. But he is just as cool after he puts the fire out because he has thought it through before he takes action. If you are just starting out or want to refresh the issues we all confront in the art of acting, read this book. If you still read Stanislavski, try Hugh's version of Earle Gister. If you are a beginner or a theater person of any kind and want to embrace the theater for the future because you believe live theater is a key to preserving and enhancing society across this world, read Hugh's book.

J. Michael Miller
Founding Dean
New York University, Tisch School of the Arts, Graduate Acting MFA
Program
Founding Director
The Actors Center, New York City

Preface

> Talent is the ability to live believably under imaginary circumstances. Everything after this is craft and technique. But we need to begin here. This is the thing that we must work on. The discipline is what we teach because acting is an art form.[1]
>
> —Earle Gister

I believe all actors want to know the secret of acting. This book addresses one of them. I am an actor. Perhaps you are, too. If so, I wrote this book for you. When I was starting as a professional, I badly wanted to know all the secrets of acting. More concretely, I wished someone had written a book explaining precisely what it is an actor does to get started in performance.

Most of the books I was given when I started were sprawling, artistic tomes; esoteric rhapsodies on the art of acting; or thick, nineteenth-century triptychs covering every aspect of the craft that were not only impenetrable but also, quite honestly, tedious and ultimately not practical. This was discouraging, as acting was what I wanted to do most. What I had longed for as a young actor was a simple how-to that explained what to do in that mystical, magical void called performance. Of course, one book cannot encapsulate an entire art form, but a primer for a specific aspect of technique, a base from which to build the core of a performance, is not only possible but also essential. *Acting Action* is that foundation. It is a place to begin. It is an attempt to write to my younger actor-self who was just starting out and needed a helping hand. I invite you to come along for the journey.

More precisely, this primer is a practical guide for actors, directors, and teachers in the technique of "playing action." Playing action is one of the essential principles of the acting system developed by Konstantin Stanislavski, famed Russian theater director of the Moscow Art Theatre, acting theorist, and the grandfather of Western actor training. This book addresses a specific need in the world of actor training. It illuminates what exactly to do in the moment-to-moment act of the acting task and serves as a basic creative manual for both the stage and the camera. In other words, this book explains how to do the doing of acting. This particular varietal of playing action is a highly specialized version of Stanislavski's action, as taught by Earle Gister (head of acting at the Yale School of Drama, 1979–1999) and Lloyd Richards (dean of the Yale School of Drama, 1979–1991) and taught to them by Paul Mann, American acting teacher and member of the Group Theatre.

Although the techniques presented in part I are primarily the discoveries of Stanislavski, they are refined and disseminated through the idiosyncratic lenses of Gister, Richards, Mann, and (in part II) Maria Knebel, an artistic associate of the Moscow Art Theatre and student and colleague of Stanislavski. The aim here is to highlight a few core aspects of Stanislavski's methodology—primarily playing action—in a clear and digestible manner to get you up and acting.

Action is the core of acting; without it, no matter how motivated, imaginative, or inspired the actors may be, they will not serve the demands of the playwright. First and foremost, it is the actor's professional and artistic responsibility to make the event of each scene happen under imaginary circumstances with precise repeatability and complete spontaneity. You, the actor, must play action to do that. Curiously, this very heart of the craft is often overlooked by actors, teachers, and directors alike.

The objective of *Acting Action* is to get you on your feet with an understanding of what exactly it is you must do to begin to act well. This book removes some of the mystery and empowers actors of every age and experience level to own their craft. The entire artistic process is elusive enough; technique shouldn't be. *Acting Action* lays out what that doing is, how to begin doing it yourself, and how to refine it over time.

Our field needs a straightforward how-to guide to one of the fundamental principles of acting. As someone who oversees an American university actor-training program, coaches professional actors in Los Angeles, and teaches internationally, I know that this work is sorely needed, even though the technique espoused here is no secret to those fortunate enough to study with Gister, Richards, or Mann.

> What is it that we're doing when we're acting well? What is it that
> great actors are actually doing when they're practicing their craft at the
> highest level?[2]

There is one thing many actors have in common: *They struggle to articulate what it is they do when they act.* When asked "Did you do what you wanted to do in the scene?" actors often reply that they are not sure. They are not sure what they wanted to do, how to do it, or even if they accomplished it. When asked "When you just *did* something now, what were you actually *doing?*" many actors again can't answer. A large percentage of professional actors work only with an approximation of what it is that they are doing. It would be one thing if their work were so full of life, specificity, power, imagination, consistency, and inspiration that they didn't need to articulate it. Genius doesn't need an explanation. However, more often than not, there is a level of self-consciousness that inhibits the work of many actors and results in a generality, a wooden mechanical quality, a stiffness and hesitancy that interferes with a full release of their acting potential. They end up playing a quality, playing the language, or outright self-generating their work, which results in an artificial representation of the character they are attempting to believably inhabit. Ironically, these are the very qualities Stanislavski was trying to correct via the development of his system more than one hundred years ago. Clearly, there is still much work to be done in our field.

At the end of the day, *Acting Action* is a book that I wish someone had given me when I was starting out. At that time, I often would stare at the performance space, eager to begin but without a tangible, reliable, and repeatable way of working. This is an endeavor to share my thirty years of experience with my younger self. I also hope to give you a peek into what it was like to be in Earle's acting classes and to impart some of his and Lloyd's wisdom, as well as that of the source himself, Konstantin Stanislavski.

Acting Action is divided into two parts. Part I, "Context," explains the underlying theories at work. Part II, "Practice," outlines exactly what to do in the rehearsal studio and performance. Ultimately, I hope you find this book useful and that it helps you release your fullest acting potential. May you fly freely and boldly through the magical door of "As if" into your imagination and soar on wings of ease, beauty, and inspiration.

Acknowledgments

I must first acknowledge my sources for this material. I am deeply indebted to Earle Gister and Lloyd Richards for sharing not only this valuable material but also their invaluable gifts as teachers in their classes at the Actors Center in New York City as part of the indispensable and inspiring Teacher Development Program (TDP) now being offered by the National Alliance of Acting Teachers (NAAT). I also must humbly acknowledge J. Michael Miller, founding director of the Actors Center, for his years of unwavering mentorship, his belief in me as a teacher, and his encouragement to write this book. I also want to thank him for his heartfelt and insightful foreword to the book. I, too, wish to acknowledge the many other teachers and colleagues with whom I have studied acting and whose teaching has deeply affected my own practice, namely Jack Clay, Joanna Merlin, Ron Van Lieu, Viacheslav Dolgachev, Mala Powers, Mark Jenkins, Judith Dickerson, Max Dixon, Catherine Madden, Connie Haas, David Zinder, Alexandra Billings, Catherine Fitzmaurice, Randy Reinholz, Declan Donnellan, Ted Pugh, Fern Sloan, Lenard Petit, Jack Colvin, John Lehne, Vernice Klier, Sharon Marie Carnicke, my performance faculty colleagues at California State University Long Beach (CSULB), Ezra Lebank, Andrea Caban, Anna Steers, Simon Brooke, Sarah Underwood, Joanne Gordon, and Brian Mulligan. I would also like to acknowledge my co–executive director of the NAAT, Amy Herzberg, with whom I attended Earle's classes in the TDP, as well as the stalwart members of NAAT's Executive Committee, the incomparable Michele Shay, Kenneth Noel Mitchell, Gerald Glackin, Peter Jay Fernandez, and Jane

McPherson. I am also deeply indebted to all the students I have ever taught, from whom I certainly learned more than they from me; all the actors with whom I have ever shared the stage and screen, especially my beloved *Remember WENN* family; my cohorts in the TDP at the Actors Center from 2003 to 2008, especially Kimberly Ross; my dear, fellow travelers in MICHA, the Michael Chekhov Association, Jessica Cerullo, Dawn Arnold, Ragnar Freidank, Anne Gottlieb, Bethany Caputo, Scott Fielding, and Craig Mathers; MCE: Michael Chekhov Europe; Uli Meyer-Horsch; Suzana Nikolic, Jesper Michelsen, Sol Garre, Jobst Langhans, and Marjolein Baars, as well as all my esteemed colleagues in the NAAT, and my colleague in performance theory, Kevin Sverduk.

At Rowman & Littlefield Publishing, I humbly acknowledge the support, encouragement, and guidance of Carol Flannery, Michael Tan, Christen Karniski, Lara Hahn, and Niki Guinan, as well as the invaluable editorial assistance I received from my colleagues in the field of actor training, Jonathan Freeman, Kerrie Brown Seymour, and David Bridel. A generous and sincere bow of appreciation goes to Gary Palmer for his brilliant artistic interpretation of the space between; I am deeply honored to have his beautiful artwork grace the cover of this book. I also want to loudly acknowledge the herculean editorial assistance of the indefatigable Julia Martin on both parts I and II. I am deeply indebted to her for her relentless, eagle-eyed proofreading; writing assistance; technical editing; language editing; substantive notes on chapters 4, 5, and 6 in particular; and unwavering moral support. To all of these angels, I am eternally grateful.

No matter how naturally talented the actor may be, he will never evolve much for his art or bequeath his own gifts to theatrical posterity if he isolates himself in that small cell of his "own technique" and devices. The art of acting can grow and develop only if it is based on an objective method with fundamental principles.

—Michael Chekhov

Introduction

How you talk about your work is how your work will happen.

—Earle Gister[1]

One can learn *about* acting from a book. However, one cannot learn *how* to act from a book. In acting, as in any psychophysical endeavor, all questions, discoveries, answers, and growth happen in the doing. That said, this book provides actors, directors, and acting teachers a crystal-clear context for one of the foundational mechanics of acting as well as some practical exercises to articulate this process in order to develop a lifelong acting practice. I hope that this guide will deepen and hone the laboratory exploration of your acting as well as add joy and specificity to your professional performances. Everything that follows must ultimately be exercised, practiced, and repeated. It is not sufficient just to read the book, for acting is not understood intellectually; it is experiential. It is understood in the body, like riding a bike or swimming. You have to get on the bike or dive into the pool to learn how to do it.

All questions for the actor are answered in the doing.

—Earle Gister[2]

These human experiences must be practiced over and over and over again. As the genius Russian actor and acting theorist Michael Chekhov notes, for the actor "repetition is the growing power."[3] The practice of practice must become your practice for life, or you will never arrive at mastery. A book can help point you there. Practice and repetition get you there.

> Repetition is the growing power.
>
> —Michael Chekhov[4]

As in any field, how we talk about the work is crucial, yet over the years, it has become clearer to me exactly how essential this is to the successful training of an actor. How actors talk about and practice their craft is vital, for this determines exactly what will happen in performance. At first glance, this seems obvious. However, very few actors speak about their work with the precision, discipline, and rigor necessary to truly divine what happens in the moment of acting. Earle Gister was an acting teacher who worked at this demanding level. Of the many lessons he taught his students, this one is perhaps the greatest: "How you talk about your work is how your work will happen."

The creative act is gorgeously elusive, always seductive, and quite often inexplicable, yet an acting technique should not be. Technique should be concrete, comprehensible, practical, and practicable. Creativity and technique are necessary bedfellows, dancing together in the liminal space between our daily selves and artistic selves. That said, technique is in service of the creative act; it is not an end goal in and of itself. No matter the size of the acting talent, actors always need a foundational technique from which to build a performance, a time-tested way of working to nurture and shape the creative impulse to give it ongoing form and precision. But this work is not prescriptive. You will need to discover your own relationship to it as an actor. Play with it in your way. Meet it on your terms. But you will have to get on your feet and do it to truly learn it. It is only a tool to serve your natural ability, as well as what Michael Chekhov calls your "creative individuality."[5] This ultimately is the goal of any technique: to serve you and your idiosyncratic artistic impulses.

How I approach acting changed forever during my time studying with Earle Gister. His grasp of technique as well as the source material was second to none, a fact to which everyone who ever had the honor of working with him can testify. Earle mostly taught playing action using the dramatic source material of Anton Chekhov. It was through these richly human and divinely sublime texts that Earle demystified the actor's craft while igniting the actor's passion to play and grow. His diagnostic eye for what to look for in an actor's work was razor sharp and delicately efficient. Earle could identify immediately and precisely where an actor needed to work; when they were fully connected to their scene partner and when they weren't; where they were playing action—the desired form of the technique—and where they were inexpertly playing the language or a quality, both of which are the undesirable results of self-generated mechanical acting. The atmosphere Earle created in the room was one of deep love and respect for the actor's craft, process, imagination, curiosity, literature, beauty, and art. Students felt free to risk, to dare, to play, to dig deeper into their creative questions and acting abilities. They felt empowered to make bold choices. Earle made his students feel that their raison d'être as an actor was vital to the health of humanity writ large. His classes were all about his students' gifts and the beauty of the work. However, it was the precise way he talked about acting that drove it all. The longer I teach, the more I appreciate this aspect of his mastery. I humbly hope to connect you, the reader, with some of the genius that was Earle's acting class, filtered through my own pedagogical lens.

If you are an actor reading this, I hope this book will help you to diagnose, articulate, and perform with surgical precision and commanding authority. If you are a director, I hope this book will shed light on what actors actually do in the moment of acting and provide you ways of communicating that will help them achieve greater depths in their performances. Finally, if you are an acting teacher, this book will provide you with a cogent and true pedagogical compass as well as a time-tested technique to teach your students how to play action—one that works—for how we as teachers talk about the craft of acting with our students is how they will eventually perform.

Summary

- How you talk about your work is how your work will happen.
- You can learn about acting from a book; you cannot learn how to act from a book.
- Acting is like swimming: You have to get in the proverbial pool to learn it.
- All questions are answered in the doing.
- Technique is the foundation for your performance. The ultimate goal of any technique is to fully release your creative individuality.
- Repetition is the growing power.

PART I

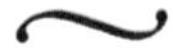

CONTEXT

The function of negative knowledge is not unlike the uses of space. The empty page upon which words can be written, the empty jar into which liquid can be poured, the empty window in which light can be emitted, the empty pipe through which water can flow. The value of emptiness lies in the movements it permits. This is why the emptiness must come first.

—Alan Watts[1]

~

CHAPTER ONE

The Space Between

Thirty spokes meet in the hub,
though the space between them is the essence of the wheel.
Pots are formed from clay,
though the space inside them is the essence of the pot.
Walls with windows and doors form the house,
though the space within them is the essence of the house.

—From *Saikontan*[1]

The Essence of Acting

The space between is where the magic happens. It is the terrain of infinite possibility, communal energy, dramatic release, and artistic inspiration. It is born of perception and reception and blossoms into radiating and receiving. Grace, humanity, and beauty appear in the space between seemingly miraculously. The space between is both a creative mystery and the direct result of the disciplined, rigorous practice of a repeated technique over time. It is a fleeting gift arising out of egoless generosity and undivided attention, one that only emerges from fully engaged listening and viewing the world through an artistic lens. The space between is where relationship is born for the actor. It cannot be created in a vacuum and only materializes through honest, vulnerable communion with another human being. This communion is a profound human connection with another, a metaphysical oneness created by two or more actors in space and time.

To go to the space between is not for the faint of heart. The space between demands courage, faith, vulnerability, and an unwavering artistic conviction from those who dare to seek it. Yet the resulting experience is ultimately why we actors put on our war paint and why the audience comes to bear witness. Actors are adrenaline junkies, artistic warriors "drawn," as Nina says in Anton Chekhov's *The Seagull*, "into the vortex." Actors are pulled into the space between because the experience of it can be nothing less than profound. Every actor who has ever found themselves in the zone before a packed house of attentive listeners knows this to be true. It's why we keep coming back. The space between is like a drug, only better—healthier, more nurturing, and profoundly rewarding. Actors feel inspired there, and so does the audience. Truly inspired acting can only live in the space between, for it is the essence of acting.

The Beautiful Game of Acting

Everything I know about morality and the obligations of men, I owe it to football.

—Albert Camus

I was twenty-one when I decided to pursue acting professionally. My mother was a Broadway actress and a Juilliard-trained opera singer, so I was exposed to the mystical world of the theater from a very young age. I performed in many productions in my youth and even took acting classes in college. Yet up until my last year of university studies, acting had been more of a hobby. I focused all my creative energies and free time on playing competitive soccer. Little did I know that those nearly two decades of the sport would help me in my career as a professional actor. For multiple reasons, across multiple artistic and professional arenas, all I learned as a soccer player served me well during my thirty years as a professional actor.

Although the life of a soccer player and the life of an actor couldn't be more different, in many significant ways they couldn't be more similar. They both demand unflinching dedication, intense training, rigorous discipline, deep-seated motivation, unwavering belief in self, and the ability to lose and not take that loss personally. Soccer players and actors alike choose to swim in the public fishbowl. They both require the nerve to withstand withering judgment from the outside and the peace of mind to wrestle with your own inner critic. They demand that you dig deep to find the courage to handle criticism as well as the fortitude to get back out on the field or stage the next day and do it all again. They both require a craving for public performance, a balanced perspective on winning and losing, the ability to absorb unnatural doses of pressure, and the mental toughness to handle it all. They demand the deft interpersonal skills to dance through a sea of superhuman egos as well as a genuine ability to trust others.

They both have a positive relationship with competition, understanding that it is a natural and necessary ingredient if you want to bring out the very best in yourself. They both insist that you work with your most healthy and engaged self across all areas of your life: physical, mental, emotional, and spiritual. Both the successful actor and the successful soccer player must sacrifice themselves in the pursuit of something simultaneously bigger than themselves and buried deep inside of who they are. Both must care keenly about their preparation and then turn that care into play at showtime. They must have buckets of hope and stadium-sized dreams. Yet most importantly, and perhaps surprisingly, both require a vibrant imagination. Besides an un-fettered love of the game, more than anything, soccer and acting demand a fertile and facile imagination.

> The man who has no imagination has no wings.
>
> —Muhammad Ali

For soccer players to rise above the journeyman level, they must work the field with a lightning-quick imagination and see the negative space, the emptiness that surrounds them with potential. They must do so while running in an all-out sprint while twenty-one other players weave around them in an ever-changing kaleidoscopic maze and their lungs scream for more oxygen. This negative space, the space between the players, is where the power lies in what is known globally as the "Beautiful Game." The magic that transpires in this negative space is what makes the game so compelling to watch. Beauty in the game is what you see if you know what to look for. The same is true for acting. The space between the players is where all the power and potential lies, yet few actors know it's there, and most actors rarely take advantage of it.

> I skate to where the puck is going to be, not to where it has been.
>
> —Wayne Gretzky

If you've ever watched an under-five-years-of-age (U5) American Youth Soccer Organization (AYSO) soccer match, you've experienced unbridled joy. It ain't pretty, and it ain't the Beautiful Game, but watching U5s play is one of the most enjoyable things you can do. Even on your worst day, a U5 AYSO soccer game will instantly slap a smile on your face and freeze it there for about forty minutes. A dozen tiny, kinetic bodies buzz across a micropitch, small limbs and hair flailing akimbo while they elicit cries of laughter and delight from players and parents alike. I like to call it "amoeba ball." The children follow the ball around the field in one huge, unorganized clump as if possessed by the ball's invisible powers. Both teams bump against each other like supercharged elements, and the ball acts like a magnet controlled by some cult leader commanding the kids, "Attack! Ball! Now!" At this age and for some years to come, both the adorable young players and their equally unaware parents mistakenly think soccer is about the ball. But the game is not about the ball. The Beautiful Game is about everything around the ball. Kids at this age simply haven't learned that yet. They must, however, learn this essential truth if they want to play the game well.

> In football, the worst blindness is only seeing the ball.
>
> —Nelson Falcão Rodrigues

Just like novice soccer players, actors initially think acting is about the ball. It is not. Just as in soccer, it is about everything else on the field. It is about everything *around* them. For the actor, in this analogy, the ball is you. You need to surrender yourself to everything happening around you if you want to win at the beautiful game of acting. Acting at its best is, perhaps paradoxically, about the other actors onstage.

Soccer, or football, as the sport is more appropriately called outside the United States, is beloved across the planet for its never-ending statistical possibilities and probabilities. All twenty-two players on the field simultaneously generate powerful combinations of potential plays. The result is a collective kinetic energy that is continually created, destroyed, and recreated again and again in negative space ad infinitum. To achieve this level of beauty in football, the players must see the field around them for all its potential, receive and read the multitudes of signals, and make split-second decisions. These decisions are not intellectual but psychophysical and have significant consequences to the outcome of the game.

The same holds for acting. You rehearse beforehand, but the performance takes on a life of its own. You either get in its flow, or you are left behind. You cannot control how a performance is going to go as an actor any more than a football player can control how a game is going to play out. You affect it, sure. But to try to control is not only futile; it actually destroys the performance.

Superior work has the quality of an accident.

—Alan Watts[2]

How we behave, both in our acting and our everyday lives, depends on at least two things: (1) what we perceive and (2) what we receive. The combination of the two is what we call our point of view. It is only from a place of intense listening, of clearly seeing what's in front of us and receiving the gift of the present moment, that we spring into any meaningful action. In other words, the way you see the world and how you process it determines how you act in it.

By the time young players are ten (U12), things begin to look a little better. They spread around the field more, hold formations, comprehend their positions, and look up from the ball as they dribble. They start to understand that the only road to success in soccer is through seeing what's around them. By U12, they stop trying to do it all themselves and start passing the ball. This is a painful lesson for the soccer player to learn, but it is necessary. It is, in fact, the linchpin that must be pulled to release the young player into the flow of the Beautiful Game. It is impressive to watch the virtuoso performance of individual players, such as Garrincha, Pelé, Hamm, Messi, Ronaldo (the Brazilian and the Portuguese), Mané, Salah, Firmino, and Marta, as they play with awesome power and dexterity. But that pleasure is nowhere near the transcendent experience of watching eleven human beings, a team, find balletic synchronicity with one another. It is then when something delphic appears between them, as if from nowhere. Let me repeat: It appears *between* them. From the negative, empty space *between them*. Why is that? How is that?

As the old sports cliché goes, "There is no *I* in *team*." Those eleven players decided that the team is more important than what they are doing individually; they created something greater than the sum of its parts. The same is true for actors. As long as actors think that acting is about themselves, about giving or generating a performance, the audience will never be truly transported. They may be impressed with that performer's talent, amazed even. But they will never bear witness to the kind of art that changes the air in a theater and transports an audience to another world.

As an actor you must learn to *get* your performance from your scene partner, not *give* a performance yourself. Your scene partner is your source of all inspired behavior. I discuss sourcing in greater detail later in the book.

> The most important person in your scene is your partner.
>
> —Earle Gister[3]

Around the age of fourteen is when young people often discover they truly love playing football, or any sport for that matter. It is at this fulcrum that their interest turns from a mere hobby into a dedicated passion. They want to take their game to the next level and leave AYSO, making the important switch to competitive academy football. Their first practice at the academy level can be a surprising and humbling experience as the young players realize they are completely lost. The game now passes them by so quickly they don't know what to do or even how to get on board the speeding train. Although they may have dominated the game at the level below with their individual skill and ability, the new club player is now relegated to the position of spectator in this ever-morphing web of possibility. They must now spend virtually all their time learning to control the ball, only to get rid of it as quickly and precisely as possible by releasing it to one of their teammates. They must learn to read the field for its negative space and follow their impulses to release into the emptiness accordingly.

The Beautiful Game is about movement into the space between players and the ball alike. The player must not only learn how to see the space between but also imagine future actions in this negative space. They must train their bodies to react without thinking and imagine what is about to happen next while also working in the moment to make that next thing happen in the now. To do this, the player must flow in harmony with everything happening around them. The same holds true for the actor.

However, the space between is not only analogous to sport. It is a universal truth, much like the laws of aesthetics, the Fibonacci sequence, and the golden rectangle. The power of the space between is found in the deepest recesses of mathematics, physics, quantum mechanics, philosophy, music, and Buddhism.

> *La musique, c'est ce qu'il y a entre les notes.* [Music is the space between the notes.]
>
> —Claude Debussy

Ma

The Japanese have a word for this space between: *ma*. *Ma* is the essential void, interval, blank, or negative space between all things. It is the emptiness where possibility dwells and the intersection of the subjective and objective experiences, the concrete and the imagined. It is an active pause, from which meaning materializes. It is through this negative space that art happens.

Ma is a place of consciousness; it is also a practice, an intention, an awareness of both form and nonform that simultaneously arises from a deeply human aesthetic understanding of life. *Ma* is the moment that appears from the compositional elements of space and time. It is a total lack of clutter. It is clarity and focus and contains the purest forms of both action and nonaction. It contains all that came before and all that is about to come. So for the performer, all roads eventually lead to *ma*.

In Japanese life and culture, *ma* is not simply a philosophy; it is a daily practice. It is always available to those who are alert and listening for it. But most people are too distracted by the noise of their everyday existences and their own egos to experience it. Life is demanding, and our daily toils pull our attention in a big way. Yet, despite that pull, *ma* is ever present, ubiquitously appearing in Japanese architecture, music, poetry, and gardening. If you have ever had the pleasure of receiving the gifts of a well-crafted Zen garden, then you have experienced *ma*. It transports the viewer into an experience. Awareness of *ma* must be developed by the actor if performance is to rise to the level of art. If you are too busy "acting," you will miss it.

Before I dive into the acting technique, keep in mind that technique itself is never the goal. Technique is in service of something greater, and that is inspired artistic expression of the highest magnitude. The artistic act forges itself from a lifetime of discipline traveling the rocky road of mastery and often appears when one least expects it.

Yet art is not random. Art is precise and specific. It requires ease, form, composition, and beauty. The seeds of these essential elements are sown in technique. The technique of playing action laid out in this book is in service of releasing the full performance potential of every actor, who in turn is in service of the mysterious process of creation. The act of creation may be elusive but never an acting technique.

> The more technique you have, the less you have to worry about it. The more technique there is, the less there is.
>
> —Pablo Picasso

The technique of playing action and *ma* go hand in hand. For the actor, the one cannot exist without the other. In acting, this harmonious communion between actors is the result of selfless listening. When this synchronicity occurs, the space between the actors becomes filled with energy, and *ma* suddenly appears, as if from nowhere. In this moment, the space between the actors ignites into compelling dramatic existence, with all its accompanying power and meaning, where the total experience is far greater than the sum of its parts.

There is a feeling of oneness in the space between—not just between the actors themselves, but also with the audience and the camera. Performance becomes possessed with a powerful ease; a sharp form; a sense of wholeness and purpose; and, ultimately, beauty. It is this moment that adrenaline rushes in, fueling actors with a sense of freedom and release, when the sensation of artistic satisfaction permeates their entire being; they perform in a state of flow, in simple and dynamic union with their scene partners. Nothing the actors could generate in isolation even compares with the power and presence of this communal creation. Ultimately, the space between is where the ordinary is forged into the extraordinary.

Acting Is Like Love

Acting is like love; you can't do it alone.

—Sean Penn

At the end of the day, acting is like love; you can't do it alone. If you know how to love, then you know what to do when you act. Loving another is an act of total surrender. Love appears only when you surrender your heart, ego, and whole self to someone else, when another human being becomes a well for you.

When you are in love, you let down your guard, take off your social masks, and "source" your partner. You give yourself to another with complete abandon, all of your attention, spirit, and energy, all as a gift. You listen to their spirit joyfully with your entire being. You delight in being in their presence and are fully present, honest, and vulnerable yourself; you put their interests on equal footing with, if not before, your own. You make them feel like they are the most special person on the planet, and they do the same to you. You let your partner truly see your unprotected self, and you take the quality time to see them without judgment in all their radiant humanity. If you do all these things, then love has a chance in hell of entering the equation. If you don't, it won't.

Through this perpetual, mutual act of sourcing and giving, you feel that you are inseparable. You are filled with their presence, and the result is you receive the gift of love. It is only through selfless giving of ourselves that we receive priceless love. If you've ever been in the presence of two people in love, any kind of love, you can actually feel this connection between them. That is the space between. The space between them both changes the atmosphere in the room and fills it with a profound existential meaning and spirit. Inspired acting arrives at this same result.

> Love takes off masks that we fear we cannot live without, and know we cannot live within.
>
> —James Baldwin[4]

When the Penny Drops

> It's not that you don't know what to do, you just don't do what you know.
>
> —W. Timothy Gallwey[5]

I can recall as if it were only yesterday the moment when the proverbial penny dropped, and I authentically experienced playing action and the power of the space between. Ironically, I had already been working professionally for many years; had studied a variety of inspiring, effective, and useful approaches to the work; and had learned from many wonderfully gifted teachers. To an extent, my prior training was working. I was making my living as an actor; booking jobs; and feeling more or less satisfied, depending on the job. I just didn't know what I didn't know. Yet, in Earle Gister's class at the Actor's Center in New York City, I was working on a scene with a sublimely talented actress named Kimberly Ross, and suddenly all my numerous years of training and professional acting jobs suddenly made sense; I had my aha moment, and the penny dropped.

Kim and I were working on the Sonya-Astrov scene from act 2 in Anton Chekhov's *Uncle Vanya*. At the top of the scene, Sonya knocks on the door to lure Astrov out of his drawing room and into the kitchen nook so she can chastise him about his excessive drinking with Vanya. Kimberly knocked on the door and called, "Astrov." I opened the door and was changed forever. Kimberly was no longer there; Sonya stood before me, alive and filled with hopes and dreams for her life with Astrov. She was *releasing* all these things onto me, and they surged into my heart, filling my entire being with the vibrating sensation of love. When that door opened and I *sourced* Kimberly, not only did Astrov's world change for me, but also the world of acting itself changed. What I *perceived* and *received* from Kimberly was so full and charged with life that I had no choice but to say Astrov's first line. Kimberly released her energy onto me so strongly that she made me act Astrov. Let me repeat that: *She made me act Astrov.* For the next ten minutes of the scene, there was no one else in the room but Astrov and Sonya, even though more than a dozen other actors were watching us. Kim became the source of all my behavior as Astrov, and accordingly, the space between us became alive with the relationship that is Astrov and Sonya in act 2 of the play. The energy between us transformed our relationship. It was effortless. We were in flow, in the moment, in the zone: We were in the space between.

The scene ended. I felt incredibly light and filled with joy, as if I had been suddenly freed from myself and the weight of my own ego, freed from my own inner critic and the pressure to *give* a performance. I felt as if I had known all along how to do this, which was indeed the case, and was simply moving Astrov's life forward under imaginary circumstances. It was terribly bittersweet, simultaneously both enlightening and frustrating.

We turned to Earle, and he said, "What were you working on, and how did it go?" For some time, I couldn't speak. I just sat there. What had just happened? After more silence, Earle knowingly smiled and said, "You just played action with Kimberly, and the work took on a life of its own." We now understood the crises in which the characters found themselves. The atmosphere was filled with the deep sorrow, pathos, and humor of the wasted lives of Astrov and Sonya but also the simple, honest, human love between them. An author's characters, the atmosphere, the soul of a script, and its theme only arrive fully embodied when the space between appears.

I exhaled the release of an actor who had been working hard on his craft and who had finally arrived at some point of freedom. All the actor-ego interference just fell away, and *Uncle Vanya* simply opened up. It was as if Sonya and Astrov jumped off the page, walked into that light-filled midtown acting studio in Manhattan, and entered our contemporary bodies. Anton Chekhov's writing played the both of us, as if we were channeling it somehow. The work to do so was effortless. It felt as if everything from the play was happening, and I, the actor, simply needed to get out of its way. I began to understand in my body, experientially, that my acting instrument was merely a vessel for the play to express itself through me. I just had to get out of the way. And I did. I got my ego out of the way, "sourced" Kimberly, and the space between showed up. She was my well. Everything was there in her. I simply had to pay attention to it and then react.

I slowly began to realize what I had done—no—rather what Kimberly and I had done together; we had cared more about the characters than ourselves, cared more about moving the characters' lives forward than we cared about our acting. And when we did, the whole world of *Uncle Vanya*, as well as that of acting, presented itself. And here's the kicker: It was so simple. It was as if I had completely forgotten myself, and Kimberly as Sonya led me to a place of deep human understanding, empathy, compassion, and artistic intimacy. It was profound but also felt like I wasn't working; rather, the scene was happening to me. We allowed it to happen from our imaginations. It was simultaneously complex and effortless, filled with ease and detail. I was changed forever.

We had played action through the entire scene, and the air not only in the space between us but also in the entire studio was disturbed with energy. We had changed the molecules of the air in the room. And here's the thing: It was so much fun. It never felt like work. Earle smiled and said, "You already knew how to do this. You did it all the time as a child. The adult you just needed a reminder."

Earle had indeed reminded me of something simple yet profound. Right before we started the scene he said, "What is it you want to make her, Kimberly, the actress playing Sonya, feel to get what you need as Astrov? She is your source; receive what she is sending you, and then release your energy back onto her. Make her feel loved like a niece."

Earle was right. It was indeed that simple. Make her *feel* something. It was this slight adjustment to my acting that changed everything for me. Up to that point in my career, I had been taught that action was a verb, something I did to make the other person do, think, or feel. But Earle's approach made action both more specific and more potent. Rather than think of the doing as a verb, which kept my attention on myself to one degree or another, he taught us that action was an exchange of energy to make the *other person feel* something.

This slight yet hugely significant adjustment allowed me to pay even more attention to my scene partner, forget about myself, and focus on one thing: changing the emotional life of the other actor in the scene. If we accomplished this, then the other person would eventually do or think what we wanted them to. The action must change how the *other* actor feels. It must create an active and real emotion in your partner that helps your character move their life forward.

> Action is energy. It must be sent and land on the other actor.
>
> —Earle Gister[6]

Finally, I had the secret.

Dissolving the Ego

If you are doing it for a result in the future, you are not doing it.

—Alan Watts[7]

We only learn the lessons we are ready to learn in the moment that is right for us individually to learn them. We can't jump ahead and speed up learning; we can't know when a moment of growth will arrive or if it ever will. In fact, the more we try to make it happen, the less likely that it will happen. We need to simply love the work for what it is, love the doing for its own sake, for in that is all. Moments of discovery and growth must arrive organically on their own accord for them to have any meaning or permanence. They emerge only after spending sustained periods of time "playing on the plateau."[8] They certainly only appear when we surrender our egos and the self-satisfaction that comes from growth. Yet, this only happens when our egos are quiet, completely dissolved in the joy of doing for doing's sake and that alone.

It is my hope that you will have a similar moment of discovery about playing action. Moreover, if you practice this work, I am certain that the space between will appear. That is my promise to you. But you've got to learn to love playing on the plateau, even across long periods without growth. You must show up each day filled with the joy of doing the work for the work's sake and cherish the opportunity to play and create. If you do this and build a practice of loving the plateau, then growth will eventually arise from the space between as if from nowhere and everywhere simultaneously.

Take it from one of the most transcendent actors to ever tread the boards: the Italian tragedienne Eleanora Duse, who almost single-handedly ushered in modern acting as we know it via her mystical and mesmerizing performances. As author Peter Rader imagines her saying in his insightful book *Playing to the Gods*,

Theatre began as an off-shoot of religion, with the singular purpose of helping us to understand what it means to be human, in all its poignancy, humor and devastation. As our ancestors gazed up at the stars trying to fathom our purpose the high priestess of the tribe, the shaman, would recount the stories of the past, enacting the different roles: the hero, the beloved, the antagonist; allowing his body temporarily to become possessed, and letting the spirit archetypes channel through him. This was the original acting. It meant dissolving the ego. I call it: The Grace. But in those moments when The Grace flows, I (Eleanor) felt connected to the entire universe.[9]

No matter where you come down in the Duse-versus-Bernhardt debate, Duse was a remarkable artist who was able to access her artistic nature in unusual ways to achieve feats of brilliant transformation. By all accounts, she was able to use herself as a medium to transmit an artistic experience to her audiences like no other. Duse's acting is legendary for being simultaneously deeply human and metaphysical. To work such artistic miracles, Duse operated as a sort of mystic in the theater, one who channeled her character's spirit in service of the play. In order to do so, she, by her own admission, needed to "dissolve" her ego. It was then that what she called the "Grace" would appear. We can take this Grace to be her inspiration, her muse. Part of your process as an actor requires you to likewise dissolve your own ego. That is the only path to true inspiration.

The Daily Self and the Artistic Self

Your higher self endows the character with creative feelings.

—Michael Chekhov[10]

Another genius in his own right, Russian actor and acting theorist Michael Chekhov breaks the actor's ego into two parts: the "lower self" and the "higher self."[11] His lower self is what I call in my acting classes the "daily self." This is the part of you that is active in all the arenas of your everyday life. His higher self I believe is your "artistic self," which is the part of you that comes alive when you are called on to create something, to access your artistic energy. They represent two different energies from the various roles we play in our quotidian and creative lives alike. However, the actor looking to find what Duse called the Grace, or what you and I might call inspiration, cannot do so from the lower self (i.e., the daily self). As Duse says, to access that shamanistic side of ourselves, to truly transform, we must develop a practice of "dissolving the ego," stepping out of our lower selves and into our higher selves (i.e., artistic selves).

There is no true artistic transformation from the lower self. You must cross a threshold every time you work, leaving your daily self and stepping into an image of your artistic self. You must find a way of working that allows you to access your artistic side so you are not simply operating from your pedestrian energy. This is not simply a recommended step in your work; this act of dissolving the ego is an essential one. The way you do this is to become more interested in your character than in your own acting. The story is never about you, and yet it is paradoxically your job to tell the story. Letting go of the ego attachment in your work is one of the true keys to inspired acting. As Rader imagines Duse saying, this is the way to the "original acting." Acting is ultimately about transformation, but you can't transform if you are locked in your everyday self.

Why start here? Why start a book on acting with a soccer analogy, a Japanese aesthetic, love, and a personal anecdote from an acting class many years ago about dissolving the ego? Every page that follows in this book is about how to arrive at the level of presence and awareness necessary for playing action, achieve inspired acting in your own work, and electrify the performance spaces you inhabit. For the soccer player, the lover, the Japanese artist, and the actor alike, all roads lead to the space between: the essence of inspired acting and where the magic happens. Let's go there.

Exercises

Slow down; you move too fast.

—Simon and Garfunkel

Building a Practice of Awareness and the Space Between

Actor training is about building a comprehensive practice of repeatable habits that increase your acting potential. Awareness training is one of the cornerstones of this practice. To improve your acting, to work from your artistic self rather than your daily self, you must increase your sensitivity to and perception of the world around you, as well as yourself in it; you will want to increase your powers of observation and become more aware of *ma*, the negative space around you, as well as the energy and the space between people, places, and objects.

The foundation of awareness training is built on breath and curiosity. Remind yourself to keep breathing and redirecting your attention outside yourself. To do all this, you will need to slow down—way down.

Developing a Healthy Inner Voice

Before we continue, I need to say a word about your inner critic, the voice in your head that judges what you do as you do it. You know the one. As you work through these exercises, please pay close attention to your inner dialogue about yourself in the work, as well as the exercises themselves. The inner critic tends to increase performance interference while simultaneously reducing performance potential.

An arguable definition of being in the "zone," "flow," or "moment" is that you are so fully engaged in your acting (doing what the character needs to do to move its life forward) that the voice of your inner critic is completely mute. In psychology this is called a "peak experience," a term coined in 1964 by American psychologist Abraham Maslow for when you are so consumed by what you are doing that there is no room left for self-criticism.[12] Maslow writes of peak experiences as "rare, exciting, oceanic, deeply moving, exhilarating, elevating experiences that generate an advanced form of perceiving reality and are even mystic and magical in their effect upon the experimenter."[13]

This is the place from which we release our fullest potential and is one of the goals of actor training: to perform in the zone as often as possible (frequency), for as long as possible (duration), and with the least amount of interference (potential). Therefore, if an uberobjective of actor training is to have peak experiences more often and longer-lasting, then you need to not only be aware of but also actively work on your relationship with the aspect of your craft that most often interferes with your acting, which is your inner critic.

Most performance interference comes from within the actor, and most is mental in nature. Our performances, peak or otherwise, are the direct result of the stories we tell ourselves about our work. Your relationship with your own inner critic is as important as any of the individual exercises or training you will do. This relationship plays a huge part in determining how the exercises will go for you and what you will get out of them. As a barometer, the degree to which you negatively judge the world around you is the degree to which your inner critic is alive and dominating your inner dialogue and, consequently, will determine the degree to which you judge yourself in your own work and the work itself.

Watch out for the sudden appearance of your inner critic. It likes to slip in, judge what you are doing, pull you out of the work, and even make fun of it while you are doing it. This distancing effect reduces the potential profundity of the experience. Our job as actors is to be as fully in the experience as possible. And you cannot be fully in the experience if you are judging it as you do it. For any exercise to be truly effective, you, the actor, must fully surrender to it. Judgment—intellectual analytical criticism—is a huge form of interference for the actor.

Yet, actors love to justify their judgment, which is really a form of fear or self-protection, and they find a myriad of really "smart" reasons to do so. But as you will learn throughout this book, to tap into your excellence (not your averageness), you must work as an actor from your unprotected self. Your excellence demands all of you in the moment, each and every time. The following practice will help you quiet your inner critic and build a performance habit that will free you even under the highest professional pressure. It is a simple, clear, habitual practice rooted in the Alexander Technique for body work; it is also an effective way to reduce self-criticism.[14] It has three parts: (1) notice, (2) stop, (3) redirect.

Notice, Stop, Redirect

Notice

Notice the arrival of your inner critic or when your attention has been distracted from what you are doing. When your inner critic is activated, judgment arrives (most often in the form of self-criticism, but it can take many forms), and your attention is pulled off an outside target and back onto you. It immediately increases self-consciousness, most often in the form of negative judgment. This heightened self-consciousness interferes with your full commitment to the act of what you are doing and simultaneously decreases your potential to fulfill the action. You will notice that your attention has left full engagement with what you are doing, and you begin to hear your inner critic, most often as negative thoughts; you also may feel your inner critic psychophysically, as sensations in the body: tenseness, fear, rigidity, holding of breath, doubt, and so on. Once you begin to realize your inner critic is present, go to the next step.

Stop

Give yourself a moment to stop what you are doing. Allow your lips to come apart slightly, let your breath drop in, and acknowledge what is truly happening. Say "yes" to the fact that your inner critic is beginning to take up some of your mental space and pull your attention from what you are doing. This may take only a nanosecond, or it may take a bit longer. It is not a deliberation; it is a simple acknowledgment of the truth of what is happening in the moment. This step reorients you in the present moment of what you are actually doing and experiencing.

Redirect

Purposefully, playfully, and willfully redirect the target of your attention to outside yourself and reengage in the exercise (or the scene, as the case may be). Repeat this three-step process as needed. It may take you a few times to get fully back into the doing.

Note: One of the arguable qualities of a professional actor, as opposed to an amateur, is not that the inner critic goes away all together, for it never will, but that the performer's relationship to it, more often than not, is a healthy one. The successful actor has not only made peace (more or less, depending on the actor) with their inner critic but also has harnessed the energy of the inner critic and brings it to the performance to more fully release their acting potential.

The inner critic loves making a fuss and finding all sorts of reasons to stop the doing and pull out: Nothing is ever right, the performance conditions are never to their liking, the other actors are a problem, the script is inadequate, the director doesn't know what they are doing, and more. The inner critic is like a multiheaded hydra. It takes many forms and manifests in a multitude of nefarious ways, always providing "legitimate" and righteous excuses.

All this, as I explain throughout this book, is nothing more than fear. For the actor, fear is ego. The professional actor knows how to turn the energy of fear into excitement. The professional is able to get back into the doing quickly, quietly, and efficiently. They are able to find success in their acting under the highest levels of performance pressure. What you may discover as you begin to work this process into your performance practice is that it takes some time to complete the three steps. It may only take a few moments, or it may take thirty seconds or more.

What will begin to happen is that, depending on the size and seriousness of the distraction, the time it takes to execute these three steps will diminish significantly the more you practice it. Experienced professionals can redirect themselves back into the moment almost instantly. That should be your goal: to find your way back into full engagement as efficaciously and quickly as possible. You can apply "Notice, Stop, Redirect" to anything you are doing to dive more deeply into the experience and get more out of it. For our purposes in this book, I ask that you specifically apply "Notice, Stop, Redirect" to the exercise work as well as your scene study (playing action) work.

Instant Forgiveness

"Instant Forgiveness" is one of the most valuable tools you can possess in your actor's toolbox and is related to "Notice, Stop, Redirect." I suggest you implement it into your acting practice immediately.

Often what happens with our inner critic is that it begins to judge itself while in the act of acting. First, we notice that the inner critic appears and judges something we are doing. Then, the inner critic compounds the problem as we begin to judge the fact that we are judging ourselves. In other words, we beat ourselves up because our inner critic showed up. And we do all this while we are still acting in a scene. This harmful habitual thought pattern increases performance interference exponentially, feeding on itself in a never-ending cycle.

One antidote to this mega-interference is "Instant Forgiveness." "Instant Forgiveness" is deceptively simple, yet it can produce some of the greatest positive results in your acting. It is exactly like it sounds and goes like this: As soon as you notice your inner critic arrive or any negative thought or judgment about yourself or your fellow actors, just instantly say to yourself without any real thought, "I forgive __________." It can be any of the following: "I forgive myself." "I forgive my scene partner." "I forgive my director." "I forgive my inner critic." "I forgive [fill in the blank]."

Note: That's it. Once you start practicing "Instant Forgiveness," especially in combination with "Notice, Stop, Redirect," you will immediately reap the performance rewards of increased potential in your acting.

Imaginary Eyes (Pools of Wonder)

Artists work from a place of perpetual wonder. Likewise, dynamic performances begin for actors from a perspective of investigative human wonderment. As professional empathizers, actors must see the world through the eyes of another human being, the character they are playing, and embrace their point of view, imaginatively and empathically. This exercise gives you a practical and practicable means to build wonder, one where you see through a set of imaginary eyes.

Begin by making a conscious decision that you are going to slow down in order to perceive and receive more fully life's gifts and the world around you. Say to yourself, "I have very little time, so I'm going to go very slowly." Repeat this three times. Notice if your habit is to rush even this simple task.

Activate this mantra by slowing down the tempo of your breath. Close your eyes, and let your lips part ever so slightly, allowing your breath to drop in more fully. Breathe in through your mouth on the count of four, and then breathe out on the count of eight. Do this eight or more times. (There is more on why actors need to breathe through their mouths later in the book.)

Now, place the palm of your dominant hand on the back of your lower skull. This is the location of the visual cortex in the brain (where information filtered from the eyes is formed into imagery that elicits action potential). Imagine that you are "seeing" from this place in the brain (you actually are) rather than from the front of your skull. Your eyeballs are merely receptive light refractors, beautiful ones but lenses nonetheless. Hold your hand on your occipital lobe (back of your lower skull) for four breaths, and then drop your hand. Imagine that you are seeing from this *slower, deeper, calmer* place.

Then, as you slow down, continue giving yourself the following prompts (depending on where you are, either silently or out loud): "I desire to become more aware of the world around me," or "I desire to build a practice of increased awareness," or "I wish to see the world through artistic eyes," or invent a statement that resonates with you.

As you are an actor and your imagination is the greatest tool you possess, *imagine* that your eyes are *pools of wonder*. Perhaps in your mind's eye, you give those pools of wonder a color, a texture, a sensation, or some other distinct quality. Play around with different choices, but allow the joy of seeing the world through lenses of *wonder*. Even give yourself permission to wonder how this exercise or a scene or a game will go.

Now, open your new "eyes of wonder." Receive your surroundings with wonderment. Take this new perception out into the world. Go for a stroll, or sit in a garden. No matter where you are, you can do this. There is no right place to try this. The now is always a wonderful (as in "filled with wonder") time to observe human beings and the environment, especially from this calmer place of enhanced awareness and wonderment. Make sure to keep noticing your lips and reminding yourself to keep them slightly parted throughout (more on that later). Allow yourself to slow down and become more curious about your surroundings; allow yourself to see beauty in even the most mundane object.

Ask yourself,

- "What am I taking for granted right now?"
- "What can I perceive more clearly?"
- "What can I receive more fully?"
- "What can I let surprise me?"
- "How can I engage life from a perpetual state of wonderment?"

Recall when you were a child, when time was slower, the days were longer, and you used to spend afternoons wondering about the shapes of clouds in the sky. Allow yourself to access that wonderous part of yourself. Then, continue seeing wonder with each new breath.

Note: If the word *wonder* doesn't do it for you, then simply play around with other synonyms until you find a word that is effective for you to engage both your imagination and how you see the world.

Note: If your inner critic rears its head as you do this, simply and calmly apply the "Notice, Stop, Redirect" process. Pay attention to any dialogue in your head about the exercise. If cynicism creeps in or your attention waivers or wanders, redirect it back into this new exploration of non-knowing with joy and playfulness.

"As If" for the First Time

> It's as if I am seeing for the first time in my life.
>
> —Tuzenbach[15]

When we work as actors, we must experience the work as Stanislavski posits: *as if for the first time; as if for the last time; each and every time*. To that end, this exercise will help you work on being "born to the moment," as it were, in life and in your acting.

Repeat the earlier breathing preparation from "Imaginary Eyes." Then, close your eyes for four breaths. When you open your eyes, open them as if you are a newborn seeing the world for the first time. It's *as if* you have never seen anything in the world before.

Continue to look and move around your environment; target your attention outside yourself, and ask yourself,

- "Can I continue to see the world around me *as if* for the first time?"
- "Can I perceive the human being in front of me *as if* I've never seen them before?"
- "Can I allow myself to be surprised by what I see?"
- "What happens when I do?"

Spend time exploring your immediate surroundings from this point of view, observing what you see, and notice any changes in your perceptions. Notice what changes for you, if anything, externally and internally.

Note: Allowing yourself to see things as if for the first time and being surprised by what you see, ideally with wonder and naïveté as well, is essential for camera work. The camera loves nothing more than capturing reactions of spontaneity, surprise, and discovery.

Note: Again, pay attention to any dialogue in your head about the exercise. If cynicism creeps in or your attention waivers or wanders, then "Notice, Stop, Redirect" it back into this new exploration of non-knowing with joy and playfulness.

"As If" for the Last Time

> Never forget yesterday, but always live for today, because you never know what tomorrow can bring, or what it can take away.
>
> —Buddha

There is a powerful Buddhist practice that builds presence, awareness, and gratefulness. It asks us to live each day *"as if* for the last time" and goes as follows: From the moment you wake, appreciate every moment as if it were your last day on earth. This doesn't mean you suddenly change all your plans because you might kick the bucket at midnight (don't fly to Vegas and run up all your credit cards!). It just means simply moving through your normal day with the humility and humbleness that it might be your last one. We never really know what may come; today might in fact be our last day. That's the truth, but this is far from a morbid thought.

This heightened existential consciousness actually helps build a practice of gratefulness, which in turn can lead to enlightenment. If today is perhaps our last, then we might as well make the most of it. Practicing this form of living meditation increases presence. For the actor, the ability to remain continuously and consistently present is one of the key components of inspired acting. Have you ever thought about why you want to watch one actor onstage more than another? It has to do with their presence.

> Presence is the present of being present.

Repeat the breathing preparation from "Imaginary Eyes." Then, add to your breathing patterns the following mantra: "With each breath, I breathe in gratefulness." Allow yourself to fill your lungs with more and more gratefulness with each breath. Simply start by breathing in gratefulness for breath itself. Allow yourself to wonder about your breath gratefully. How wonderful it is to breathe! Repeat this four times.

Target your attention outside yourself, and ask yourself,

- "What changes in me if I imagine this is my last day on earth?"
- "What if I see the world around me *as if* for the last time?"

Notice:

- What changes inside of you, if anything, when you do this?
- How does your relation to the outside world change when you do this?
- Is there a melancholy that is released in you somewhere? There is no beauty in life without simultaneous joy and sadness; the yin and yang of existence must be present for us to be fully present.

Spend time exploring your environment, your work, your family, and your day from this shift in perspective. Continue breathing in gratefulness with each new breath.

Note: Track any judgmental dialogue in your head about the exercise itself. Watch out for your inner critic. It likes to slip in and pull us out of the work. "Notice, Stop, Redirect" back into the exercise.

Eyes of Compassion

> Compassion may be called the fundamental of all good art because it alone can tell you what other beings feel and experience. Only compassion severs the bonds of your own personal limitations and gives you deep access into the inner life of the character you study without which you cannot properly prepare it for the stage.
>
> —Michael Chekhov[16]

Begin by repeating the breathing preparation from "Imaginary Eyes." Next, imagine it's *as if* your eyes are *pools of compassion.* Perhaps in your mind's eye you give those pools of compassion a color, a texture, a sensation, or some other distinct quality. Play around with different choices, but allow yourself to experience the freedom of receiving the world around you through the lens of compassion. Allow your empathic impulses to flow. Allow yourself to see through these newfound eyes of compassion. Now, observe the outside world *compassionately.* Continue to use this same framing device of seeing through the eyes of a particular lens for the following exercises. Make up your own, as well!

> *Those who are without compassion cannot see what is seen with the eyes of compassion.*
>
> —Thich Nhat Hanh

Eyes of Innocence

Even though it is often devalued and mocked by society at large, naïveté is an essential quality for an actor. The word *naïve* means that which is natural, free of artifice, unaffected, and unjudgmental. There is a deep well of freedom to be found for the actor in the effective use of naïveté. This exercise helps develop a courageous and useful practice of artistic naïveté.

Begin by repeating the breathing preparation from "Imaginary Eyes." Next, imagine it's *as if* your eyes are *pools of innocence.* Perhaps in your mind's eye, you give those pools of innocence a color, a texture, a sensation, or some other distinct quality. Play around with different choices, but allow yourself to experience the freedom of receiving the world around you through the lens of innocence. Allow yourself to not have to know. We feel so much pressure in life to have the right answer or get it right, yet so much more contentment comes to our existence when we maintain the beginner's mind-set, which is one of innocence. Allow yourself to see through these newfound eyes of innocence. Now, observe the outside world *naïvely*.

Eyes of a Child

Repeat the breathing preparation from "Imaginary Eyes." Now, imagine it's *as if* you are seeing the world through the eyes of a young child. Observe.

Eyes of an Artist

Repeat the breathing preparation from "Imaginary Eyes." Then, imagine it's *as if* you are seeing the world through the eyes of an artist or perhaps your favorite actor. What does the world look like when you see through these imaginary eyes? Do things shift for you? If so, what? Why? Observe.

Note: Finally, begin to build into your daily practice the habit of consciously noticing the space between things, people, time, and space. As an artist, it is your professional responsibility to do so. Once the space between makes itself known to you, it will be a joy to behold, and your acting will become more engaging, dynamic, and human.

Summary

- The space between is the essence of acting, where the magic happens. This is where relationship is born for the actor.
- *Ma* is a Japanese word for the space between, the negative space, the void, the emptiness in which all potential lives. It is present in Japanese art, culture, and daily life.
- Technique is in service of the space between.
- Superior work has the quality of an accident.
- Imagination is your most valuable commodity as an actor.
- Acting is a beautiful game. Like football (soccer), the game is not about the ball and not about you; it's about everything around you. Also like football, you need to be able to see and read the negative space around you to be successful.
- Acting is like love: You can't do it alone. The most important person in the scene is your partner. You need to learn to *get* your performance from your scene partner, not *give* a performance. You have to learn to *source* your partner. You must surrender to your partner.

- Action is an exchange of energy to make your scene partner *feel* an emotion. Playing action is born of perception and reception and blossoms into radiating and receiving. It is a *release* of energy outward. It must be sent and land on the other actor.
- It's not that you don't know what to do; you don't do what you know.
- You must care more about moving your character's life forward than how well you are doing as an actor.
- The proverbial penny will drop for you when you are ready for it and not before. You can't make that happen. Until then, you must love the work for the work and nothing more. You must love playing on the plateau more than experiencing growth.
- You have two selves: the lower self, which is your daily self, and the higher self, which is your artistic self. You can only experience the space between from your artistic self. You can't truly transform from your daily self. You must learn to dissolve your ego to experience the space between.

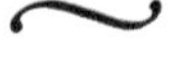

CHAPTER TWO

Acting Is Action

Action creates character. Certain kinds of characters will make certain kinds of action decisions.

—Earle Gister[1]

All roads for the actor originate with and return to action. Since the dawn of time, theater practitioners and theorists have understood that character is born of action. Fittingly, the word *drama* in ancient Greece, *dran*, means "to do." *Drama*, by definition, is doing. Doing is action; acting is drama. Therefore, acting is action.

As we actors are storytellers, our ultimate charge is to animate the human condition under imaginary circumstances in service to a story. Actors are professional human beings, behavioral alchemists mixing a playwright's fictional creation with our own human elixir in the crucible of the imagination. Actors literally breathe life into an author's text through the characters we perform. We are called "*actors*" because our work lifts text into *action*. The question quickly becomes, How do I actually do that?

Let's start by dividing action into two parts:

1. reading the action written in the script, which I baptize "invisible action," and
2. playing the action in performance, which I name "visible action."

The Two Actions

Declan Donnellan, in his seminal tome *The Actor and the Target*, separates the actor's work into two parts, the "invisible" and the "visible."[2] The invisible work is the part of the actor's process that the audience never sees: the preparation. The visible work is the actual performance the actor gives onstage—or in front of the camera—that the audience watches. I find this a practical way to think about not only the totality of the actor's process but also playing action more specifically.

It follows that action for the actor itself can be divided into similar subcategories: "invisible action" and "visible action." Invisible action is strategically woven into the text by the author. Actors must uncover this textual action for clues on how to inhabit their characters. They need to know how to read a script for the action embedded within it and must do this before they get on their feet.

> Action shapes the play.
>
> —Earle Gister[3]

Visible action is that action that the actor performs, in front of either an audience or a camera. The first action, the invisible, is the textual manifestation of the author's energy; the second action, the visible, is the energy generated by the actor to lift the action off the page—the word made flesh, if you will. The audience witnesses visible action.

We can, therefore, say that there are two types of action with which you, the actor, must concern yourself: (1) invisible action—the action on the page and (2) visible action—the action on the stage.

The Script and Invisible Action

> Invisible action is the action on the page.

In preparation for any performance, you must know how to read a script for the actions you will eventually bring to life. As these actions are invisible; you must become a keen, investigative, and facile reader of dramatic texts, not just a passive consumer of them. Many journeymen actors only read the script to learn their lines. There is an old saying in the business that makes this clear: An actor reading the script in preparation for their performance says to themselves, "Bullshit, bullshit, bullshit . . . my part," as if the rest of the script and what everyone else has to say is of little or no importance to that actor. The only thing that matters are "my lines." In fact, nothing could be further from the truth.

Although dialogue is clearly important, what we say in life is born from deeper roots of behavior, human circumstances that drive us into action. It is out of this subtextual reality that language eventually emerges. In fact, it is what the *other person* is saying and doing that propels your behavior. In essence, you should really highlight the *other actors'* lines, as they are the genesis of your behavior.

Action is subtext; subtext is action.

Acting is not ultimately about the words. We are not what we say; we are what we do. Of course, words matter, but the truth of human behavior is embedded in the action between the lines, in human *inter*action, in what transpires *between* the two characters, as discussed in chapter 1, what I call the space between. This space between I call the subtext, which means "below, or under, the text." Subtext conveys the true meaning of what's going on between the characters, no matter what they are actually saying.

In the genre of psychological realism, which comprises more than 90 percent of what you will most likely experience as a professional actor, subtext is action; action is subtext. It is what you do, then, your action, that conveys the true meaning of the scene, not what you say. In fact, the action, or subtext, is what determines the actual relationship. It can then be said that a relationship is born out of action, not words. The exception to this rule is playing Shakespeare, where the action is embedded in the lines themselves.

Action is not solely about the words, unless you're playing Shakespeare.

—Lloyd Richards[4]

It follows, then, that if you are to be successful in your acting, you must also know how to read a script to identify and comprehend the varied dramatic events in the text because it is your job to make those events happen. As many actors don't truly know how to read a script for their characters' actions, Stanislavski developed a precise and practicable method to divine the flow of action from the author's given circumstances.

Studying the script is the first step of a vibrant, dynamic, creative process, one that injects life and energy into the text, facilitating the translation from ink to human behavior. At the first encounter with the text, you must read it carefully and artistically to manifest the author's intentions. You must be able to read source material for playable actions, as well as their corresponding events, and then activate these actions during performance. Part II of this book deals more with invisible action.

Performance and Visible Action

Visible action is the action the audience sees.

Your charge is to turn the invisible action from the script into a playable, visible action in front of an audience or a camera. These two actions are different manifestations of the same uberaction: One exists on the page; the other, onstage. As Hamlet says in his advice to the players, "Suit the action to the word, the word to the action."[5]

Visible action is part of the second stage of what Stanislavski baptizes "active analysis" and is uncovered in rehearsal with the actors on their feet. You can only discover this form of action in the studio, as all questions about acting are ultimately answered in the doing. Your job is to translate one action to the other action—to make the invisible, visible. Why? Because it is first and foremost your responsibility to make the event of the scene happen in service to the story. You need to play action to do that.

In pursuit of a deeper, corporeal understanding of action, the formidable American actor and teacher Sanford Meisner honed Stanislavski's concept of action, developing a series of exercises to train the actor in visible action. This work was born out of his own work with the American theatrical company the Group Theatre. From his forays into action, Meisner writes, "The foundation of acting is the reality of doing."[6] This doing is a direct derivative of Stanislavski's action. The doing an actor must *do* is play action. But to what end?

You yourself know from life that where you place your attention is where your energy—and consequently your actions—go. Therefore, to make the action of the story happen, you have to make the other actor(s) the target of your attention and change them in order to move your character's life forward. You do this to achieve the character's objective in each scene. What experienced actors actually do onstage to change their scene partner is called "playing action," which is the visible doing of the play.

If they aren't affecting their partners, then they are usually self-generating a performance. Self-generating happens when the actor's attention is on themselves while acting. If their attention is on themselves and they are self-generating, then nothing is happening between the actors, and the events of the story aren't manifesting. If the events aren't happening, then the story isn't being told, and the script isn't being served. Therefore, an actor who isn't playing action isn't doing their job. It all boils down to this: Actors are doers; they must play action at all times to make the story happen.

Advertising executives and dictators alike have known this for a long time: If you can make a person feel a certain way, then you stand a good chance of manipulating their thoughts and actions. Throughout our lives, we are endlessly bombarded with commercial images and catchy slogans geared toward changing how we feel about certain products. The advertising industry knows all too well that if they can make you *feel* desirous of a product, then you are more likely to *buy* it. They manipulate your feelings to affect your actions—feelings to action. Using the actor's vocabulary of the *objective*, the objective of the advertising agency is to get you to purchase the product they are advertising. They make you *feel* something so you will *do* something.

The same is true for the actor onstage. Your character/you must make the other character/actor *feel* something in order to *do* something. This goes back to Aristotle and beyond. The art of rhetoric, or persuasive speech, is a potent weapon. Once you change how a person *feels* about something, you can more easily change their *thoughts* and *actions*. At the end of the day, you must make them *feel* in order to *do*. The process of doing this is called playing action.

> Tell me what someone does, and I'll tell you who they are.
>
> —Uta Hagen[7]

Examine, for a moment, your own life. Recall a time when someone made you feel happy, sad, or loved or perhaps when you made someone else feel special, guilty, or embarrassed. This is what we do all day, every day of our lives: We play action onto other human beings. We walk through a never-ending gauntlet of relationships and, therefore, a river of exchanged energy, which results in feelings. With each twist and turn along life's meandering path, we are made to feel different ways; we, in turn, make other people feel things. Making other people feel things is the natural by-product of human relationships; in fact, it defines relationships. The total sum of a person's inter*actions* with another person is known as a "relationship." Relationships are defined by our inter*actions* with other people, the action that passes back and forth between us and other human beings.

Actors must do the same thing onstage. They must first analyze their scripts to identify the characters' overarching superobjectives, as well as the series of objectives in each scene of the play. Then, they choose corresponding actions to play in order to achieve those individual objectives. When strung together, a story begins to emerge, and we see the characters more clearly. Action is, therefore, character.

Nomenclature

I want to return to the quote "How you talk about your work is how your work will happen" for a moment. At this point we need to get on the same page about the language we use when talking about acting. This is vital and will end up shaping the performance. To that end, let's get specific about action: *Action is action.* It is helpful if actors, directors, and acting teachers talk about acting this way. Action is action, period. Why is this important?

Actors play action. Actors do not play intentions; they do not play tactics; even worse, they do not play objectives or any other such misleading approximation of doing. None of these words are action. The use of such inaccurate nomenclature will lead you astray in your acting. Worse, it will put you "in your head," increase your self-consciousness, and pull your attention from your scene partner.

To point, the word *intention* implies the future and intellectualizes the act of acting. One cannot play the future in the present. If a character intends to do something, they are not actually doing it; they are *intending* to do it. What they want to do is something that they will actually do in the future, in the eventual now, which is not now, yet.

> Don't use the word *intention*. *Intention* equals *thinking*. Thinking is not action; it is not doing.
>
> —Earle Gister[8]

How would you actually "play an intention"? What I often hear in answer to this question is convoluted and circuitous or, ironically, a description of the process of playing action using different vocabulary. But words matter. Art is not sloppy; it is precise. Therefore, we must be precise in how we talk about our art form.

Usually, imprecise descriptions are removed from the actual acting experience and tend to be metaphoric or intellectual in nature. They fail to articulate with precision and detail the exact mechanics of what the actor is doing in the moment. You would never, for example, hear a car mechanic talk metaphorically about the carburetor, fuel pump, or any other part of the engine. They talk in specifics, as it is their job to do so. The same level of rigor and precision should hold true for acting. One of the core tenets of being a performing artist is how you talk about your work is how your work will happen, so we should simply call what we do by its correct name, which is action.

Likewise, a tactic is a means of achieving something, a vehicle to do something, but it is not the actual doing itself. A tactic is not an action; it is *how* you play an action; it is a qualifier of action. One must say, "My tactic is [fill in the blank]," but it is not the actual act. This is an important distinction, as *tactic* is quite often used erroneously by acting teachers, directors, and actors themselves.

The word *tactic* by definition is one step removed from the act itself. Sometimes *tactic* is used as a synonym of *action*, but it is not what happens in the actual moment. In the moment itself, something else happens—and that something is action or energy. You can't play the plan of the moment or the idea of the moment. You can only play the action of the moment. You don't *tactic* in a moment. You *do* something. That doing is the actual act that happens in the moment. A tactic, however, is *how* you do it.

The moment of engagement turns a tactic or plan into *action*, which ultimately is *energy*. For example, a SWAT team is comprised of highly trained law enforcement officers who are skilled in a variety of tactics. The word *tactic* is even embedded in the title of their elite force: Special Weapons and Tactics. They learn a host of tactics to operate across a spectrum of highly dangerous, confrontational scenarios. Yet, in the moment they get the call, they don't "go into tactics." They go into action. They are "called to action." Action is what happens when the doors of that armored vehicle fly open and they leap into *action*.

As acting also only happens in the moment, you need to be in action in your acting. What SWAT agents are actually doing is *re*acting to a set of given stimuli (i.e., their given circumstances). And that re*action* is what happens when the plan of what to do, the tactic, is transformed in the moment to the doing, to action. This isn't just an opinion; it is one of the laws of physics itself, Newton's Third Law of Motion. Action, which is motion as energy, can only happen in the present moment, and according to Newton, "To every action there is always opposed an equal reaction."[9]

In part II of this book, I explore this concept further with Stanislavski's "Five Questions." There you will see that the word *tactic* aligns not with part A of question 4, which is the *action* you play in a scene, but more precisely with part B of question 4, which is *how* you play your action in the scene. Part B of question 4, the "how," is an adverb, for adverbs qualify verbs.

If my action is to make my scene partner feel loved, then the "how"/tactic can be many adverbs: tenderly, romantically, or playfully or similarly, like a friend, like a lover, or like a niece, as there are many ways to make someone feel loved. Additionally, these words, *loved* and *tenderly*, are only used to get you started in the scene. They are active offerings you bring into the top of the scene to affect your scene partner. Once you are in the circular give and take of energy with the other actor, then you must source and respond to what they are doing to you. It is at this point that the river of action takes you into its perpetual flow, and the words you wrote in your prompt book (*loved* and *tenderly*) become spontaneous psychophysical behavior that aligns with the given circumstances from the script.

If actors are trying to act their plan for the scene (i.e., to act their tactics or intentions for the scene), then they are *thinking* about what they are doing *while they are doing it*, instead of doing what their characters are doing to move their lives forward. Working this way increases self-consciousness, which is performance interference. The actors are unable to be the moment of what transpires between them, as they are thinking about what they are doing while it is happening; this act distances the actor from the moment. They are not, therefore, in the moment.

As one often hears in acting classes, they are "in their heads." What is technically meant by this ubiquitous phrase is that their attention is on themselves. They are the target of their own attention. This self-consciousness is crippling to the actor and keeps them from targeting their attention outside themselves, which is necessary to play action. Actors who are "in their heads" recirculate their own energy back onto themselves in a never-ending cycle. Thus, the behavior is self-generated.

The First Law of Thermodynamics, the conservation of energy, dictates that "energy can neither be created nor destroyed"; accordingly, energy, action, must live in the present moment.[10] The all-too-frequent use of erroneous language by actors, directors, and acting teachers has the direct or indirect effect of putting the actors' attention back onto themselves because the language they use is not about what is actually happening in the moment. They are usually talking about a plan for the moment rather than the moment itself. This never goes well, just as trying to make a football match go a certain way never works. You can't do it. You can only respond to what is actually happening in the moment. You have to *react* to the stimuli in the now, for that is where all energy exists, and action is energy. Of course, you must have a plan going into the game, but then you activate it via reactions to what happens in real time. Accordingly, as the actor's performance takes place in the moment, action should be talked about as such by all involved.

Additionally, a director doesn't say, "Lights, camera, tactic!" or "Lights, camera, intention!" or, worst of all, "Lights, camera, feel!" They say, "Lights, camera, action!" Hamlet's advice to the players is not "Suit the intention to the word," nor is it "Suit the tactic to the word," nor is it "Suit the emotion to the word." It is decidedly written by Shakespeare, who was first and foremost an actor and who was writing for actors, to have Hamlet's advice to his actors be "Suit the *action* to the word, the word to the *action*."[11] Let's get this right. We say *action* for good reason. It's what we do as actors to bring the drama on the page to life. We act. Drama, *dran*, is doing. Doing is acting. Acting is action.

Feelings

It is not your job to feel but to make the other actor feel something.

—Earle Gister[12]

Before I go on, a word about feelings and their relationship to action is necessary. Actors love to feel. Admit it. If you are an actor, you love to feel things deeply, or you wouldn't have gotten into acting. One of the fun parts of acting, and there are many, is that you get to feel a wide variety of emotions in the safety of fiction. It isn't your life, but you get to feel *as if* it is. However, there is a catch: Just as in life, feelings arise as a result of what happens to the actor; feelings arise from action. This is true from the actor's perspective, as well as the audience's.

Feelings are born out of the movement of our lives, out of the moment; the heart of any moment is what we are doing in it. However, novice actors often mistakenly start with feelings; even experienced actors can fall into the trap. They consciously try to feel, and the result looks fake or, at least, produces a generalized emotion. No one in real life is going around trying to feel. Ask yourself right now, "Am I trying to feel something? Or, rather, am I simply living my life, doing what I am doing, and feelings arise from it?" Let me repeat: It has been my experience that the only people trying to feel something are actors either preparing to enter a scene or acting in a scene. The rest of us are just living our lives. Feelings arise from the action of our lives.

If, as an actor, you try to generate a feeling, you are, by definition, "self-generating." You have made yourself the target of your own attention to create an emotion or a desired state of being. Your attention is not on your scene partner. If your attention is not on your scene partner, then you are disconnected from the person with whom the author strategically put you in the scene. Consequently, you are not playing action, and the story isn't being told. Hence, you are not doing your job.

> An actor cannot be caught up in their own feelings; they must be caught up in the feelings of the other.
>
> —Earle Gister[13]

Feelings are, of course, part of the actor's "state of being" work. Actors *have* a state of being when they enter a scene from what is ubiquitously called the "moment before," and then they *play* action in that scene. Literally, it is that simple. First you *have* a state of being (feelings/sensations), and then you *play* action (energy). Part 1 is part of your preparation work, the invisible work, which the audience never sees. It is appropriate and necessary during this part of the work to have your attention on yourself, your instrument, and all that that entails: to align your nervous system, body, emotional life, breath, voice, and imagination with that of the given circumstances of your character. More on this in chapter 7.

However, once you are into part 2, the visible work, acting in the scene itself, then the totality of your attention must be on your scene partner, not on your state of being or your emotional life. This is a hugely important bridge, one that actors fail to make time and time again. It is essential that as soon as your character crosses the threshold from the liminal space between the moment before and the action of the scene, your attention must shift from yourself to your scene partner.

> You must be coming from some place; have a state of being when you enter the scene. Then you are here to do something that is important and immediate.
>
> —Lloyd Richards[14]

One of the frequent problems in acting is that actors tend to believe that acting is *demonstrating* the character's state of being or feeling the feelings. Returning to the football analogy, actors think that the game is about the ball, about themselves. It's not, or at least not primarily. Remember: It is about everything outside yourself, the world around you and what your character is seeing, perceiving, and receiving. Sure, you need to have ball skills.

Feelings and emotional expression are both certainly a part of your craft and, in fact, part of action itself and are dealt with in more detail in chapters 6 and 7. It's not that you don't feel things in acting. Of course, you feel when you are acting as your character would according to the given circumstances in which they find themselves. But those feelings arise from the action you play and from what you receive from your scene partner.

Creating feelings for their own sake is *not* what you should do in the moment of performance. Your job is to do what the character is doing to move their life forward in that particular moment. And they/you need to change someone else (your scene partner) in order to do that.

> On the stage there cannot be, under any circumstances, action which is directed immediately at the arousing of a feeling for its own sake.
>
> —Konstantin Stanislavski[15]

Think of it this way: If your character is not trying to feel something in the scene, then you shouldn't be trying to feel, either. Your attention should be on what your character is seeing, perceiving, and receiving from the other actor and stimuli in the scene. Your action is born out of a *reaction* to the river of action already flowing. If you are thinking about yourself, about whether you are feeling what you have predetermined your character should be feeling in the moment, then you have left the world of the script. If your attention is on yourself, then it is not on trying to change your scene partner. It is not on playing action, and then the story isn't being told. If the story isn't being told, you're not doing your job. You see how this works. It is a syllogism that bears repeating: Drama is doing; doing is action; therefore, the doing of drama is action.

Exercises

> I spent a lifetime in a garden one afternoon.
>
> —Buddha

Artist's Slow Walk

"Artist's Slow Walk" is a very simple yet profound exercise you can do to develop your powers of artistic perception. Ideally, this exercise is performed in nature, in a park, on the beach, or in a part of town where there aren't a lot of people and you won't be self-conscious about walking so slowly or fear running into someone you know.

Simply turn off your phone, put away any other electronic devices that might distract you, and walk silently in super-slow motion for thirty minutes straight. Set a timer, and don't stop until you've reached the thirty minutes. Put one foot immediately in front of the other at the pace of tai chi. Refrain from talking to anyone, unless you absolutely have to, or listening to music. You might not get very far, perhaps one hundred or two hundred yards, but you will be amazed at what transpires during this time. Remember it is not about the distance you travel but the journey you take. Slow down—way down. Open your senses, and notice what you perceive and receive.

Immediately upon finishing the walk, sit down and write in stream-of-conscious freehand about your experience. Don't edit. Just write until you have nothing else to record. Write down your honest reactions to the walk, no matter how strong or tepid they are. Notice how your body feels. Notice where your thoughts are. Notice your breathing pattern. Notice your overall state of being. Notice your senses.

At first you might find this exercise awkward; your habits may scream loudly, "We don't like this!" However, I have found that, eventually, people find this walk very meditative. Feel free to repeat it often. Treat yourself to your own "Artist's Slow Walk" once a week or so. I do an alternative version of this when I walk our dog, Minnie. I try to go to a new spot and simply walk very slowly, perhaps throwing a bone or ball to let her run while I walk. Develop your own version. Make it yours. Have fun with slowing down, and notice what happens to your powers of perception.

- **Who:** This is a solo exercise.
- **Tools:** A notebook and something with which to write.
- **Place:** A remote location away from your home neighborhood where the chances that you will run into anyone you know are slim to none. An ideal place would be somewhere in nature, away from an urban environment, like a beach or a secluded path in the woods. However, if you live in a major metropolitan area, try to find either a large park or quiet area of your town.
- **Time:** In total, both parts of this exercise take about one hour. Set aside thirty minutes to do the walking component and thirty minutes to write afterward.

Activities

Part 1: Once you are by yourself in your selected location, turn off your mobile phone or any other electronic device that could possibly distract you—no electronics whatsoever, besides, perhaps, a watch. Set an alarm for thirty minutes.

Begin by letting your lips separate ever so slightly, allowing your breath to drop in. Then repeat to yourself a minimum of three times, "I have very little time, so I am going to go very slowly." Now start to walk at a very slow pace, as if you were walking in slow motion. The pace will most likely feel unfamiliar and even somewhat uncomfortable at first. Keep going, as this is normal. Simply keep walking at this slow pace.

Notice what begins to happen as your body adjusts and you gain full balance and motor control. Keep checking in with your breath to make sure you are not holding it or tensing up. Simply remind yourself to keep your lips slightly parted, and as you walk, notice both your internal experience as well as the world around you. Continue walking this pace for the entire thirty minutes, until your alarm sounds.

Part 2: Once the thirty minutes have expired and while you are still in your chosen location, begin to write what you noticed during your walk. Simply write down your experience as fluidly as you can. What did slowing down do to you physically? Emotionally? Mentally? Did you find you were in harmony with the world around you? Or in harmony with yourself? Or perhaps you fell out of harmony with yourself as the exercise started but then slowly rediscovered it anew? Were you in flow? Or did you experience interference? Did your inner critic show up? If so, how? Why? When? What was it saying to you? How did you deal with it? Allow your writing to be complete stream of consciousness. This is purely for your edification. Punctuation, spelling, grammar, and other writing components don't matter. Just write freely and truly from your soul.

Crazy Names

The original version of this exercise appears in David Zinder's seminal book on actor training, *Body Voice Imagination* as "Crazy Names and Variations," a book I highly recommend you have on your actor's shelf.[16] It is filled with enumerable valuable tools, exercises, and wisdom on how to effectively train your instrument and is essential reading for anyone serious about growing their craft. The following series of exercises are used as ice breakers. However, I have adapted and expanded them to align more specifically with the mechanics of playing action. Virtually all the core, rudimentary, structural components of action are present in this seemingly innocuous yet playful suite of human interactions. In fact, they are microscenes disguised as playful exercises. I have found they are best suited for a group or class environment, but two actors can also perform these at the top of a first rehearsal or whenever they need to jump-start their connection. "Crazy Names" quietly works on multiple structural components of action:

1. Visual, physical, and verbal contact
2. Breath
3. Presence
4. Energy exchange

Note: This suite of exercises is a primer for playing action and scene work.

Version 1: First Name Only
1. **Visual:** Make visual contact with someone in the room.
2. **Physical:** Walk toward them, and extend your hand; begin to shake hands.
3. **Verbal:** You say, "Hi, I'm [your first name]."
4. **Verbal:** They say, "Hi, I'm [their first name]."
5. **Physical:** Keep shaking hands.
6. **Verbal:** You say, "Hi, [their first name]."
7. **Verbal:** They say, "Hi, [your first name]."
8. **Physical:** Stop shaking hands.
9. **Physical:** Walk away.

Repeat the sequence. Meet everyone in the class this way. Don't leave anyone out.

Note: Keep strictly to this text as written. Don't improvise other greetings or slip into casual conversation. Use this script only.

Version 2: First and Last Names
Use the same visual, physical, and verbal framework as in version 1.

1. Make visual contact with someone in the room.
2. Walk toward them, and extend your hand; begin to shake hands.
3. You say, "Hi, I'm [your first and last name]."
4. They say, "Hi, I'm [their first and last name]."
5. Keep shaking hands.
6. You say, "Hi, [their first and last name]."
7. They say, "Hi, [your first and last name]."
8. Stop shaking hands.
9. Walk away.

Repeat the sequence. Meet everyone in the class this way. Don't leave anyone out.

Note: Keep strictly to this text as written. Don't improvise other greetings or slip into casual conversation. Don't leave anyone out.

Version 3: Movement and Sound
Use the same framework as the first two versions.

1. Make visual contact with someone in the room.
2. Walk toward them, and extend your hand; begin to shake hands.
3. You say, "Hi, I'm [make a large physical movement and loud sound]."
4. They say, "Hi, I'm [make a large physical movement and loud sound]."
5. Keep shaking hands.
6. You say, "Hi, [their large physical movement and loud sound]."
7. They say, "Hi, [your large physical movement and loud sound]."
8. Stop shaking hands.
9. Walk away, and go meet someone else this way.

Repeat the sequence. Meet everyone in the class this way. Don't leave anyone out.

Note: both parties should repeat back the other person's movement and sound as precisely as possible!

Note: As you move on to others, *never repeat* the same movement and sound. Each time you meet someone, you must generate a new movement and sound combination.

Version 4: Famous Names
Use the same framework as previous versions.

1. Make visual contact with someone in the room.
2. Walk toward them, and extend your hand; begin to shake hands.
3. You say, "Hi, I'm [famous person]."
4. They say, "Hi, I'm [another famous person]."
5. Keep shaking hands.
6. You say, "Hi, [their famous person]."
7. They say, "Hi, [your famous person]."
8. Stop shaking hands.
9. Walk away.

Repeat the sequence. Meet everyone in the class this way. Don't leave anyone out.

Note: As you move on to others, *never repeat the same name.* In other words, you will use the name of a *new* famous person with *each person* you meet. And once a famous name is used in the room, it shouldn't be repeated by anyone else in the room.

Version 5: Made-Up Names
Use the same framework as previous versions.

1. Make visual contact with someone in the room.
2. Walk toward them, and extend your hand; begin to shake hands.
3. You say, "Hi, I'm [made-up name (e.g., Tommy Two Toes)]."
4. They say, "Hi, I'm [made-up name (e.g., Sally Backwards)]."
5. Keep shaking hands.
6. You say, "Hi, [their made-up name]."
7. They say, "Hi, [your made-up name]."
8. Stop shaking hands.
9. Walk away.

Repeat the sequence. Meet everyone in the class this way. Don't leave anyone out.

Note: As you move on to others, *never repeat the same name.* In other words, you create a new made-up name with each person you meet (e.g., you can only be Tommy Two Toes once). And once a made-up name is used in the room, it shouldn't be repeated by anyone else in the room.

Version 6: Gibberish Names
Use the same framework as previous versions.

1. Make visual contact with someone in the room.
2. Walk toward them, and extend your hand; begin to shake hands.
3. You say, "Hi, I'm [gibberish name]."
4. They say, "Hi, I'm [another gibberish name]."
5. Keep shaking hands.
6. You say, "Hi, [their gibberish name]."
7. They say, "Hi, [your gibberish name]."
8. Stop shaking hands.
9. Walk away.

Repeat the sequence. Meet everyone in the class this way. Don't leave anyone out.

Note: You must repeat their name back *exactly* as they pronounced it. Demand precision from yourself.

Note: As you move on to others, *never repeat* the gibberish name. In other words, you create a new gibberish name with each person you meet.

Version 7: First Name Only (Chaos Version)

Use the same framework as previous versions, but in this version, all members in the class must meet one another under a highly compressed amount of time, one that is appropriate to the group size. If the group took five minutes to complete version 1, then have them do this in two and a half minutes, then one minute, and then thirty seconds. Unleash the chaotic energy of fun.

Version 8: First and Last Names (Chaos Version)

Use the same framework as previous versions, but in this version, all members in the class must meet one another under a highly compressed amount of time, one that is appropriate to the group size. If the group took five minutes to complete version 1, then have them do this in two and a half minutes, then one minute, and then thirty seconds. Unleash the chaotic energy of fun.

Going Deeper into the Space Between

Up to this point, all eight versions of "Crazy Names" have served as a collective ice breaker to create human contact between all individuals in the class or ensemble. So far, everyone has literally seen one another, touched one another, sent sound to one another, exchanged energy with one another, played with one another, invented with one another, imagined with one another, and solved problems with one another. They have shared not merely their names but different parts of themselves, and they have done so multiple times.

The room is now changed. The group is now changed. Social masks have fallen. The proverbial ice has melted, and human connections are beginning to be built. The groundwork for the space between, for playing action, which is an exchange of energy between two people, has been laid. If this were a business conference, we might stop here and get on to other work at hand, as people now feel more at ease with one another. But actors must go deeper, for the fabric of the actor's craft is woven from human connection. The connections we are professionally required to make with one another must be more vulnerable than mere social greetings. Therefore, use the previous

"Crazy Names" templates and go deeper into human connection with the following suite of exchanges.

Version 9: First Name, Lips, and Mutual Breath
Use the same framework as previous versions.

1. Make visual contact with someone in the room.
2. Walk toward them, and extend your hand; begin to shake hands.
3. Before you say anything, both actors notice their own lips and let their lips separate slightly.
4. Now, take a breath together at the same time. Breathe in the other person, together.
5. After the mutual breath, you say, "Hi, I'm [your name]."
6. They say, "Hi, I'm [their name]."
7. Keep shaking hands.
8. You say, "Hi, [their name]."
9. They say, "Hi, [your name]."
10. Stop shaking hands.
11. Walk away.

Repeat the sequence. Meet everyone in the class this way. Don't leave anyone out.

Note: Keep strictly to this text as written.

Note: Notice what the added breath has changed for you, if anything.

Version 10: First Name, Two Breaths
Use the same framework as version 9, except now add a second mutual breath before you end the handshake and part. Meet everyone in the class this way.

Note: Notice what this has changed for you, if anything.

Version 11: First Name, Two Breaths, and "Nice to Meet You"
Use the same framework as version 10, except now as you take the second mutual breath at the end, add the thought "Nice to meet you." So, you both are thinking, "Nice to meet you," at the very end before you separate. Meet everyone in the class this way.

Note: Notice what this has changed for you, if anything.

Version 12: First Name with Imaginary Heart

Use the same framework as version 11, except in this version, begin by sourcing the image of your heart as you approach someone. Imagine that you are opening your heart to this person at the very beginning. Imagine sending them the image of your heart or that you are opening your heart to them. Also realize that they are doing the same for you. Meet everyone in the class this way.

Note: Notice what this has changed for you, if anything.

Version 13: First Name with Open Gesture

Use the same framework as version 12, except in this version, begin by physically opening your body in as large a gesture as you possibly can make before you shake hands. Reach your arms to the sky, and kick your legs out wide. Make yourself as open as possible. Both actors remain in the open gesture for ten seconds or longer. Take a deep breath together. Open the image of your heart to your partner. Also realize that they are doing the same for you. Then, continue with the exercise as before: shake hands, exchange names, and so on. Meet everyone in the class this way.

Note: Notice what this changed for you, if anything.

Version 14: First Name with Hug

Use the same framework as version 9, except now, if you have the impulse to hug the other actor after introducing yourselves and you sense they share that impulse, you may hug one another. Meet everyone in the class this way.

Note: Hug each other physically heart to heart. Quite often when we hug, we do so with the opposite side of our chest. Make a conscious decision in this case to hug heart to heart.

Note: Notice what this changed for you, if anything.

Version 15: First Name with Eyes of Compassion

Use the same framework as version 9, except this time, add imaginary eyes filled with compassion. See your partner through these eyes of compassion. Meet everyone in the class this way.

Note: Notice what this changed for you, if anything.

Summary

- The word for *drama* in ancient Greek, *dran*, means "to do."
- Acting is action. It is not intention, strategy, or tactic. Don't use the word *intention*. *Intention* equals *thinking*. Thinking is not action; it is not doing.

- Actors are professional human beings who tell stories via playing action. Playing action is changing your scene partner. Action (our human interactions) determines our relationships.
- Action shapes the play and creates character. Certain kinds of characters will make certain kinds of action decisions. Tell me what someone does, and I'll tell you who they are.
- Action has two parts: the action embedded in the script (invisible action) and the action in performance (visible action).
- Subtext is the meaning "below" or "under" the words, which is conveyed by playing action. Action is subtext; subtext is action.
- It's not about the words, unless you're playing Shakespeare.
- The foundation of acting is the reality of doing. The doing an actor must do is play action.
- Feelings come along in the doing. They are a by-product of action. Onstage there cannot be, under any circumstances, action that is directed immediately at arousing a feeling for its own sake. An actor cannot be caught up in their own feelings; they must be caught up in the feelings of the other. It is not an actor's job to feel but to make the other actor feel. If you are trying to create a feeling in yourself, then you are "self-generating."
- You have a state of being when you enter; you play action in the scene.
- Syllogism: Drama is doing; doing is action; therefore, drama is action.

~

CHAPTER THREE

Acting Defined

Acting is the life of the human soul receiving its birth through art.

—*Richard Boleslavsky*

What is acting actually? It's not tangible. You can't touch it; you can't bottle it; you can't pour it into a cup like coffee. It's not a commodity per se. How do we know what it is? How do we know it exists? Can we even define it? I think I must before I go on.

Across your career, you will tackle a wide variety of genres, from ancient Greek drama, Shakespeare, psychological realism, farce, and even magical realism. You will also probably perform in a wide variety of mediums: proscenium stage, three-quarters thrust, in the round, outdoor festival, single-camera drama, single-camera comedy, multicamera comedic television, feature film, video games, green screen, voice-over, and on-camera commercial, just to name a few. Therefore, a generous and all-encompassing definition of *acting* is called for, one that is as inclusive as possible. I propose the following definition:

> Inspired acting is living believably under imaginary circumstances with precise repeatability and complete spontaneity.

In a nutshell, this is what acting is and what we do as actors. We live believably under imaginary circumstances, whether onstage or in front of a camera. We do it repeatedly and with professional precision. Paradoxically, we also do it as if for the first time, each and every time. Let's examine this definition more closely and start with the word *living*.

Living

Acting is fine. Just don't get caught at it.

—Spencer Tracy

Acting should feel like life, not like acting. If it feels artificial or mechanical in any way, your work is off the mark. It might not feel like your personal, idiosyncratic life per se, nor should it. But it should feel like you're *living* the life of your character. When you are in a state of flow as an actor, the work feels effortless, like it's simply *happening to you*, like you are living the fiction yourself, which, in a sense, you are.

Whether onstage or on-screen, our artistic objective as actors is to entertain, enlighten, or inspire the audience. For that to happen, the audience needs to be swept up by the story. They need to be taken deep into the world the author imagined. In order to take them there, actors must inhabit the lives of the characters in that world. Characters indeed have lives, albeit fictional ones. They are living beings in their own fictional world. Actors must treat it as they would any life—as if it was a real life. Living is, therefore, in the DNA of the writing.

Conversely, as actors we do not "demonstrate" believably; nor do we "indicate," "show," "approximate," or "perform" believably. It is our job to *live* the character's life *as if* it were our own. To do this, we must be inspired by the script, the totality of its imagery and given circumstances, and our character. The degree to which we are inspired is the degree to which both our scene partner and audience will be inspired. Therefore, we need to have the sensation in our bodies that feels as if we are actually *living* that *life*, even though rationally we know we are acting; hence the use of the word *living* in my definition of *acting*.

Verisimilitude

Michael Chekhov made me realize that truth, as in naturalism, was far from the whole truth. In him I witnessed exciting theatrical form with no loss of inner content, and I knew I wanted this too.

—Sanford Meisner[1]

A word about verisimilitude before I go on. Quite often, living believably gets confused with living naturally. Especially in psychological realism plays from the late nineteenth through the early twenty-first centuries, present-day actors often try, mistakenly, to act natural. Let's be clear: Characters are not trying to act naturally, unless for some reason that is their objective in the scene. What they are doing is living their lives in the worlds they inhabit. Our job as actors is to go to their worlds via our imagination and live as believably as possible.

What is natural anyway? I occasionally hear from actors, "My character would never do that." How would you know? Apparently, they *do* do that because the author wrote it. Or sometimes an actor will exclaim, "I'm afraid of being too much" or "larger than life." What's too much? Let the director be the judge of that. Or the audience. And "larger than life"? Have you lived life lately? Life is large—very large. Talented authors don't write scripts about small moments in life; they write about important, quite often highly disturbing moments that are filled with meaning and dimension. Even if the scripts seem quiet, they are not small in their humanity. If you, the actor, are spending energy trying to be natural, then that, in fact, is what you are doing; your character is consumed with trying to move their life forward. Do that instead.

Believably versus Truthfully

> Truth on the stage is anything we can believe in with sincerity, whether in ourselves or in our colleagues. Truth cannot be separated from belief, nor belief from truth.
>
> —Konstantin Stanislavski[2]

A word about the word *truth*. Many acting teachers use the following definition of *acting*: "living *truthfully* under imaginary circumstances." I did as well for quite some time. That's fine. It works for many actors and teachers alike. At the end of the day, it's what you connect to most as an artist that will work for you. I agree with Stanislavski that in an ideal world, truth and belief should coexist harmoniously.

However, I personally have come to the conclusion many years later, as did Earle Gister in his own work, that the word *truth* can become problematic for the actor, and what is more actable and accessible than truthfulness is whether the performance was believable for both actor and audience alike. This may seem like splitting hairs, but that is exactly the point. How we talk about our work is how the work will happen. I have come to realize over the years that truth is relative. Truth means different things to different people. What Stanislavski is really after is the sincerity of the acting. This, I believe, is the heart of the matter.

Seemingly paradoxically, the word *truth* can actually create interference for the actor and keep them from fully expressing the character. The search for truth can become acting baggage that holds you back in your process. Actors often waste a lot of time and energy wringing their hands over whether their acting is truthful. However, more practical questions are, Do I myself *believe* what I just did? Was I *sincere* in the acting of it? If not, go back and do it again. Keep rehearsing your part until you feel as if it's really happening to you and believable to you in the act of doing it. Make believe, sincerely. Make yourself believe; make the audience believe. If you are committed to what you are doing and sincere about it, then the audience will believe you, too.

It doesn't need to feel familiar at all, just believable. There is a significant and important difference between familiar and believable. Much of the time it doesn't feel familiar, as the character's life may be very different from our own. But we can imagine that if we were dealing with similar circumstances, we could do what the character does, and it would be believable that we would do that. It's the fun part of the beautiful game of acting. We get to live a variety of imaginary lives in addition to our own. That's the agreement we all sign up for: All participants—doer and viewer—know we are all part of a game, a theatrical fiction.

Imaginary Circumstances

This part of the definition is pretty straightforward. As far as I know, two things are always true for you as an actor when you act: (1) You will always be in your own body, and (2) you will always be under imaginary circumstances. This is the intersection where acting plays out, where your body meets your imagination. Even if you are working on a reality television show, it is not your real life—far from it—and you will still need to engage your imagination, perhaps more than ever, based on the "reality" television I have unfortunately wasted my time watching.

Clearly in any scripted piece, the circumstances given to you by the author are not from your own personal life. They are imaginary, and yet you need to use your body, your voice, and your imagination to bring it to life. We need to engage our imagination to enact those facts presented to us in the script. How do we do that? We use Stanislavski's "magic if" or, more commonly, the "as if."

The "As If"

Our work on a play begins with the use of "if" as a lever to lift us out of everyday life onto the plane of imagination.

—Konstantin Stanislavski[3]

Use of the "as if" magically opens the door into your imagination. For example, if I say to myself, "I *am* Macbeth," my mind retorts, "No you're not. You're Hugh O'Gorman. You were born in New York City at Mount Sinai Hospital," and so on. But if I say, "It's *as if* I am Macbeth," then my mind goes, "Great! We are playing a game. It's *as if* we are Macbeth. This will be fun," and we are off to the races. It is so simple and so elegant and, more importantly, so reliably effective each and every time you act. You were born to imagine. The magic "if" takes you there.

Precise Repeatability

The more constraints one imposes, the more one frees one's self. And the arbitrariness of the constraint serves only to obtain precision of execution.

—Igor Stravinsky

Acting needs to be precise and repeatable. But what do we mean exactly by these words? I find it helpful to think of it this way: Art is never sloppy. Even a wildly improvised work of art, like a jazz solo, contact improv dance, or a Jackson Pollock painting is born of precision. Deep within the bones of the improvisation, there is a high level of rigor exercised by the artist, one that is grounded in a lifetime of exacting technique.

The "What"

Three major factors provide this precision, which when combined determine what you actually do while acting. These shapers of acting behavior are (1) the script, (2) the direction, and (3) your scene partner. Together they make up the "what" of acting. Let's take them one at a time.

The first is the script, as it is the original source material. It sets the boundaries of behavior for the genre of performance via the style of the writing. We as actors need to be able to read and divine these parameters as they are intentionally set by the author. More crucially, the script is the map of actions, the blueprint of behavior of the characters. It is precise, and as actors, we need to read it with the same level of precision as it was written. The author creates a specific world in which to inhabit and constrains our behavior in a helpful, creative, and specific way.

Next, a director comes along and engages us with their vision of the script. We receive their creative input, assistance, and inspiration while crafting a common vision with the ensemble. We work with the director to marry all of our individual artistic choices. Accordingly, the boundaries of our behavior as the characters get more specific and refined based on the director's vision for the script.

Finally, our scene partners, as well as the other members of the cast, bring their choices to the performance, and that, in turn, makes us even more precise, as we are compelled to *respond to what they are doing*. Likewise, we elicit responses from them, helping to shape their performances. In the Meisner technique, this is called the "pinch and the ouch."[4] The degree to which my scene partner figuratively pinches me is the degree to which I will say, "Ouch," and it must be in direct correlation to the strength of the pinch. If I "Ouch" loudly to a soft pinch, it won't be believable. The audience will question what I did based on what they actually saw me receive from my scene partner. When this happens, and it does more often than it should, we say that an actor is "self-generating." They are generating the "Ouch" on their own as part of their *idea* of how the scene and their acting should go. But as I have already stated, you can't act an idea, strategy, tactic, intention, or plan. You can *have* a plan, but you must *play* action. That means, if you want the audience to believe you, you must *react* directly to what you receive from your scene partner and in proper relation to the size, scope, and dimension of that stimulus.

> Acting to me is always reacting.
>
> —Spencer Tracy

Often, I'll say to an actor working in the studio, "Your partner threw you an orange, and you threw back a grapefruit." If someone throws you a metaphoric orange, that's what you toss back. If they throw you an apple, throw the apple back. Don't try to turn the orange into a grapefruit, even if you think that's the way the scene should go, because it's not going that way. When you do that, you're trying to fight the current of action by turning the moment into something it isn't. You are trying to act your plan for the scene or how you think the scene should go. You are trying to act your homework. But homework must be left at home. You can't act an idea if you want your work to be believable. You can only *react* to the actual stimuli in front of you, both imagined and real. The audience will detect the inherent behavioral lie in what you are doing. And if you do that while on camera, God help you. The camera is the world's biggest lie detector and will catch you acting your plan each and every time.

At the end of the day, we have three precise parameters that give shape and substance to our acting: the script, the direction, and our scene partners. Then, if we are in the theater, we repeat this night after night; and, if we are on camera, we repeat it take after take. All this comprises the "what" of the doing. It is precise and repeatable.

The "How"

Here's the sticky wicket: That doesn't mean that how you perform is the same from night to night or take after take. The "how" always changes. According to the Second Law of Thermodynamics, how you play the action in any scene can never go the same way twice, as time moves constantly forward.[5] The same can be said of a soccer match. It is impossible to repeat how the game went. Certainly, games can be played over, yet they will never be the same from the moment of the first whistle onward. Scenes can be repeated and must be done so precisely, but they will never go the same way twice. Just like you can't take a photograph of the future, neither can you relocate yourself back in a moment that already happened and relive it, at least not until time travel is mastered. Yet actors try all the time to do just this, with staggeringly poor results.

Accordingly, the "how" of the scene always changes. The "what" does not change. The "what" is always precise and repeatable. The "how" is always spontaneous. This brings us to "complete spontaneity."

Complete Spontaneity

Inspired acting is always spontaneous. At its best, acting is free play; it is an improvisation within a set of boundaries. Those behavioral boundaries, both real and imagined, comprise the "what" of your performance: the script, the direction, and your scene partner's performance. However, your *reactions* in the moment to all real and imagined stimuli must always remain fluid and spontaneous. Great actors working at the top of their game are akin to a jazz ensemble riffing off one another; listening with an otherworldly acuteness, responding to each and every rhythm, note, and beat change; deeply curious about what their colleague is going to do next. Just like accomplished jazz musicians, or soccer players for that matter, actors at the peak of their abilities understand that their work is lifted to new heights by the mere fact that they have no idea what is going to happen next. If you know for sure how it is going to go, where's the thrill? True artists and athletes embrace the unknown. In fact, they seek it. Releasing into what Declan Donnellan calls the "actor's faith" is the only road to inspiration in performance.

As Donnellan clearly lays out in *The Actor and the Target*, you have two choices as an actor, and the choice is a highly uncomfortable one: You can choose "certainty," or you can choose "faith," but you can't have both simultaneously.[6] You must choose. Of course, it is only through faith that your work can remain spontaneous. What's more, a great actor, a jazz musician, and a soccer player all implicitly trust their abilities, their bodies, their imaginations, and their experiences to handle the task at hand. They trust that their instrument will deliver what is necessary for the scene, as will their colleagues. The more you work as an actor, the more the improvisatory nature of the work becomes desirable rather than something to fear.

> Acting is an improvisation within a set of behavioral boundaries, fictional and real.
>
> —Lloyd Richards[7]

Of course, this spontaneous behavior is contained within certain boundaries. Life is the same. Even now as you read this sentence, you have no idea what exactly will happen next—not with 100 percent certainty. You might have an idea, but everything is possible at all times, within certain boundaries, which are your current given circumstances. You think you will be able to finish reading this chapter and then make a pot of tea and check your e-mails before reading the next chapter. But you may get a call saying that a friend has been admitted to the hospital, or especially if you live in Los Angeles, the earth might start shaking and change your plans. Life is ultimately unpredictable.

This unpredictability is both powerful and liberating once you embrace it. It allows for the element of surprise. Great acting is filled with constant and ongoing surprises, and nothing likes surprises more than the camera. If your acting isn't surprising to you, to your scene partner, and to the audience, then you aren't fully in the moment, you aren't fully in action, and it probably isn't your best, most inspired work.

Inspired acting happens as if for the first time, each and every time.

—Earle Gister[8]

Control freaks have a tough time with acting. Usually they are not very good at it. After a spell toiling in the acting trenches, they either get out of the business altogether or become directors, who love being in control. Control freaks are looking for "certainty" in performance, and they will never find it. Control is an illusion at best or delusional at worst, even in life writ large. Control in performance is what we simply call "bad acting"; it's wooden, mechanical, and disconnected from the spontaneous nature of life. Inspired acting asks the actor to embrace the improvisatory nature of the moment and let go of any desire to control. Actors must willfully release into their artistic energy and joyfully invite spontaneity.

However, like for the soccer player, this spontaneity is not random. It has certain parameters. It lives like a flowing river within the banks of behavior orchestrated by the script, the director, and what you are *perceiving* and *receiving* from the other actors in the scene.

The River of Action

The action of acting is like the current of a river. Like any river needs banks, acting needs boundaries in order to flow with purpose and direction. When we talk of a river, do we talk only of the water? Or do we also talk of its banks, shape, power, flow, and size as if it were alive? A river has an energy; a source and a terminus; a beginning, a middle, and an end. So, too, we talk of acting. In this analogy, the river's current is the actor's action. Like water in a river, if you put your proverbial acting vessel into it, you may have an initial *idea* of the direction you are headed, but once you actually hit the water, the experience of the current is going to take you where it wants, no matter what. The same is true in acting. Your idea of the flow is not the same thing as the actual flow itself.

You certainly have a final destination in mind, which is downstream (the character's superobjective). You have various rest stops or landmarks along the route (scene objectives). And you have a certain path you follow determined by the shape, size, pitch, and contour of the river banks (given circumstances, direction, and the other actors), which is the structure dictated by the script. Yet once you jump into that current of action, *it takes you* along for the ride. No matter how experienced and sure a sailor you are, no matter how steady your steering and navigation, the river has the power, and it will take you spontaneously downstream. You must play inside the structure of the script, which are the banks, but it is the power of the energy of the flow of the current of action that takes you along for the ride. Let me repeat: The current takes you along for the ride. So, too, in acting. What you can do, however, is steer within the experience of it. Playing action is the steering mechanism.

> The river of action takes you along for the ride, and you can never enter it in the same place twice.

Once you breathe, release the desire for control, and allow for spontaneous impulses, then and only then will your acting take on power, freedom, and beauty. A true sailor knows how to read the current and tides. So, too, must the actor. The true sailor knows how to harness the power of the natural movement around them. So, too, must the actor. Just like the soccer player, once the referee blows the whistle, the game begins, and it takes on a movement of its own. The footballer can only respond to what actually happens on the field. As an actor, you not only must read the movement of action, both invisible and visible, but you also must learn how to get yourself in flow, in the service of both your character and the play.

To recap:

> Inspired acting is living believably under imaginary circumstances with precise repeatability and complete spontaneity.

This, then begs the question, what does one actually do to live believably? This takes us to playing action itself.

Exercises

> Transformation—that is what the actor's nature, consciously or subconsciously, longs for.
>
> —Michael Chekhov[9]

Crossing the Threshold

You are the instrument you play when you act. To live believably under imaginary circumstances with precise repeatability and complete spontaneity, you must be the most finely tuned version of yourself that you can be. Just like a musician who tunes their instrument before a concert, you, too, must develop a habitual process of tuning yourself before you play. If transformation is the ultimate goal in your acting, then you must be as in tune with yourself as possible. You are the artistic zero point for all the characters you will ever inhabit; you are the material you mine when you imagine and give shape to a role.[10] Accordingly, the degree to which you are in tune with yourself and can take active stock of and make use of all your assets is the degree to which you will be able to reliably summon yourself in service of the characters you play.

Michael Chekhov is clear that true transformation is not possible from your daily self (lower self). You can only transform from your artistic self (higher self). The following is a series of exercises to help you transition from your daily self into your artistic self. Together they comprise a Chekhovian process called "Crossing the Threshold." This process follows a flow of first gathering your attention, then engaging your imagination and incorporating imagery, which leads you to inspiration. It is the path of:

Concentration → Imagination → Incorporation → Inspiration

Beauty awakens the soul to act.[11]

This is where we are headed: beauty. Beauty awakens our soul and inspires our acting. As our objective is to make a work of art, each and every time we start our work, it is helpful to remind ourselves of this noble mission. As actors, we are missionaries in service of beauty.

Start by Stopping

Like in a martial arts dojo, you will start your process from "off the mat." Lean against a wall or find a spot along the periphery of your acting studio, and give yourself a couple of minutes to simply stop and "be" off the mat. In the center of the room, on the mat, is where your art lives. For now, you are standing in the quotidian wings of your work, looking into your dojo.

First and foremost, acting is about showing up, and you showed up. You can't act if you're not there. Your daily self got you here. That's good. You're here. Give yourself a pat on the back for that, for showing up.

Start by stopping: Just stop for a moment and "be." Remind yourself that you don't need to prove anything; you don't need to get anything right; you can simply give yourself a few minutes of "being" before you begin your work. You have nowhere to go, nowhere to be, other than right here, right now. Simply stop and breathe. Simply start by stopping.

Hopes and Dreams

Then, after a few minutes (or however long you need), allow some space in your consciousness for your hopes and dreams to visit you. What are the images of yourself in the work? Do you see yourself on a Broadway stage, taking a bow? Do you see yourself on a film or TV set? Starting your own theater company? Writing a new script? What you do today in the room is in service of these long-term goals. Hopes and dreams get us out of bed in the morning. They keep us going, they fuel us, and they are images that we can source for motivation. Spend some time with them. They are ultimately why you are training today.

Today's Goal

Then, give yourself a specific, intrinsic *goal* for being in the room today. Why are you here today? What impulse brought you in the room today? Why are you here right now? This goal can be an image, a thought, an idea, or even a psychophysical sensation. It should not be academic or analytical in nature but more a desire to work on a specific aspect of your work. Think of this work session as an *opportunity* to discover something about yourself in your work, and what a gift that is. Ask yourself, "How can I move my art forward today, right now?"

The Last Acting Class

Visualize yourself standing here and now in your daily self. Ask yourself, "What might shift in me right now if this were the only opportunity I ever had to work on my acting?" Then ask yourself, "What might shift in me right now if this were my last acting class ever?" Breathe in some gratefulness for the opportunity to work on your craft.

Instrument Scan/Right Here, Right Now (Head, Heart, Will)

Stanislavski divides the actor's instrument into three trainable areas: the head (intelligence and imagination), the heart (emotional life), and the will (desires and doing). We always must work from where we are, no matter what is happening to us in our lives at that moment. As humans, we have no other choice. Acting always happens in the intersection of your body, the imagination, and the moment. You need a process of self-analysis to determine where you are in your head, heart, and will when you arrive at the theater or on set. The following is a simple way to check your instrument in each of these discernable areas before beginning your work:

- **Head:** Place a hand on your forehead and ask yourself, "What's in my head today? Where are my thoughts right now? Are my thoughts in the past, present, or future? Are my thoughts positive or negative? Are my thoughts short or long? Are my thoughts calm and centered or frantic and chaotic?" Simply listen to your thoughts, and notice them with objective observation, without judgment (more on this in chapter 5).
- **Heart:** Next, place your hand over your heart. Ask yourself, "Where are my emotions right now? Are my emotions aligned with my thoughts?" Simply listen to your emotional life, and notice where you are today with objective observation, without judgment.
- **Will:** Next, place your hand on your will center (in the middle of the pelvic girdle). Ask yourself, "What am I desirous of right now? What is it I really want and need to do right now? Are my desires aligned with my emotions and thoughts?" Simply listen to your desires, and notice them with objective observation, without judgment.

Then, feel what it's like to be in your body overall kinesthetically. Are you energized? Relaxed? Stiff? Tense? Tired? Alert? Ready? Lethargic?

Then ask yourself, "Where is my overall energy level today? Are my desires, thoughts, and emotions connected or are moving in different directions?" This is where you are right here, right now, in your daily self. And this is always just perfect because it's exactly where you are.

Note: Remind yourself that there is no right or wrong when scanning.

Note: Simple, honest, objective observation of the daily self is the goal.

Engine of Energy/Your Inner Rhythm

Actors are sculptors of energy under imaginary circumstances. Accordingly, you need to be acutely aware of your own engine of energy, which is the combination of your heartbeat and your breath. You can't go more than six minutes without this combo. The combined beats of your heartbeat and breath comprise your inner rhythm, the energy source for your creative individuality.

Heartbeat. Direct the target of your attention to your heartbeat. If you need to, place your fingers on your opposite wrist or on your neck to feel your pulse, or place one hand directly on your heart. Listen to your heartbeat. Notice the expansion and contraction of the beat. Breathe in some gratefulness for this gift of a beat. Your heartbeat is one-half of your inner rhythm.

Breath. Direct the target of your attention to your breath. Listen to your breath. Notice the expansion and contraction of your lungs. Feel the temperature of the air you breathe in and out. Breathe in some gratefulness for this gift of breath. Your breath is the other half of your inner rhythm.

Total Inner Rhythm. Now allow your attention to hold space for both your heartbeat and your breath simultaneously. This combination of heartbeat and breath make up your entire inner rhythm. This is the core source of your energy, your ki, chi, or prana. This is the dance of the divine inside you, the engine of energy for your creative individuality.

Note: If your attention wanders, and it likely will, as you're human, simply practice "Notice, Stop, Redirect."

Heat Circles and Social Mask

Now that you have gotten in touch with your engine of energy, your inner rhythm, you will want to get some heat and energy moving throughout your body. Come off the wall, and stand with your feet a little wider than shoulder width. Bend your knees slightly, and begin to rub your hands together, creating some heat between them. As you continue to rub your hands together, circling your hands in front of you, make four large circles to the right between your head and pelvic region.

As you continue to rub your hands together, reverse directions and make four large circles to the left. Once your hands are sufficiently warm, place the heels of your palms over your eye sockets, completely blocking out any light. Allow your eyes to fully relax for fifteen to thirty seconds. Next, slide your fingers and palms down your face, massaging your forehead, nose, cheekbones, and jaw, pulling off your social mask as you go. Repeat this three times.

> A simple way to woo the reluctant or impatient urge within you might be to create a vision based on the method, a vision of yourself as already having acquired all the techniques. Such a vision will set to work within you of its own accord. The suggested vision will facilitate and speed the absorption of the technique, which in turn will facilitate and speed your professional work.
>
> —Michael Chekhov[12]

Imagine It, See It, Be It: Stepping into Your Artistic Self

Part of your practice involves visualizing your artistic self and then incorporating that image into your body. This is an image of yourself completely free of interference, possessing all the desirable qualities you wish to manifest in your acting. It is an image of you at your fullest artistic potential. It's the part of you called on when you perform. It is not the daily self, not the side of you that goes grocery shopping. Rather, it is the energy in you reserved and dedicated to creating beauty.

To build new habits, you need to replace the old ones with images of the new habits you want to develop. You must visualize the aspects of your work, or habits, that you want to change and replace them with healthy, positive, more productive ones. Your body, given this new direction in which to grow, will respond almost immediately to this new imagery. Given consistent, disciplined practice over time, your body will eventually incorporate them fully into your acting. Your acting will accordingly improve. But you need to show it the way, through your artistic self and imagery.

Imagine It. Close your eyes, and imagine a deep, dark night, one so black it is free of any imagery. Do this for at least thirty seconds. Then, onto that blank black screen in your mind's eye, visualize a positive image of yourself in your acting. Imagine a version of yourself the way you want to see yourself in your work. This image represents your artistic self.

See It. Refine the image of yourself. In your mind's eye, zoom in on particular aspects of yourself in your work that you want to address in today's work. Add to this imagery certain qualities that you want to possess in your acting. See yourself adding these qualities to your work. The composite imagery represents your artistic self, the self you want to be in your acting.

Be It. To "be it," you will need to incorporate this new image into your body, which brings us to the next step of literally crossing the threshold and stepping into that image.

Crossing the Threshold/Incorporating the Image

Imagine a threshold between where you now stand (along the periphery) and the center of your studio. The center of the space is where your artistic work lives. You are about to step out of your daily self and go there, into your artistic self. In your mind's eye, give that imaginary threshold a color, texture, or sound. This is the imaginary membrane that separates your daily life from your artistic life. It's like stepping onto the mat in a dojo. In a moment, you will step through that imaginary translucent wall.

First, visualize your artistic self on the other side of that wall, in the work. See yourself in the center of the room; see yourself in your art; see yourself in beauty. Perhaps you see yourself on the top of an alpine mountain on a gorgeous summer day, arms stretched to the sky, radiating joy, ease, confidence, spontaneity, form, faith, permission, wholeness, freedom, and beauty. See yourself in the zone, in flow, fully in the moment, radiating in the space between.

In your mind's eye, visualize this image as a life-sized hologram standing about three feet in front of you. See it looking at you. Imagine it reaches out its arm as if to say, "Let's begin. Let's play!" If they are not already, now open your eyes, and imagine that you are stepping *out* of the image of your daily self. Like a superhero taking off its costume, you leave the image of your daily self standing there for the duration of your training session. Not to worry: It will always be there to come back to!

Now move through the imaginary wall, and step *into* the image of your artistic self. Let your body *incorporate* the image of your artistic self. "Listen" to the image kinesthetically with your body; allow it to feed you with the qualities it possesses. Let the imagery do its work and resonate throughout your body. Then take your artistic self for a walk around the room, incorporating other positive imagery as you go. Your artistic self is always ready to work, play, and grow. Only your daily self habitually gets in the way of your work.

Stop and look back to where you crossed the threshold. Imagine you can see your daily self standing there. Realize you are now standing in your art, in your beauty, in your artistic self. You are standing in a sea of creative freedom and permission. Imagine it's *as if* you are now weightless, and the image is lifting you upward. Imagine now that the image begins to walk you around the room.

Note: some actors are very visual and will have a sharp picture of their artistic self in their mind's eye; they will have no problem visualizing the qualities of their other they want to improve. Other actors work more kinesthetically and experience imagery in their bodies as a sensation rather than an image. In sports psychology this is called a "feelmage." For you, *feel* the *image* (feelmage) in your body more than you see it. Some actors toggle back and forth between those two relationships with imagery depending on the circumstance. All are equally valid.

Expanding and Contracting

Continue to move about your studio in your artistic self. Then make yourself as big as possible. Allow your whole body to expand into an enormous open gesture, expanding your limbs as far as they can go, your chin floating up ever so slightly as you look up at a forty-five-degree angle. Sustain this gesture by imagining that your limbs continue forever. Take up as much physical and vocal space as you can. Imagine that the image of your artistic self expands you beyond your physical limitations. Imagine that you go on forever. Say to yourself, "I awaken the sleeping muscles of the body."

"Listen" psychophysically to what this gesture does for you internally; let it fill you, and listen to it when it's done:

- Your mind will wander, or
- Your body will tell you it's done.

Go back to a neutral position, and then make yourself as small as possible. Do the same in the opposite direction by contracting your body. Move back and forth between expanding and contracting physically and vocally. Listen to the sensations in the body! Take your artistic self for a walk around the studio with lightness and ease. If the sensations fade, reignite with a new gesture.

Layered Walking

All acting plays out at the intersection of the body and the imagination. You will always be in your body when you act, and you will always be under imaginary circumstances. This exercise layers into your body slight physical adjustments along with imagery as you simply walk in your studio, or anywhere for that matter. You can use this, for example, as you walk from your car across the studio parking lot as you arrive for an audition. Fundamentally, the way it works is that as you walk, you make a physical adjustment with your body or you incorporate a new image in your body or both. You then notice the effects of those adjustments to your artistic energy. The overall objective of the exercise is to create performance-level energy and readiness in your body.

Imagery: Before you begin walking, take a moment to reconnect with your purpose, which is to perform. Now imagine your performance as a gorgeous cliff high above an endless sea off in the distance, for as we transition from preparation to performance, we must always take the final leap of faith off that proverbial cliff. The sea below represents your creativity. As an actor you are always heading toward a "performance": an audition, rehearsal, opening night, filming, interview, PR junket, or even acting class. How you prepare your body, imagination, and energy to approach the performance cliff will determine how your leap of faith goes. Showtime, "go time," always arrives. You want to positively prepare the energy in your instrument accordingly for that moment.

Imagery: In your mind's eye, see your "performance cliff" off in the distance. That's where you are headed.

Physical: Start walking toward your imaginary performance cliff, and don't stop walking until you reach it at the end of the exercise.

Imagery: Source the image of your artistic self as you walk. Incorporate the image into your body (step into it), and imagine that it is this part of you (your artistic side) that walks you around the room, not your daily self. Let this image take you for a walk. Imagine that it is doing the work for you and lifts you up as you go. Your artistic self is always ready to work.

Physical: As you walk, let your chin physically float up ever so slightly, and notice what happens. Your mother was right: "Keep your chin up." It's harder for the brain to hang onto negative thoughts when you are physically looking up.[13] Keep your chin up.

Imagery: Continue walking as you add an image of a large, bright, hot sun in the center of your chest; this is the image for your engine of energy, what Michael Chekhov calls the actor's ideal center. Allow the positive imagery of this sun to expand you as you walk. Imagine that you are radiating luminosity and lightness of being to everyone and everything around you from your ideal center.

Physical: As you walk, notice the gaze of your eyes; keep your eye line up off the ground (hopes and dreams don't live on the floor). Look toward the horizon, off toward your imaginary performance cliff in the distance. Eyes up.

Imagery: Imagine that you are being pulled by a magical wire attached to your sternum. The image can be anything: rope, wire, chain, laser beam, leather, a sound, string of pearls, and so on. It pulls you forward effortlessly and with ease. It's as if you are being pulled through life with no effort on your part. The image does the work.

Physical: As you walk, notice your lips, and if they are touching each other, let them now part slightly, allowing your breath to drop in more fully as you walk.

Imagery: Imagine it's as if the performance cliff is getting closer and closer with each step you take. Hear the stage manager saying, "Places everyone"; it's almost showtime.

Physical: Take a slightly larger step than you normally do, and notice what happens. Literally step out of your habitual walking pattern. Step out of your habit. Cover more ground with each step.

Imagery: Imagine it's as if you are walking with the quality of movement of joy or confidence or ease or beauty or power or whatever quality you want to possess for your performance. Allow the quality of that movement to infuse your body and affect how you approach your performance cliff.

Physical: Roll through your foot, pushing off with your toes. You are actively moving forward into life, not sinking back on your heels. Your purpose is strong, so let your walk be, too. Your toes propel you forward as you move toward the ever-closer performance.

Imagery: Imagine you are being pushed from behind by a strong, steady wind: "May the wind always be at your back." It's as if the wind effortlessly lifts you as you walk. It lifts your feet, your legs, your arms, your back. You're simply being blown through life with no effort on your part. Allow the image to do the work for you.

Physical: Get your arms physically involved in your walking motion; pump with the feeling of the form as you walk.

Imagery: Imagine you have long, inner limbs that live inside your physical limbs—arms and legs that are attached to the image of the sun in the center of your chest. Give them a fun and dynamic color or texture. Let the imaginary legs take the physical legs for a walk. Let the imaginary arms take the physical arms for a walk.

Imagery: Now walk as if you are weightless.

Imagery: Allow an imaginary inner smile begin to form. You are smiling on the inside, excited to perform. You live for this. Your desire for the space between is alive in you.

Physical: Pick up your tempo until you are almost running, and then, in your mind's eye, as you arrive at the lip of your imaginary performance cliff—

Physical: Jump up into the air as if you are jumping off the imaginary cliff. Let go into trust, intuition, surrender, faith, and the creative subconscious.

Physical: When you land, immediately expand your body as much as possible in an open gesture and say, "Yes!" out loud. Take your space unapologetically. Say, "Yes!" to your performance, your ability, your experience, your preparation, your faith in your talent, and your trust in how your performance will go.

Physical: Say to yourself, "I'm ready," for you are.

Summary

- Acting is fine. Just don't get caught at it.
- Inspired acting is living believably under imaginary circumstances with precise repeatability and complete spontaneity. It happens as if for the first time, each and every time. It is always improvisatory within behavioral boundaries; at its best, it is free play. The more constraints one imposes, the more one frees one's self. And the arbitrariness of the constraint serves only to obtain precision of execution.
- The key to unlocking your imagination is Stanislavski's "magic if." You *live* the character's life *as if* it were your own. It is not your job to be natural. Your job is to move the character's life forward.
- The word *truth* can sometimes create interference in acting.
- If you believe what you are doing, then the audience will, too. Keep rehearsing until you believe it yourself, until it feels as if it's really happening to you.

- When you act, (1) you will always be in your own body, and (2) you will always be under imaginary circumstances.
- The three major shapers of your acting are (1) the script, (2) the direction, and (3) your scene partner. Together they make up the "what" of acting. The script is the map, the blueprint of behavior for the actor. Acting becomes more specific based on the director's vision. You are compelled to respond to what your scene partner does. You can only *react* to the actual stimuli in front of you, imagined and real; acting is always reacting. This "what" of the acting is what you do as the character in your scenes night after night, take after take. It must be repeatable.
- The "how" of acting is always spontaneous. The "how" of the scene always changes, so it can never go the same way twice. The "what" does not change.
- Acting is like a river; its current is action. The river of action takes you along for the ride, and you can never enter the same place twice. You navigate within the experience of its banks. Playing action is the steering.

CHAPTER FOUR

Playing Action

The foundation of acting is the reality of doing.

—Sanford Meisner[1]

If a workable definition of *inspired acting* is "living believably under imaginary circumstances with precise repeatability and complete spontaneity," and if acting is doing, then as an actor, you must next ask yourself, "What do I actually *do* to 'live believably'?"

Twentieth-century American actor, acting teacher, and theorist Sanford Meisner states, "The foundation of acting is the reality of doing."[2] Doing is how we live believably. More concretely, acting is not the approximation of doing or the imitation of doing or the demonstration of doing. Acting is the *reality* of doing under imaginary circumstances. However, this then begs another question: What exactly is the reality of doing? The answer is *playing action.*

Have you sat across a room from someone you find attractive when suddenly that person looks right at you? Your heart skips a beat, your palms start sweating, and your breath quickens. The French call this a coup de foudre, and it is a striking example of energy exchanged between two people, or what actors call playing action. This energy exchange is when the space between comes to life, crackling with humanity and electricity. It's what we mean when we say two people have great chemistry. There is a connection between them that can be noticed and felt by others. Actors also describe this as "sending and receiving" or "exchanging energy." Our bodies experience both a *release* outward while—and here's the catch—simultaneously *receiving* what the other person is sending us. It is a mutual *radiating* and *receiving*, born of listening and perceiving, creating communion between two or more actors. Cumulatively, this exchange of energy produces the connection between two people, or what we call a relationship.

The "reality of doing" is playing action. As an actor, you already know that the currency of the actor's craft resides in the moment. Your work as an actor happens in the now. Stanislavski names this moment-to-moment work "action."[3] But what is that exactly? And how do you do it? If you want to arrive at a professional level of specificity in your work, you must take a closer look.

The Action

The reality of the doing is playing action.

As action is doing, *action* exists as a verb for the actor. Accordingly, beginning acting classes introduce *action* as a verb, and this is how most actors understand it. At first, this is appropriate. However, with experience, we arrive at a more precise understanding of *action* and realize that a verb is a vehicle of change. It is, in fact, your scene partner who is changed by the verb.

If you are acting in a seduction scene, you might rightly assume that the corresponding verb is *seduce*. But what happens when two people seduce each other? There is a cause-and-effect exchange of energy between those two people that results in a change of feelings, which then drive behavior. If the feelings of both characters are changed, then the corresponding event (the seduction) is successful. If the feelings are not reciprocated, then the event (the seduction) is not successful. Either way, the resulting emotional shift, due to the exchange of energy, drives the resulting behavior.

However, if you are acting a verb, then much of your attention is still on yourself: "I seduce." The focus is still on the *I*, on what *I* am doing. You need to turn the verb into action and release that action onto your partner. To do this, you must ask yourself, "When I seduce someone, what is the effect I have on them?" This slight but incredibly important adjustment in turn redirects the target of your attention off yourself and onto your scene partner, onto the person you are seducing. If you seduce someone, it is their state of being that is ultimately affected. You want to make them feel special, turned on, sexually excited, and so on. They, the other, are the focus of all your attention. In order to do this, you need to move beyond the idea of action as a verb. It is, in fact, the *energy* you release onto your scene partner that activates the seduction.

This brings us to our initial definition of *playing action:*

> Playing action is an *exchange of energy* to *make the other actor feel something.*

This exchange of energy must change the other actor, not alter your *idea* of the other character in the scene, but *affect* the other *actor.* Your job is to make the *other* actor, who is the other character, *feel* what you need them to feel so they will do what you want them to do. This exchange of energy is not random. Playwrights attach a specific purpose to it, and Stanislavski calls this purpose, or motivation, the objective.[4]

The Objective

Every objective must carry within itself the germ of action.

—Konstantin Stanislavski[5]

As I have established, actors perform actions under imaginary circumstances. Everything you do as an actor (or character) onstage must be for a reason, what is called the objective. Otherwise, why are you there? Your character's behavior is not arbitrary. The author carefully crafted the character's objective for each scene, and that objective drives your behavior. The character needs you to identify with the objective and add your acting impulses and imagination to lift it into the dimension of a fully realized human being. The objective provides the purpose for each scene; the action gets it done. In well-written scripts, there is only one objective per scene per character, as there is only one event.

The Need

See the result achieved. That is the objective for me.

—Michael Chekhov[6]

The objective can also be called the character's need. They need something to improve their lot in life, to move their life forward, as it were. In fact, I prefer the vigorous word *need* over the intellectual word *objective* or even the less forceful word *want. Need* is more human, relatable, and active, providing behavioral fuel for the actor's fire. Something you *need* is stronger, more immediate, and more palpable in the body than something you merely *want.*

As an actor, you can psychophysically drop a need into your body through the use of imagery, or what Michael Chekhov calls the psychological gesture. The energy of the need is generated off-stage before the scene begins. You can induce it at a visceral level so that you enter vibrating with the character's desire. This preparation creates "where the character is coming from," or the "moment before." Then, that force gets *released* outward onto your scene partner as the visible action during the scene. There is more on how to do this in the second part of the book.

You must use the other character(s) in the scene to satisfy that need. Characters don't move onto new actions until they achieve their need or give up. This point is explained further in question 5 of the "Five Questions" in chapter 7. It follows, then, that you, the actor playing the character, must pursue that goal until the end. You and your character together will either succeed or fail, and you will have one action to play per scene to meet that need. How you play that action depends on the beat changes in the text, the director's input, and how your scene partner affects you. How that action is played changes all the time, moment to moment. The "what," the need, stays the same while the "how" is ever-changing. This understanding refines our definition of *playing action* even further:

> Playing action is an exchange of energy, *purposefully directed,* to make the other actor feel something *in pursuit of a need.*

On a final note, it is not enough to understand your character's need in a scene analytically or intellectually. You must transfer it from the page of the script into a psychophysical experience in your body. An effective way to do this is to ask your imagination to create images for the need in each scene. As Michael Chekhov suggests, visualize the result achieved. Find the image of the desire, the need. This image will awaken your will to act. Imagery works on our subconsciouses and changes us physically, emotionally, and intuitively.

Have fun imagining vibrant images of what your character needs in each scene. Then source those images in your imagination before the scene begins. Imagery is one way to turn an idea into a playable action. Pictures are energy and can be measured as electrical impulses in the brain. As soon as you begin to source an image, you move into action. Images are electric. Use them. However, a character's needs are always themselves in the service of the larger event of the scene.

The Event

Stanislavski suggested actors should begin their work on a play by studying the important events in the story that forms the basis of the plot.

—Maria Osipovna Knebel[7]

Each well-written dramatic scene has only one principal event. The event is the reason the scene is in the script. It is the scene's purpose. In other words, the author wrote that scene for that particular event to happen, to force all characters in the scene to move through the event together, react to it, and be changed by it. There is no dramatic conflict without an event. The conflict in the event changes the characters when it happens along with their actions. The bulk of the scene is spent with all characters trying to make that event come to fruition. We know that an action is inseparable from a specific need, and we can say that the change of one action to a new action is a new event. Thus, needs and events are also inextricably intertwined.

Stanislavski says the primary action of each event is determined by the "leading circumstance."[8] Out of all the given circumstances from a scene, the leading circumstance is the principal or primary circumstance that dictates everyone's behavior. If the event is a funeral, then everyone more or less knows how to behave. If the event is a wedding, then everyone will behave differently than at a funeral. If the event is a rock concert, then they will again behave differently than at a wedding. The leading circumstance for any event is the same for all the characters in the scene. It is objective. *How* each person *responds* and acts in this event is what makes the characters individuals. Their *reactions* to the event are *subjective*. We go to the theater or cinema to watch characters react to certain circumstances.

The simplest way to think about events is to realize they are always a noun, and there is only one per scene: a class, a match, a ceremony, a show, a seduction, a confession, a fight, a discovery, and so on. That event (noun) determines how everyone will behave (verb) due to its leading circumstance. Events, therefore, dictate our behavior, hence the objectivity of an event. How each individual *reacts* in the event determines their individual character, or how each of the characters differ from one another, hence the subjectivity.

Furthermore, as events are things, or nouns, they have an entry point and an exit point. For example, it is easy to recognize that a class is an event. All classes have a beginning, middle, and end. In other words, the experience of the event called a class has temporal boundaries that work on all the characters. The participants of a class are universally clear when they enter the class, when they exit the class, and what roles they play during that event. They know, more or less, how to behave and that the leading circumstance of any class is to move knowledge forward, to learn. Everyone participating in a class is engaged in the action of the class, no matter their role, teacher and student alike.

Think about any of your classes from high school. You can go person by person through that class and identify your classmates' characters, who they are, by *how* they behaved in class. The class clown was joking around all the time, which pissed off the nerd, who was trying to pay attention and actually learn. The stoner stared out the window or slept through class with headphones wrapped around their tinted glasses. The artist was drawing on the cover of their textbook, while the musician was writing songs in theirs, and the theater kid was singing sotto voce in the back corner. The bully was jealously staring down the cheerleader, who was playing with her hair and kicking the chair of the jock in front of her, who in turn was passing love notes to the valedictorian sitting front row center in the hopes of getting her help on the upcoming exam. Everyone collectively behaved a certain way because they were all students in an event called a class. Everyone was *objectively* in an *event*, a *class*. But who they are, their *character*, was determined by *how they reacted* to that *event*. Their reactions to the event are *subjective*.

Other examples of events as a noun are reconciliation, confrontation, goodbye, welcome, birth, kiss, and robbery, among others. As your first job as an actor is to make the event happen in service of the play, you must ask yourself, "What is the event in this scene?" The reason for this is that all linear storytelling is simply a sequence of events. A story, at its bare bones, is nothing more than one event after another. For example, if we were able to take an X-ray of a story and see its skeleton, it would be clear that it is composed of a series of events. These events are what hold the story together structurally. It can't stand on its own, as it were, without all the events.

Even if you are speaking all your character's lines and moving around the stage in space in time, if you don't know what the event of the scene is, then what are you really doing? You have to answer the question "Why am I (as the character) here? What am I here to do that is immediate, important, and moves my life forward?"[9]

Another way to think of it is this: If a scene isn't about one event, then what is a scene? You will be hard-pressed to answer that question. If your job as an actor isn't to make the event of the scene happen in service of the play, then what is it? To only say the lines, feel emotions, and move around the stage? Of course not. Dramatic structure has a purpose to it. The event provides that meaning and purpose to every scene ever written.

> You must be coming from some place to do something immediate and important that will move your character's life forward.
>
> —Lloyd Richards[10]

You can't effectively play the scene if you don't know the reason the scene exists in the overall story. Events are active, dynamic environments that further the dramatic action. Therefore, the leading circumstance of each event determines your character's action. If you are going to act the scene, then you need to be able to read the blueprint for what to do, to know exactly why your character is there and what they need and what they are there to do.

To be more precise, the event is the point of the highest dramatic conflict between the characters in every scene. It is the change of one action into a *new* action. This moment usually happens right at the end of the scene. Conflict doesn't necessarily mean the event is a bad thing. The highest point of dramatic conflict in the scene may be a kiss, for example. When two characters kiss, especially for the first time, they are both changed forever at that moment. The characters immediately have new objectives and new actions, for their relationship has changed.

A new event begins a new action, which begets a new need for your character. Everything in that scene is the buildup to that change. Characters either achieve their needs, or they don't. If their need is satisfied, then they move onto new needs with new actions toward the next new event, usually in a new scene. Be aware, though, that this change isn't necessarily immediate. It is a *process* that can either be long or fast or some time in between, which is why scenes take time to play out. Events take time. Great writers have the skill to develop this dramatic tension over the course of a scene, which is why they usually only deliver one event per scene.

> It is important to remember that each event generates a new action, which in turn generates a new event.
>
> —Maria Osipovna Knebel[11]

It is essential to examine how characters strive or connive to move their lives forward in a specific moment. This way of thinking helps to reveal the characters' actions. For example, your character may be ironing clothes while chatting with their spouse about their respective days. In this context, ironing and chatting are what we call activities. But what your character might really be doing is preparing to tell their spouse that they are leaving them for their best friend. That particular event, a confession (a noun), will have a specific beginning, middle, and end, with a leading circumstance, an action, which is to confess. To do that, your character might be playing the action to make their spouse feel loved. When it is over, both characters will have new objectives with corresponding new actions to try to move their lives forward until the next event changes their strategies or their goals. In this case, the new event could be a fight, silence, a separation, divorce, or even a reconciliation in the form of lovemaking.

Just like people, characters often think one thing but say another or promise one thing yet do something else or even do things that they don't want to do. We do this all the time. People exhibit a range of behavioral contradictions and paradoxes, yet that is what in part makes us interesting; complex; and, ultimately, human. Divining characters' motives can be tricky, yet it always comes down to how they think they are helping themselves, no matter how misguided the behavior can be.

At its most elemental level, life itself is arguably nothing more than a series of events. Yet this series of events, at times seemingly innocuous and inconsequential, is everything for us human beings. Samuel Beckett, the Irish existentialist, recognized this perhaps better than any playwright in the Western world. He understood that events comprise the existential fabric of our lives. Events, especially the insignificant ones, make up our existence. Even waiting for an event can be an event.

If we think of an average day as a series of quotidian events, then we can see how the corresponding leading circumstance shapes our behavior and, hence, the action of each of those daily events: sleep, meditation, exercise, breakfast, commute, work, meeting, lunch, class, interview, cocktail party, commute, dinner, concert, reading, lovemaking, sleep. Your fundamental job as an actor is to identify in each scene where your character appears in the event in which they are participating and work to make that event happen. This brings our definition of *playing action* to:

> Playing action is the exchange of energy, purposefully directed, to make the other actor feel something in pursuit of a need, *to make the event of the scene happen.*

The Superobjective (Hopes and Dreams)

In a play the whole stream of individual, minor objectives, all imaginative thoughts, feelings, and actions of an actor should converge to carry out the super-objective of the plot.

—Konstantin Stanislavski[12]

Stanislavski calls the ultimate goal of your character the superobjective; it is what your character needs in every scene in the script. It drives their behavior through the entire arc of the story and never changes. They are always in pursuit of it. For me as an actor, the term *superobjective*, like *objective*, is a bit too analytical. I prefer the words *hopes and dreams*; I find them more artistic. Like all of us, characters are filled with hopes and dreams that get them up in the morning and spur their behavior throughout the play and beyond. Your characters are always trying to move their lives forward, all the time, in every scene. They are driven by their ambitions, just like you are in real life.

Luckily for us as actors, hopes and dreams are images. Imagery is the currency of the craft of acting. Just as you can use images to give form and energy to the need of your scene, you can also develop a cache of images for your character's hopes and dreams. Then, you can source them before and during the show to help you get into character and motivate your performance.

We also now know from neuroscience that imagery is the lingua franca of the intuition.[13] The way to speak to our intuitive side is to provide it with strong imagery. These images fuel all the individual needs your character has in each scene. The need to achieve these goals is the inner motivation you must incorporate into your actor's instrument, your body, before each scene. The moment before, as it is colloquially referred to in our business, must be a visceral experience for the actor; it is the palpable, raw predicament that the character must extricate themselves from during the scene. To alleviate this human predicament, you must get the other character in the scene to do what you need them to do. To do that, you must make the other actor feel something. Thus, we now arrive at the following final definition of *playing action*:

> Playing action is an exchange of energy, purposefully directed, to make the other actor feel something in pursuit of a need, to make the event of the scene happen, *in service of your character's hopes and dreams.*

At the very least as an actor, you must be able to play action in pursuit of a need. If you are going to live believably under imaginary circumstances with precise repeatability and complete spontaneity, then you must also make the event of the scene happen in every scene your character appears. This is achieved only through the exchange of energy that alters the other actor in pursuit of a need, in service to your character's hopes and dreams. This is what you actually do onstage: *make the other actor feel something*. That is the doing of playing action.

Play's the Thing

> This is the real secret of life—to be completely engaged with what you are doing in the here and now. And instead of calling it work, realize it is play.
>
> —Alan Watts[14]

The beautiful game of acting must be played, not worked. What we actors do in performance is play action. We use the word *play* on purpose, for we do not work action. The thing we do, more than anything, as actors is play. The script itself is called a play. The audience says, "I'm going to see a play tonight." In Shakespeare's time and since, actors have been called players. Play is what you do as an actor, always. Never forget this. Acting is not work. Acting is play, so play. *Play* action; don't work action. Action should always be light and free, infused with ease, beauty, and the simple joy of doing, no matter how intense or heavy the subject matter of the scene. It should not be heavy and laborious. No one wants to watch you work hard. An audience does, however, want to watch you play imaginatively.

One of the ancillary benefits of remaining in a state of play is that when we play freely, our attention is completely engaged in the power of the now. There is no need or time to worry, to be anxious or upset, or to judge yourself when you are playing freely. The act of free play is inherently in the present, filled with positive imagery, and fully engaged. There is no room for fear in play. Fear for the actor only exists when you're not fully engaged in what you are doing; additionally, you can't fully play if your thoughts are focused elsewhere. The game will then pass you by. Play only happens in the now, and fear dies in the now. This is fortuitous for us as actors, as our work also happens in the now. Keep the spirit of play in your heart space at all times when you act. Play, and do so freely.

When you learn to play action, you discover such ease and flow in your acting that you will wonder what you were doing before. When this joyous exchange of energy begins to move back and forth between you and your scene partner in an uninterrupted current, unimpeded by ego, flowing with the freedom of childlike play, then and only then will the space between come to life. *Ma* suddenly appears, and the world of the play, like a sculpture, begins to take shape.

Exercises

The second half of this book, "Practice," is entirely dedicated to developing a professional practice of playing action. That said, the following exercises are simple, effective, and informative tools for developing a corporeal understanding of playing action—the sending and receiving of energy.

The first exercise is the ubiquitous ball toss. No respectable teacher of the Michael Chekhov acting technique would start a class without it! Fundamentally, it is a basic dyad or circle ball-toss game. But like everything in actor training, this exercise can mean nothing (it can simply be a ball game), or it can be ripe with meaning (highly illustrative of the core mechanics of playing action). It all depends on your perspective, how you approach it, and how you play it.

The second exercise uses the universal neutral scene but in a very specific way, with precise objectives related to a corporeal understanding of playing action. It actively demonstrates the expression "It's not about the words" by allowing actors to experience playing action as an exchange of energy to make the other person feel something, which is the true meaning of what is happening, otherwise known as subtext.

The Ball Toss (Sending and Receiving Energy)
- **Who:** Two or more people.
- **Tools:** Any small ball will suffice; however, I recommend using a juggling ball or hacky sack, as they don't roll all over the place when dropped. You don't want to spend your time chasing bouncing balls around the studio.
- **Where:** An acting or dance studio, stage, gym, school all-purpose room, or large enough open space, indoor or out, with a not-too-low ceiling. Stand a comfortable tossing distance from one another. If you have a group, find the integrity of a circle appropriate to the space you are in.
- **How:** For the purposes of this exercise, all tosses are *underhand only*. The objective is not to be as inventive with how many ways you can toss a ball. It is decidedly to be consistent and reliable with the quality and care of your tosses. The gesture of your underhand toss should be precise and repeatable.

Note: Many actors have a complicated relationship with ball games. In fact, many actors got into theater as young people specifically to *avoid* athletics and as an escape from ball games in particular. Not to worry: As in all things in life, we have a relationship with ball games, and luckily, relationships are fluid, malleable, and ever changing. If you are one of these people who hates ball games, decide that now, at this point in your life and artistry, you are open to the opportunity of building a new relationship with ball games, just like you are open to creating a new, healthy relationship with your inner critic. For now, the ball-toss game is a positive vehicle with the artistic end of furthering your growth as an actor. Simply decide that the ball is your new friend.

Sending (The Toss)

Notice your lips. Allow them to separate slightly. Breathe in with the feeling of *ease*. Let this sensation of ease permeate your entire body. Imagine or decide that the ball you are about to toss to your partner is a precious *gift* and that the gesture you are about to make is one of *giving*. Both the toss and the gesture are gifts for your partner. It is not about you. You are about to give your partner these precious gifts, and they need to receive them successfully.

Target your attention onto your partner. Reach into the space behind you, your back space, with the ball. Make sure to make eye contact with your partner. Only toss the ball to them when you sense that *they are ready* to receive your toss.

Once you have established a connection with your partner, toss the ball *underhand* carefully and intentionally with only the amount of force necessary to reach your partner, exhaling as you do. Ideally the ball will arc halfway between the two of you and land gently in the lap region of their body. Part of the gift you are sending them is that they should be able to catch the ball with little to no effort while standing.

Sustain the gesture of *sending* beyond when the ball leaves your hand until they have received it. You want to make sure that your gift has been *received*. Don't drop your arm or pull back until they have received the ball. Allow yourself to see your partner as someone who has just received your gift and the swift moment of satisfaction that comes with that.

Now allow yourself to assume the role of the *receiver*. Ask your body to stand with the quality of movement of *readiness*, and target your attention outside yourself, following the movement of the ball and the other players in the game. Do all this with the feeling of ease while breathing fully and gently.

Receiving (The Catch)

Make eye contact with your partner as they prepare to toss the ball to you. Radiate energy of readiness to them, letting them know you are prepared to receive the toss. Keep your eye on the ball as it moves through the air. Attempt to actually see the seams of the ball as it moves closer to you. Watch the ball all the way into your hands. Don't take your eyes off it until you can feel it touch your skin and you hear the contact.

When receiving the ball, see if you can catch it with *soft hands*, silently, so that the ball doesn't make any noise when you catch it. Move *with* the ball like a shock absorber as it arrives in your hands. Have a good look at the gift you have received. Allow yourself a small moment of satisfaction in catching the ball. Then look up and find the next person to whom to toss the ball. You are now the sender. Do all this with the feeling of ease while breathing fully and gently.

Alternative Versions of the Ball Toss

You can build on the basic ball toss with various versions.

Version 1: Your Name

Say your name out loud as you toss the ball, sending the gift of your name. Attach the beautiful energy of the sound of your name to the tossing gesture. This helps you practice "sending yourself out," which is what we do as actors in scene work, only under imaginary circumstances.

Note: Practice saying your name out loud as you actually make the physical gesture of tossing, not before or after you toss. Say your name during the toss. Gesture and sound go together in the same moment. Then, make sure your partner has received your name.

Note: You are always sending out your energy, even when you are playing a role. The real energy from your life is in service of the fictional character's life. This is also good practice for sending on text, for as actors we breathe through our mouths when we have something to say.

Version 2: Receiver Says Your Name

This is the same as version 1, but in this version the receiver also says the name of the tosser after they have received the ball: (1) You, the tosser, say your own name as you toss. (2) The receiver then also says your name upon receipt of the ball.

Note: Add a flare of celebration to your name as you say it. Celebrate yourself when you say your name.

Version 3: Group Says Your Name

This is the same as version 2, but if you are in a group, after the receiver has said your name, the ensemble says your name all together. It's a way to reinforce the name and add energy to the room.

Version 4: Receiver's Name

In this version, you say the name of the person to whom you're tossing as you toss the ball. You now say their name instead of yours. Send them the gift of their name as you make the tossing gesture.

Note: Practice saying their name out loud as you actually make the physical gesture of tossing, not before or after you say the name. Gesture and sound go together in the same moment. Then, make sure your partner has received their name.

Version 5: Receiver Says Their Own Name

This is the same as version 4, but now the receiver also says their own name out loud. The tosser says the name of the receiver as they toss. The receiver then says their own name after they have received the ball. Both celebrate the receiver's name when they say it.

Version 6: Group Says the Receiver's Name

This is the same as version 5, and if you are in a group, the group can then say the name of the receiver all together after the receiver has said their own name. It's a way to reinforce the name and add energy to the room.

Version 7: Tosser's Name, Your Own Name, Receiver's Name

Now, in this version, there are three steps—once you have received the ball and before you toss the ball to someone else:

1. You say the name of the person who tossed the ball to you.
2. Place your hand on your chest, and say your own name.
3. Then say the name of the person to whom you are tossing.

So, it goes in the order tosser's name, your name, receiver's name.

Note: This version has the desired effect of slowing everyone down because the receiver can't simply go on and toss to the next person without first acknowledging the person who tossed to them and then themselves. It forces the receiver to target their attention longer outside of themselves, which sustains the human connections longer.

Version 8: Qualities of Movement

Practice tossing the ball with different physical qualities of movement. Toss with the feeling of ease, joy, care, love, playfulness, sensuality, confidence, power, expertise, mischief, and so on.

Version 9: Imaginary Qualities

Imagine that the ball itself is composed of different imaginary qualities: expensive crystal, a raw egg, a tomato, a hot potato, Jell-O, the last drink of water, diamonds, and so on.

Version 10: Imaginary Stakes

Give yourself the imaginary prompt "Dropping the ball is unacceptable."

Note: Acting always takes place in high-stakes environments. It is important that once you have the basics of this game down, you find ways to increase the pressure on yourself. You need to build a practice that includes both deliberate practice and training for adversity. This will prepare you for the professional road ahead. As you sense yourself arriving at a plateau of competence in your ability to play this game, increase the performance pressure to ensure you train out of your comfort zone.

Version 11: Imaginary Characters or People

Imagine you are the world's greatest ball tosser. Now toss the ball! Imagine you are an Olympic-level ball catcher. Now receive the ball. Or imagine that you are your favorite actor, athlete, or celebrity playing the game. Endow your body with their expertise, power, and ability.

Note: Eventually you can do the ball toss in character as part of your rehearsal process.

Version 12: Imaginary Circumstances

Lastly, as we always play action under imaginary circumstances, imagine different fictional high-stakes scenarios where dropping the ball costs you or your partner something. For example, the ball contains lifesaving information, and your partner must catch it. If the ball is dropped, the message is not received, and all is lost (as in the film *Midnight Express*), or if you drop the ball your partner is executed (*The Deer Hunter*), or if you drop the ball, you lose one of your children to the Nazis (*Sophie's Choice*).

The important thing is that you begin to get into your body the gestures of sending and receiving, for this seemingly innocuous game is in fact a strong behavioral analogy, if you will, for the technique of playing action. The ball represents the energy you will be sending in your scene. It is a paradigm for playing action: *sending and receiving.* The more you do it, the more your body will incorporate it, and the less you will have to think about it. You will be playing "out of your mind," which is a desirable thing for a performer.

The paradigm:

1. You must make contact with another human being.
2. You must breathe with them.
3. You must send them something (the ball = energy).
4. You must deal with a moving object whose trajectory is unpredictable and unknowable. Accordingly, you must stay in the moment to deal with the moving projectile. If you check out mentally, the ball will strike you, or you will drop it.

This simple game demands you remain present and send and receive. You can't act if you're not present.

Instant Forgiveness

Any of the previous ball games are a wonderful opportunity to practice instant forgiveness.

Note: for more on "Instant Forgiveness," see the exercises section from chapter 1.

Celebratory Bow of Failure!

A simple yet important practice you can add à la carte into any of the previous ball games is the "Celebratory Bow of Failure!" It works like this: Any time you drop the ball or throw the ball errantly to your receiver, you step into the middle of the circle; look everyone in the eye; and take a proud, enthusiastic, and joyful bow! You do all this while everyone else in the group cheers and applauds vigorously!

Note: This begins to do a jujitsu move on your relationship with failure and consequently your inner critic by training you that failure is something to celebrate, be proud of, and worthy of applause—not feel negative about in any way, shape, or form. Failure comes along with the game of acting, and you can't succeed or fail if you're not in the game. But if you are in the game, it is certain you will fail at some point, if not often. So, go for it, and then celebrate the results, come hell or high water. Take back the power from failure.

Note: This is an example of an exercise from the "Training for Adversity" performance philosophy. It works to prepare the student for the road ahead rather than prepare the road for the student, which is, sadly, all too ubiquitous these days.

"It's Not about the Words" Neutral Scenes (Action as Subtext)
One of the simplest and clearest ways to learn how to play action is to use the time-tested neutral scene. However, here the framework of neutrality is used to hang the hat of action on: how you make your scene partner feel, which is accomplished in a mutual exchange of energy. This energy exchange conveys the true meaning of any scene, which is subtextual, below the text. If action is energy, then energy is the subtext of the scene. The objective of this series of exercises, therefore, is to help drop action into your body by receiving and releasing energy in relationship with your scene partner using a simple text. It is the first textual exploration of "It's not about the words."

Version 1: Discovering the Text Together
Pick one of the following two neutral scenes (or any other neutral scene):

Neutral Scene 1: "Isn't it almost time?"

ACTOR A: Isn't it almost time?

ACTOR B: It is.

ACTOR A: Are you ready?

ACTOR B: Are you?

ACTOR A: I guess so. You?

ACTOR B: As I'll ever be.

ACTOR A: What time is it?

ACTOR B: It's time.

ACTOR A: It's time?

ACTOR B: It's time.

ACTOR A: Okay.

ACTOR B: Okay.

Neutral Scene 2: "Good morning."

ACTOR A: Good morning.

ACTOR B: You think so?

ACTOR A: Don't you?

ACTOR B: That depends.

ACTOR A: Depends on what?

ACTOR B: On you.

ACTOR A: On me?

ACTOR B: Yes, on you.

ACTOR A: Alright then.

ACTOR B: Alright then.

ACTOR A: Have a good day.

ACTOR B: You, too.

Decide who is A and who is B. Sit in two chairs facing each other, feet flat on the floor, with your knees almost touching. Read the text to one another, giving yourself permission to take your time and discover it with your partner. There is no rush. Repeat this several times until you have a feel for the scene. Discuss what you noticed. Ask yourself, "Where was my attention? What was I actually doing?"

Note: This is a great opportunity to practice "I have very little time so I'm going to go very slowly."

Note: This is a great opportunity to practice "Notice, Stop, Redirect."

Note: This is a great opportunity to practice "Instant Forgiveness."

Note: Most often, when students perform this first round, their attention is naturally down on the text and not predominantly on their scene partner. The reason for this is that they, perhaps unconsciously, believe that the words are more important than their scene partner. I explore this in more detail in part II of this book; however, perhaps unexpectedly, often the greatest form of interference for actors is the actual text itself. The text (the words themselves or even remembering the words) pulls the target of the actor's attention off their partner and back onto themselves, causing an increase in performance interference in the shape of self-consciousness.

Version 2: Giving My Partner the Target of My Attention

This is the same framework as version 1, however in this version, you are only allowed to say your text when you have eye contact with your partner. Decide that you are going to willfully give your partner the gift of your attention. Make your scene partner the target of your attention by deciding that your scene partner is more important than the words. In other words, you are much more interested in your partner than the words you must say to them.

Begin to source your scene partner. Then, simply look down and get your line. Once you have the line, bring your attention back up onto your scene partner, and release the text onto them but only while you have eye contact. If you are unable to remember the entire line, go back down, get the rest of the line, then retarget back up, and share the rest of the line with them. They do the same. If you find yourself being pulled down to the paper, "Notice, Stop, Redirect."

Repeat several times. See if you can release the energy of the words onto your scene partner rather than simply read the lines. Discuss what you discovered.

Note: Pay attention to your attention. Did you want to look at the words more than your partner or vice versa?

Note: There is a difference between reading lines and releasing your text onto your scene partner. What was your experience of this difference?

Version 3: First Action Choice

Building on version 2, now add an action in the form of how you want to make the other person feel. Start with simple, common actions to make the other person feel good, bad, special, welcomed, unwanted, loved like a friend, guilty, like a sibling, and so on. Decide this is how you want to make them feel as you read the text, and release your energy onto your partner accordingly.

Note: If you are a teacher in a class, you can whisper the choice to each actor, and then ask the class afterward what they saw and experienced. Check in with the actors. If you are working alone with your scene partner, choose an action and release it onto your scene partner without telling them. Check in with them afterward, and ask them what they were feeling. What was their experience of your action choice?

Version 4: Opposite Action Choices

Building on version 3, now add opposite action choices in the form of how you want to make the other person feel. One actor's action is positive (warm), while the other actor's is negative (cold): happy and sad, heavy and light, big and small, accepted and rejected, alive and dead, and so on.

Note: If you are a teacher, you can do this clandestinely, without telling the other actor, and then check in at the end to see what they both experienced. Did they in fact experience opposite energies? How did that change their own action?

Version 5: Compatible Action Choices

This is the same as version 4, but now the action choices are either both positive or both negative: loved and special, smart and supported, guilty and wrong, stupid and dumb, confident and empowered, talented and gifted, frustrated and annoyed, and so on.

Note: If you are a teacher, you can do this without telling them their action choices, and then check in with your students at the end to see what they experienced. Did they in fact experience compatible energies? How did that affect their own action?

Version 6: Bold Action Choices

This is the same as version 3, but now the action choices are strong, bold choices, such as turned on sexually, frigid, worshipped, incompetent, sensual, annihilated, saintly, like shit, like a god, and so on.

Version 7: Color Action Choices

This is the same as version 3, but now explore and play around with colors as action choices; discover what happens: blue (sad), green (envy), pink (happy/light), yellow (warm), and so on.

Note: At first blush, colors may seem an odd option, but play around with them, and see what they bring out in the acting. The word choice of the action is less important than the corresponding energy that is aroused by that word. And colors have very strong corresponding energies.

Version 8: Relationship Action Choices

This is the same as version 3, but now add relationships to the action choices:

- mother and son: loved and rejected
- father and daughter: big and small
- husband and wife: guilty and wrong
- boss and employee: small and confused
- doctor and patient: relieved and worried
- two lovers: turned on and sensual

Or mix and match at will, or make up your own

Version 9: "As If" Given Circumstances Action Choices
Add to the relationships by exploring defined given circumstances:

- a doctor's office
- a first date
- an important job interview
- the morning after someone stayed out all night with no explanation
- a cancer diagnosis
- the day of a funeral
- the morning after an affair
- a prison camp in World War II
- a last goodbye

Play around with public and private locations and different high-stakes situations.

Summary

- Playing action is an exchange of energy, purposefully directed, to make the other actor feel something in pursuit of a need, to make the event of the scene happen in service of your character's hopes and dreams.
- The foundation of acting is the reality of doing; the reality of doing is playing action. As action is doing, it exists as a verb for the actor. The result of a verb is that the other person is changed. However, the use of a verb as action retains the target of attention on the self; the target of action must be the other actor, as the goal of action is to change the other person. Verbs must, therefore, be translated into an exchange of energy to make the other person feel something.
- Everything your character does is motivated by a goal. Stanislavski calls this goal the character's objective. In good writing, there is only one objective per character per scene. Using the word *need* in place of *objective* is more visceral and active. You *need* to get the other person in the scene to feel something to move your character's life forward.
- Images are electrical currents in the brain that change us physically, emotionally, and intuitively. Imagery is the language of intuition. Hopes and dreams are images that represent your character's superobjective.
- Every scene also has only one event, which is the purpose of that scene; it is usually at the very end of the scene. An event is always a noun and

is the change of one action into a new action; it is also the highest point of dramatic conflict in the scene. Conflict can be a positive thing. The leading circumstance of any event determines the action.

- Free play is the real secret to being in the here and now and is an essential element in playing action. Play action; don't work it.

Sculptors of Energy

Everything is energy. And that's all there is to it. Match the frequency of
the reality you want, and you cannot help but get that reality.

—Albert Einstein

Actors are sculptors of energy under imaginary circumstances, and energy is
the clay of our craft. It is what we mold, carve, and shape across space and
time. In other words, energy is the raw material with which we literally ply
our trade. Accordingly, if you want to raise your acting game above that of
the journeyman level, you need to refine your ability to sculpt your energy
toward creative ends. Attention is the tool we use to shape that material.
Your attention directs your energy to meet the specific artistic demands of
the script.

In sculpting terms, your attention is the chisel. If playing action is an
exchange of energy, then the degree to which you can harness your own
energy and direct it toward a target, your desired frequency, is the degree to
which you will find freedom, facility, and power in your acting. It is also the
degree to which the space between will crackle to life with power, texture,
and dimension.

All forms of actor training work to develop these two areas of our voca-
tion: energy and attention. They do it through a variety of different exercises,
methods, and approaches. Acting technique gives you a means to manage
your energy; it provides a container, a shape, a purpose for that energy and
directs it toward a goal.

Because playing action is an exchange of energy under imaginary circumstances, you need to learn to take care of that most precious commodity: your energy and, by extension, your attention, which drives it. You will need both at your beck and call to play action in performance. If you are to stand a chance in hell of surviving this Sisyphean business and producing inspired and constructive performances over the course of your career, then healthy energy management needs to become part of your daily practice.

The Life Force

> You, yourself, are the eternal energy which appears as this Universe. You didn't come into this world; you came out of it. Like a wave from the ocean.
>
> —Alan Watts[1]

In this context, energy is your life force, or your body's vitality. In yoga practice, this vital force is called prana, the Sanskrit word for "breath" or "vital principle." This subtle energy is called qi or chi in Chinese and ki in Japanese. By any name, energy is an essential element of living. It is the life force within us all, linked to our heartbeat and breath.

Your breath and heartbeat comprise your engine of energy. These combined rhythms circulate your prana, which is part of the divine dance of life called Lila in Sanskrit. You can't go much longer than three minutes without this combo delivering oxygen to all areas of your being before you cease to exist. The more you care for your breath and cardiovascular system, the healthier you will become in both your daily and artistic lives.

You can develop a meditative awareness of this inner moving energy. Ancient Chinese movement meditations, such as qigong or tai chi chuan, are highly recommended practices to cultivate well-being in qi or prana and skill in energy management. This is so important to us as actors because we send and receive that energy in the act of playing action, so you need to take care of it.

Attention

> The simple act of paying attention can take you a long way.
>
> —Keanu Reeves

I want you to do something right now. For the next ten minutes, every time your attention wanders from reading this book, I want you to raise your hand.

Once your attention returns to reading, lower your hand back down. You'll most likely discover your mind bounces in and out between this book and other random thoughts. Our minds wander about 47 percent of our waking hours.[2] That's almost half the time! Research shows that the more your mind wanders, the less happy you are, never mind productive. Our attention is feeble, beset by both internal and external distractions, but it's essential to harness it. Quality work only gets done when you focus on one thing at a time.

For the next week, notice how your thoughts affect your mood and energy. Also observe how challenging it can be to stay present in your life. If you are not present in what you are doing, you will only be content about half the time. However, when your mind is fully engaged in the activity at hand, your happiness quotient shoots up to almost 70 percent (e.g., making love is the activity where the mind wanders the least, and there is the greatest amount of happiness—no surprise there!). This happiness-to-attention ratio is true no matter what you are doing, be it sitting in traffic or eating a gourmet meal.[3]

The actor's visible work happens in the present. As an actor, it is vital to cultivate a practice of mindfulness meditation. You must observe where your thoughts go and where you spend your mental time and energy. The more you practice meditation, the more your attention will improve, and the more compelling your performances will become. As your focus learns to stay in the now, your presence will deepen. Stable attention refines your ability to play action. Combined with a personal investment in the imaginary circumstances, it also commands the attention of your audience.

Before I explain how mental focus and imagination are essential to playing action, let's first examine how they create the artist you will become.

Paying Attention

No matter where you go, there you are.

—Buckaroo Banzai[4]

We have the expression "pay attention" in English. We use the word *pay* because attention has intrinsic value. Your attention is worth something. It has currency, as it were. Even if you were ridiculously wealthy, you wouldn't indiscriminately toss away hard-earned money, but people do this with their attention all the time. If you don't throw away your money, then don't throw away your attention, either. It's valuable. Treat it so. Your attention is the conduit through which your energy flows. Where your attention goes is where your energy flows.[5]

One of the foundational elements of actor training is awareness. If you want to grow as an actor, you must apply awareness to that aspect of your craft in which you want to see change. The degree to which you develop awareness is the degree to which you will see growth. Developing a keen sense of self-awareness is key to artistic growth as an actor across all areas of training. Where you place your attention in your acting process is where you will see the most growth: voice, movement, scene work, script analysis, action, imagination, dialects, characterization, energy work, auditioning, and so on. In chapter 9 I explain the four stages of acquisition of any technique.

When we pay attention, what is it we actually do? We give ourselves a singular point of focus—a target, if you will. We direct our attention onto the task or subject at hand. And where our attention goes, our energy flows. Developing your ability to pay attention to your attention is, therefore, essential.

If your energy flow is determined by where you place your attention, and if playing action is an exchange of energy released onto your scene partner to make them feel something, then it is vital that you master the ability of willfully targeting your attention. You must be able to move the target of your attention to where you need it at any time, no matter how much pressure is on you. Most people are able to sing well in the shower because there are no eyeballs on them, the stakes are low, and there is no pressure. We know that self-consciousness rises in direct relationship to the stakes of the action being performed, the perceived value of the action to the agent. You, as a professional actor, must be able to target your attention outside yourself at will under withering performance pressure.

Excellence is born of habit. Therefore, you must develop healthy mental habits that increase your performance potential and reduce interference. You do this by building a reliable and repeatable practice that supports these goals. You can't wait until the day of the performance to begin to pay attention to your attention. There is too much at stake, literally.

Talent Is a Lifestyle

> We are what we repeatedly do. Excellence, then, is not an act but a habit.
>
> —Aristotle

Taking care of yourself physically and mentally is paramount for the actor. As W. Timothy Gallwey writes in his seminal sports psychology tome *The*

Inner Game of Tennis, "Talent is a lifestyle."[6] It is not enough to rely on your acting ability alone. You have to have a talent for your talent; you need to nurture your gift. Everything you do in the combined arenas of your life shapes how much energy you will have available to accomplish your acting goals.

You are a walking, breathing composite of all your daily practices. For the actor, habits do one of two things: They either (1) *add* energy to your craft or (2) *subtract* energy. If you reflect across the varied arenas of your life, you can easily sort your patterns of behavior into one of these two buckets. Just like a soccer player training for the World Cup or an athlete preparing for the Olympics, you will begin to see that everything you do from the moment you wake up to when your head hits the pillow at night either contributes to or detracts from the amount of energy and attention you can bring to your work. If you want your acting to rise to the level of excellence, then you need to treat yourself, your body, which is your instrument, like the Stradivarius that it is.

Properties of Thought

The world as we have created it is a process of our thinking. It cannot be changed without changing our thinking.

—Albert Einstein

Each thought you have is powerful. We live life one thought at a time, one image at a time, one breath at a time. In essence you are a manifestation of your thoughts. While cultivating mindfulness in these areas can be challenging, it's essential for the professional actor. Luckily, there is a vast amount of research in neuropsychology, sports psychology, and the human potential movement to help us gain more control over our thought patterns and develop a healthy and productive relationship with our inner narratives.

For the purposes of this book, and specifically for the technique of playing action, the skill with which you manage your thoughts is the driving force behind all you do as an actor, both onstage and off. At the end of the day, more than what others say about you, *you are a composite of the stories you tell yourself.* You are the living, breathing manifestation of your own thoughts. The precursor to "how you talk about your work is how your work will be" is, How you *think* about your work determines both how you will talk about it and how you will do it. Your acting process, and playing action in particular, starts with your thoughts and the stories you tell yourself. Where your attention goes, your energy flows.

What are the stories you habitually tell yourself about your acting? What is your homegrown narrative? Is it healthy? Productive? Positive? Optimistic? Useful? Is it grounded in what sports psychology calls a growth mind-set? Does your inner narrative increase your potential as an actor? Or, are your thoughts negative, filled with judgment and doubt, visions of failure, doom and gloom scenarios, all that interfere with your performance? Let's take a closer look at the power of thought and the habitual narrative you have running in your mind. How you *think* will determine how you *do*.

The Three Reactions

What we think, we become.

—Buddha

A thought is an electrical impulse between two neurotransmitters in the brain that can be measured by functional magnetic resonance imaging (fMRI) and other machines. Literally, science and technology can see our thoughts. Thoughts are electric, and electricity is action, and action is energy. If playing action is an exchange of energy under imaginary circumstances, then this is hugely important to us as actors. We know from Newton that each action has an equal and opposite reaction. The reactions in your body to a single thought are threefold: (1) physical, (2) emotional, and (3) intuitive.[7]

When human subjects are asked to "imagine" instead of "think," the data captured by fMRIs were the same as that captured of thoughts.[8] Like with thought, the process of imagining produces electrical impulses between two neurotransmitters. Whether a person experiences imagery visually, aurally, or kinesthetically, the images are caused by similar electrical impulses in the brain. Both your thoughts and imagination constantly and consistently change you physically, emotionally, and intuitively. Both work on you all day long—each thought, each image, and each moment of each day. You literally are a living composition of your collective and habitual thought patterns.

1. Physical Reaction

A thought changes you physically. If you think a positive thought or source a funny image, you may smile or even laugh. Your body physically changes in direct relation to this positive image. If you source a negative thought, you may hold your breath, become tense and rigid, or even tremble. Your thoughts manifest physically in your body for all to see, one negative thought at a time. What we call a poker face, the attempt to not show what we are thinking or feeling, may reduce the amount of physical response to some degree, but the body still experiences thought physically, even if not fully outwardly expressed.

2. Emotional Reaction

A thought changes you emotionally. Your thoughts also directly affect your emotional life. If you think a negative thought or source a deeply sad memory, you may feel sad or even cry. Conversely, if you source the image of someone you love or who makes you happy, you will feel an immediate and measurable positive shift in your emotional life. You feel what you think as you think it. You feel what you imagine as you imagine it. This may seem obvious, but these experiences manifest in the body emotionally by changing the landscape of our feelings, which is incredibly important for acting.

3. Intuitive Reaction

Thoughts affect your intuition. We also now know from advances in neuroscience that the lingua franca of the intuition is imagery.[9] In other words, the way to communicate with our intuitive side is to "talk" to it with images. This is the side of us that trusts our gut or has a funny feeling about something. If the actor's process is all about subconscious release via conscious technique in order to tap into the creative subconscious and act from your intuitive self, then the use of imagery is one of the most important conscious tools we have to reach the subconscious.

> The best decisions aren't made with your mind but with your instinct.
>
> —Lionel Messi

Time and Place

> The past is already gone. The future is not yet here. There's only one moment for you to live, and that is the present moment.
>
> —Buddha

Your thoughts can be focused in one of three places: (1) the present, (2) the past, and (3) the future. They cannot be in two places simultaneously.[10] That's huge. Think about that. Your thoughts only have three temporal targets. The question for the actor is, How long are you able to remain in the present without shifting to the future or past unwillingly?

When we are fully engaged in what we are doing, we are in the present. This can include thinking about how to solve a problem or analyze a situation. If your thoughts tend to the past, we call that a memory. If your thoughts move out of the present into something that may or may not happen, then we are in the future. The important part here is to realize that they cannot be in both places simultaneously. So where do you spend most of your time mentally? Where do your thoughts reside habitually? This is helpful information. The actor's work happens in the now, the present. You must be able to stay there for extended periods of time, consistently, and have control over that ability.

Duration

> There is only now. The now is all that there ever was, and all that there ever will be.

> —Alan Watts[11]

Thoughts also vary in length. A single thought can be as short as a nanosecond or as long as sixty seconds.[12] Thoughts of the greatest length, more than one minute, have been measured in Buddhist monks in the act of prayer and mathematicians and philosophers thinking through a problem. Although there is no definitive science on this, it is estimated that the average person has about 12,000 thoughts a day; up to 85 percent of those are recurring negative thoughts filled with chaos, jumping all over the place from moment to moment. On a typical bad day, you can have 70,000 thoughts or more, most of which are comprised of short, negative thoughts focused on the past or future and not engaged in the present moment.[13] Buddhists call this the "monkey mind," meaning a mind that is unsettled, restless, or confused, the part of the mind that is easily distracted. This creates interference and is not helpful for an actor.

Unsurprisingly, elite champion athletes have significantly fewer thoughts per day. Their thoughts are primarily in the present, attached to positive imagery, and longer in length, just like Buddhist monks in prayer. Also unsurprisingly, children under the age of six have fewer thoughts per day, and those thoughts, too, are in the present, positive in nature, and longer in length. Children live in the now. We humans learn more than 50 percent of all that we will ever learn by the time we reach the age of six, so it is no coincidence that there is a direct causal relationship between the amount of learning done during early childhood and the power of presence.[14] Learning takes place in the now. This brings us to the final property of each thought: quality.

Quality

Lastly, thoughts have an inherent quality and are mostly attached to negative or positive imagery but not both simultaneously. Positive imagery triggers the release of endorphins into your body, increasing a sense of well-being, hopefulness, and possibility. Negative thoughts trigger the release of cortisol and serotonin into the body, increasing the sensations of stress, depression, or sadness. Again, this is important information, as each thought changes you physically, emotionally, and intuitively in either a positive or negative fashion. You can see where this is headed. Let's put together the possible combinations of properties.

Habitual Thought

> No matter who you are, we are creatures of habit. The better your habits are, the better they will be in pressure situations.
>
> —Wayne Gretzky

Habitual thought combinations that *increase* performance potential:

- Positive, long thoughts or images in the present = ultimate training goal
- Positive, short thoughts or images in the present = very helpful
- Positive, short thoughts or images in the future = helpful (goal setting)
- Positive, long thoughts or images in the future = helpful (hopes and dreams)
- Positive, short or long thoughts or images in the past = helpful (confidence)

Habitual thought combinations that *decrease* performance potential:

- Negative, short or long thoughts in the present = interference (stress, anger, frustration)
- Negative short or long thoughts in the past = interference (guilt, shame, regret)
- Negative short or long thoughts in the future = interference (worry, anxiety, fear)

The question you must answer for yourself if you want to compete as a professional actor at the highest level is, where do you spend most of your time mentally? What are your habitual thought patterns? Remember, no matter where you go, there you are. One thought is powerful. They all are. Your composite thinking creates your reality. Your thoughts change you physically. They change you emotionally. They change you intuitively. Thoughts can be focused in either the present, past, or future but only one of those places at a time. Your thoughts are either long or short. They are either positive or negative. Those are your options, full stop.

The combination of all your thoughts and where you spend your mental time comprise the stories you tell yourself, affect your energy, and determine how you will act. But as your thoughts and images are electrical impulses, energy, and action, they need a target for your attention in order for you to play action.

Targets of Attention

Where your attention goes, energy flows.

In his seminal book *The Actor and the Target*, theater director Declan Donnellan posits that freedom in acting depends wholly on the placement of attention. As a professional actor and acting teacher, my experience is that this is definitely true and one of the most important concepts you can ever learn to empower yourself and your acting. The book's core concept is, Your attention needs a target. As with most important theorems, his postulate is simple yet elegant.

Donnellan develops the concept, claiming that if the actor sources a target outside themselves, they are liberated in their work. Only then do they truly begin to see the world from the character's point of view and inhabit the fiction effortlessly, reaching their fullest potential as an actor. Donnellan's premise is grounded in one of the fundamental principles of acting, which is to target your attention on either your scene partner or on an image at all times. Yet in practice, this simple truism is routinely forgotten by student and professional actors alike.

Another way to think of it is that the degree to which your attention is *on yourself* when you act is the degree to which you will literally be *self-conscious* and, therefore, inhibited. Self-targeting, as it were, creates performance interference. It is ultimately fear that pulls your attention from your scene partner and back onto yourself. Fear is the fundamental cause of interference in performance. And as Earle would often say in class, "Fear, for the actor, is ego." Let me repeat: Fear is ego.

Donnellan elaborates, claiming that a target provides freedom in your acting, but it does so only when the following criteria are met:

- There is always a target.
- The target is always outside you at a measurable distance.
- The target is there before you need it.
- The target is always active.
- The target is always changing.
- The target is always specific.

The most important premise with playing action is that the target must always be outside the actor, for the many reasons already established; perhaps the second most important element then is that the target is always changing. This is vital, as it demands that the actor work in the moment.

If something is always changing, you can't predict ahead of time how you are going to deal with it. You can only react to it as it changes. Like a ball being passed around the pitch by twenty-two football players, you can't know where it is going to go next, for it is always moving. Accordingly, you have to keep your eye on the ball, as it were, and follow its ever-morphing trajectory. You must respond spontaneously, reacting to each new shift it makes, or you will fail. You have no other choice. In fact, your ability to maintain your attention outside yourself and on a moving target is arguably one of the key components of successful acting. This practice, however, is liberating and represents the complete opposite of "self-conscious" acting. Once you have found a target for your attention outside yourself, the next step is to keep it there as it moves, changes, and simultaneously reacts to what you are doing.

Curiosity

Curiosity is desire of the mind.

—Catherine Fitzmaurice

Curiosity is the glue that adheres your attention to the target. It is also one of the foundations of actor training, if not all art. Master voice teacher and theorist Catherine Fitzmaurice says, "Curiosity is the desire of the mind." Absolutely. Without curiosity, the mind is feeble and easily distracted. As an artist, you must be deeply curious about the world around you. In performance, you must be deeply curious about your scene partner, as well as your source imagery. Essentially all work flows from this indispensable skill. At the end of the day, if you can't keep your attention on your scene partner, you won't have much success.

As I have already established, your ability to grow depends on the target of your attention. The amount of growth you experience is determined by your ability to remain connected to that target. Your ability to keep your attention on the ever-moving, changing target is directly correlated to your ability to be curious about it. The more curious you are about the target, your scene partner, your imagery, the more you will free yourself from self-consciousness in performance. You can't be curious about a target outside yourself if you are worried about how you are doing. Paradoxically, the more curious you are about the target outside yourself, the better you will do.

One of the simplest things you can do to sustain your curiosity and maintain a robust connection to the target is to *slow down*. It's hard to be curious about something quickly. To slow down your overall operating system, you must slow down your breathing. Slowing down your breath cycle will allow you to see the object of your curiosity in greater detail and spend more quality time with it. When you slow down your breathing, you also slow down the movement of the target, enabling you to see it with greater clarity. If you simply slow down and breathe more fully, I guarantee your acting will improve and you will enjoy performing more.

We have very little time; go very slowly.

—Buddha

Sourcing

Your target is the source of your action. In French *une source* means a "well." Your scene partner is the same. They are your source, the well from which you draw your artistic energy. Just like a power outlet, you need to plug into your scene partner. Your attention is the tool by which you do that plugging and make that connection. If you are curious enough about your scene partner (and from your character's point of view you better be because your character needs them to do something in order to move their life forward), then your attention will remain plugged into this artistic target. If your attention is plugged into your scene partner, then your ego dissolves, for they have become your source of inspiration. Then, as the great Eleanora Duse said, the Grace appears, and you begin to receive your performance from your scene partner, from your source.

The script is obviously the original source material. It is the source of the invisible action of the story. However, the source of your visible action is your scene partner. They will provide you with what you need to do. And what you need to do can only be in *reaction* to what they are already doing. Like a river, the action of a scene is already taking place when you step into its current. An essential element of playing action is learning to source your scene partner. If they are not the target of your attention and the source of your behavior, then you are self-generating your acting.

Self-generated acting is producing an idea of how the scene should go rather than responding to how the scene is actually going in real time. The more you have faith, the more your source will provide all that you need in the scene. You will then receive your performance from your partner. When the target of your attention is outside yourself, when your breath is slow, and when your curiosity is high, you will receive your performance from your source; they will make you act the part, and you will discover liberation, ease, and freedom in your work. When you are able to do all this without thinking about it, you are then ready to release.

The Release

Playing action is the release of energy onto the other actor.

—Earle Gister[15]

Once you have plugged your attention into your source, you are connected to them. Like electrical lines strung between two poles, the energy is ready to pass between. But how do you make another person feel something? The answer is by *releasing* energy. Playing action is an exchange of energy between actors. To exchange energy, both actors need to *release* it onto one another.

If playing action is how you make the other actor feel, then you simply target your attention outside yourself, and where your attention goes, your energy flows. When you *release* your energy outward, it flows along the lines of your attention toward the target (i.e., your scene partner) and affects them, making them feel something. When you step out onstage or in front of the camera, you must be actively engaged in sending your energy outward. This is the doing you must do in performance. This is the reality of doing.

To do this, you must breathe fully and *allow* your energy to be released outward. As soon as you hold your breath in performance, your attention flies off the target back to you, increasing self-consciousness. Holding your breath immediately increases interference in your performance. The more you hold your breath the more self-conscious and inhibited you will be. The more your breath is fluid, the more you will be able to effortlessly sustain your curiosity and pay attention to your target.

To do this, practice keeping your lips parted, ever so slightly. It is impossible, or nearly so, to hold your breath while your lips are slightly parted. When we speak, we breathe through our mouths, not through our noses. When we have the impulse to say something, we inhale through our mouths. As acting almost always involves text, practice breathing through your mouth in your training, and it will increase your fluidity of breath. All you need to do for this practice, a habit that adds energy to your acting, is to keep your lips parted ever so slightly at all times while you are engaged in the acting task. You don't have to have your mouth wide open, just parted enough for air to pass between your lips, even imperceptibly so.

A corresponding benefit of this practice is that the fewer breaths you take each day, the fewer thoughts you have.[16] Therefore, if you want to end up with fewer thoughts per day, like the elite champion athlete, then *slow down your breathing*. Slower breathing through slightly parted lips creates longer, more positive thoughts that live in the present moment. This practice, which is really a form of meditation, over time will improve your acting. If you develop this into a habitual practice, not only will your acting improve, but you also will most likely experience an increased sense of well-being in your life overall.

The Allowing

It is clear that where our attention goes, our energy flows and that playing action is fundamentally an exchange of energy to make the other actor feel something in pursuit of a need. It then follows that to play an action, you must technically do the following:

1. Separate your lips slightly and breathe.
2. Direct the target of your attention outside yourself onto your scene partner (or an image if your character is alone onstage).
3. Source your scene partner by simultaneously allowing yourself to *receive* their energy and *react* to it with your own energy—sending your energy onto them to make them feel something. As energy is action, all you have to do at this point, like an electrical conduit, is *allow* the energy to flow between yourself and your source, your scene partner; you will now be in the give and take of energy, the releasing and receiving of action.

The playing of action is really a sense of allowing it to happen to you. In this way, acting is as effortless as it is for children. When you engage with the spirit of play and allow for spontaneous reactions, your acting becomes imbued with what Michael Chekhov calls the "feeling of ease." You will then be in the river of action, as it were, as designed by the playwright. Just as you can't force a river to go the way you want it, neither can you force your action. You need to trust that if you target the precious commodity of your attention and source your partner by breathing them in, activating your curiosity about them, and allowing them to affect you, then you will find yourself in a deep and powerful current of action, one that will ignite the space between you and your scene partner, electrifying the air in the room. This takes faith in yourself and in your partner.

You allow the action to be played and your scene partner to affect you. You *allow* yourself to be changed and for your unimpeded energy to flow out of you onto your source target. You *allow* yourself to play freely and fully. When you do so, the space between comes to life.

Exercises

The secret of your future is hidden in your daily routine.

—Buddha

Habit Training

Fundamentally, actor training is habit training. It involves first becoming aware of the habits that have carried us through life thus far, edifying the ones that increase our performance potential and retooling the ones that interfere with our abilities. As we know, habits either add energy or detract energy from our lives. If up to 40 percent of all our daily actions are habitual, and if our habits begin as thoughts, then we need to track our habitual thought patterns to have any luck changing our habitual behavior.

Habitually, many actors are not present in their work as they work. If you are going to master the sculpting tools of our trade and play action with command and consistency, then you must develop a practice of perpetual mindfulness, and if you have not already, you must master your awareness, thoughts, attention, and energy with repeatable intentionality. This is required of a professional actor. The following exercises can be classified as presence training: You will work on maintaining your attention with precision, ease, wholeness, and beauty on a target in the present moment. All the exercises should be engaged in with a spirit of attentive joy and playfulness, where listening and responding are paramount and your breath is free and full.

Habitual Thoughts Journal

Over a one-week period, track your habitual attention patterns in a journal. Pay attention to your attention, and throughout each day write down where you spend your mental time. Track your thought patterns based on the following criteria:

- In the present, past, or future (only one of these places at a time)
- Negative or positive
- Short or long

Ask yourself,

- "Where do I habitually spend most of my mental time? In the present with long positive thoughts? Or elsewhere? If so, where?"
- "What is the habitual inner story I tell myself about myself in the work?"
- "Does my habitual inner dialogue add energy to my life and work, or does it subtract energy from my life and work?"
- "Do my habitual thought patterns release my potential (as positive thoughts or energy) or interfere with my work (as negative thoughts or energy)?"
- "If Buckaroo Banzai is right and 'Wherever you go, there you are,' where am I most of the time?"

Be exacting on yourself. Really hold your feet to the fire on this.

"Talent Is a Lifestyle" Habits Analysis

On a piece of paper, draw a vertical line down the middle. On the top left of the line, write "Adds Energy." On the top right, write "Subtracts Energy." Then ask yourself, "Across all the arenas of my life, does what I'm doing *add* energy or *subtract* energy?" Write them out:

- Going to the gym, practicing yoga, attending acting classes, eating a balanced diet, meditating, journal writing, and getting eight hours of sleep are examples of healthy habitual practices that *add* energy to your life.
- Drinking excessive alcohol, smoking weed regularly, partying in general, eating junk food, practicing negative self-talk, procrastinating, and not getting enough sleep are examples of habits that *subtract* energy from your life.

Once you are done, take a step back, and have a good look at which side is longer, more robust. In which arena do you spend most of your habitual energy?

Moment Tracking (Hand-Raise Exercise)
This exercise can be done in a variety of ways and applied to many different training scenarios. Fundamentally, it tracks when your attention disengages the target of engagement, or, more colloquially, when your mind wanders. You can do this yourself, or ask your fellow actors or students to do it. You can apply it to a specific exercise, scene work, rehearsal, or class.

Whenever your mind wanders or your attention moves off its target of engagement in the present, raise your hand. Then reengage in the task at hand. Do this every time your mind wanders. It's that simple. What you might begin to see is that you spend less time actually in the moment than you think.

Note: You can apply the "Notice, Stop, Redirect" practice from chapter 1 to this, as well. In this version, you raise your hand not just when your inner critic appears but also any time your attention moves out of the moment.

Note: As explained in chapter 5, our attention can be in one of three places: the present, the past, or the future. As an actor's work is incumbent on being present in the present moment, this ritual will help you practice coming back to the moment.

The Mirror Exercise
This classic exercise still merits use by both actors and teachers alike and can be done in pairs or groups.

Dyad Version 1: Simple Mirror
Two actors stand facing each other about three or four feet apart. Imagine a line between them. One person, the leader, slowly originates movement. The other, the follower, mirrors the leader's movement. The objective is to be so in sync with one another that an outside observer wouldn't be able to tell who is leading and who is following.

Allow your breath to be free and full. Move with the feeling of ease. Look to find flow and synchronicity between both moving bodies. See if you can create a feeling of the whole, as if you are two bodies moving as one entity. After some time, switch roles.

Dyad Version 2: Tempo Mirror
In this version, the leader is free to change the tempo, speeding up and slowing down randomly to see how they can challenge their partner. The

objective is not for the leader to lose the follower but to remain in complete synchronicity with each another, even with changes in speed.

Dyad Version 3: Leader Mirror

In this version, the two actors switch who is leading and who is following without saying or indicating anything to one another. The understanding to switch should be done psychophysically. The objective is to be so in sync with one another that an observer wouldn't be able to tell who is leading and who is following or when the switch happened; the switch should happen organically and seamlessly.

Dyad Version 4: Space Walk Mirror 1

In this version, the two actors move freely around the room on their respective sides of the line. The objective is to mirror accurately depth, distance, and movement between each other on their sides of the mirror line.

Dyad Version 5: Space Walk Mirror 2

In this version, the two actors move freely anywhere around the room, irrespective of the original mirror line. The objective is to mirror accurately depth, distance, and movement between each other throughout the entire studio space.

Group Version 1: Group Mirror

In this version, half the class lines up on one side of the line, and the other half lines up on the other side, facing one another. One group leads, and the other group mirrors. Each actor picks an actor in the other group to lead and mirror. Pairs start mirroring each other one at a time until all pairs are moving simultaneously. Pairs will have to physically navigate around other pairs during the exercise.

Group Version 2: Shifting Group Mirror

This is the same as group version 1, except now, once all the pairs are moving, pairs begin to switch off with one another, exchanging partners as they mirror.

Group Version 3: Random Group Mirror

Add, mix, and match à la carte the elements of tempo, leader exchange, and space from the dyad versions.

Group Version 4: Diamond Mirrors

The group splits up into sets of four actors each as best you can (groups of three can work, as well). The four actors stand in the shape of a diamond, all facing the same way, with about four to six feet between each of them. The front of the diamond (the actor with their back to the other three) begins to move. The other three actors behind them mirror and move in complete synchronicity with the front actor. The front actor is free to move as they wish without "losing" the three actors behind him and should explore levels, the ground, tempo, rhythm, walking, and so on. The front actor "passes" leadership of the group by turning either to their right or left and "handing off" the movement to the person (on the right or the left), who is now the front of the diamond, as everyone is now facing that direction. Leadership of the diamond can be passed back and forth or across the diamond accordingly.

Note: Again, the objective is to be so synchronous that from the outside, it is hard to tell who is leading and who is following; transitions of leadership should be smooth and seamless.

Dyad Vocal Mirror Exercise

In this version of the mirror exercise, it is language that is mirrored, not physical movement. Two actors sit in chairs facing one another. One actor is the talker; the other actor is the vocal mirror. The talker begins to talk slowly, speaking comfortably, and clearly out loud about any topic they wish. The vocal mirror must say out loud *exactly* what the other actor is saying *as they say it*. The objective of the pair is to find a tempo where the talker and the vocal mirror are in complete sync and speaking at as close to normal pace as possible. Ideally there are no pauses or lapses between what the talker and the vocal mirror are saying. The words should appear to be coming from both of them simultaneously. Then switch roles.

Point, Nod, Go

This fun group attention exercise is played exactly as it sounds. All versions are played with the group standing in a circle.

Version 1: Point and Nod

One person, the pointer, points at someone else in the circle, the receiver. The receiver of the point acknowledges that they have been pointed at by nodding their head "yes." After nodding, they then turn to someone else in the circle and point at them, and so on. This continues until the entire group has been engaged and finds a smooth, uninterrupted flow.

Version 2: Point, Nod, Walk

One person, the pointer, points at someone else in the circle, the receiver. The receiver acknowledges that they have been pointed at by nodding their head "yes." That nod gives the pointer permission to leave their spot in the circle, walk across the circle, and take the receiver's place. (*Note:* You can't move or walk until the receiver has given you permission to do so by nodding their head "yes.") The receiver, after nodding "yes," becomes the new pointer. They then point to a third person in the circle, who is the new receiver. That new receiver then nods their head "yes," and the new pointer leaves their spot before the original pointer arrives; the cycle is off and running. Each pointer, once given permission to walk by the receivers' nods, walks across the circle to take their place, so it's a continuous flow of people taking the place of the person who received their point, which should be free by the time they arrive, and so on. This continues until the entire group has been engaged and finds a smooth, uninterrupted flow.

Version 3: Point, Yes/No, Go

One person, the pointer, points at someone else in the circle, the receiver. Now, in this version, the receiver has the *option* to either nod their head "yes," accepting the point (as in all the previous versions), or "no," rejecting the point. If the pointer's point was rejected by the receiver, then the pointer must quickly find another person in the circle and point to them. That new person also has the option to respond with a "yes" or "no," to either accept or reject the new point.

The pointer cannot move or walk until they have found someone in the circle who will accept their point. Once the pointer receives a "yes" nod, they walk across the circle to the receiver and take their place in the circle as in previous versions. But they can't walk until the receiver has given them permission to do so by nodding their head "yes," nor can they take the place of the new pointer until they have received a "yes" from someone else, and so on. This continues until the entire group has been engaged and finds a smooth, uninterrupted flow.

Note: Too many "no" nods in a row slows down the flow of the game too much. There should be about ten or so "yes" nods (to build up momentum) for every "no" nod.

One-Word Story Circle

This can be done with a group or a dyad.

Version 1: Group Circle

The group sits in a circle on the floor or in chairs and decides on an innocuous topic: pizza, rainy days, animals, colors, the moon, and so on. Once a topic has been agreed upon, one person, the starter, starts the story with the first word but one word only. The story of that topic now moves around the circle to the *right*, one person/word at a time, with each new person offering only one new word. The sequential words must make sense in relation to the words before them and build the story logically. Each person develops the story with the addition of their new word. The idea is to achieve a flow that resembles normal conversation. Work to have no pauses between each word. Reverse the direction for the next story. Work with the feeling of ease. Keep lips slightly parted and your breath full and smooth.

Note: this is a wonderful game to practice "Notice, Stop, Redirect" and "Instant Forgiveness."

Version 2: Dyad with a Scene Partner

Sit opposite your scene partner in a chair. This has the same parameters as the group version; decide on a given circumstance or topic. One person can only say one word at a time to tell that story. Then, after a while, each person can say two words at a time. Then, after a while, three words, and so on. See if you can find seamless synchronicity with each other. Work with the feeling of ease. Keep lips slightly parted and your breath full and smooth.

Note: This is a wonderful game to practice "Notice, Stop, Redirect" and "Instant Forgiveness."

One Person Walking

This is a group exercise, ideally done in a large dance studio, on a theater stage, or even outdoors.

Version 1: Always One Person, Only One Person

The group spreads out across the space. Everyone stands in alert stillness to begin, lips slightly parted, with soft focus. Then, without deciding ahead of time, one person suddenly begins walking. This first walker will continue to walk until someone else in the group randomly starts to walk, at which point the first walker will immediately stop walking. The new walker can either stop themselves at any time or wait until someone else from the group starts to walk. If a walker stops suddenly for any reason, someone else in the group must start walking, as there must be one person walking at all times. There must be one person, and only one person, walking at all times.

Version 2: Always Two People, Only Two People

This is the same as version 1, but this time, instead of one person walking at all times, there must be two people, and only two people, walking at all times.

Version 3: Random Numbers Walking

This is the same as version 1, but this time, one person in the group (or teacher) calls out a number between 1 and 5. Whatever number they call out is the number of people walking at all times. Randomize number sequences and durations.

Version 4: Limited Steps

This is the same as any of the previous versions, but whoever is walking only gets to take a certain number of steps before they must stop. Usually one to eight steps work the best. Randomize the number of steps or work sequentially up and down. Use in combination with a randomized number of walkers.

Version 5: Walking and Talking Story Improvisation

This is the same as version 1, with only one person walking at a time. However, this time, the group will tell a story as they walk. The group can decide on a topic ahead of time or not. The first person begins walking and talking simultaneously: "Once upon a time, I tied my shoe in a lighthouse on the moon." They will continue walking and telling the story until someone else starts walking and picks up telling the story from the exact spot where the exchange took place. There must be one person walking and talking at all times. After everyone has walked and talked at least once, the group will find a conclusion to the story by stopping the walking and talking simultaneously.

Note: Each walker/talker must build on the logic of the story as it develops.

Summary

- Acting is fundamentally energy work. Actors are sculptors of energy under imaginary circumstances. Everything is energy, and energy is vitality. It also goes by the name prana, qi, chi, ki, and life force. Match the frequency of the reality you want, and you get it.
- Your heartbeat and breath comprise your engine of energy, your inner rhythm.

- Attention is the tool that shapes your energy. Your attention needs a target. To free your performance, the target must be outside yourself. Curiosity is the glue that holds your attention to the target. Where your attention goes, your energy flows.
- We are what we repeatedly do. Talent is a lifestyle. Excellence, then, is not an act, but a habit. Habits either add energy to your work, or they subtract energy from your work.
- Thoughts are powerful. They affect you physically, emotionally, and intuitively. They exist in either the present, past, or future. They are either long or short, positive or negative. The champion performer and children under the age of six have fewer thoughts per day. Those thoughts are in the present, longer, and attached to positive imagery.
- Playing action is experienced as allowing your energy to radiate outward while simultaneously receiving your scene partner's energy and letting it affect you. It is the release of energy onto the other actor.
- Practice breathing with your lips slightly parted.
- No matter where you go, there you are.
- We have very little time; go very slowly.

⁓

CHAPTER SIX

Deeper, Not Wider

Play is a musical thing. It is a dance. It is an expression of delight. You don't dance because it's good for you. You dance because you're happy.

—Alan Watts[1]

The landscape of acting technique is only so wide. At a certain point, your growth as an actor depends less on acquiring more technique and more on your commitment to the technique you already have. In a nutshell, you eventually need to go deeper into yourself, not wider across technique.

Technique itself can only do so much. It is in service of your artistic will and bravery. Ultimately, technique asks, How far are you willing to take your work? Are you going to play it safe in performance or take bold risks? Will you work with control or faith? Are you courageous enough to disengage your ego, leave it all on the artistic field, and risk abject failure? Or will you always look to be told you're good?

This chapter focuses on some essential aspects of acting that are perhaps less tangible but to which you must fully commit if you want to rise above the ordinary and ignite the space between. They are elements of the craft that deepen your technique and release your creative individuality.

Intimate Harmony

Beyond technique, acting requires intimate harmony with your scene partner. If you are to vibrate your entire nervous system artistically with a frequency worth watching, and if your acting is to have any imaginative dimension, texture, or humanity, then you must be able to harmonize with your scene partner. That is, you need to play multiple complementary notes of your humanity simultaneously to a pleasing effect while maintaining a personal relationship under imaginary circumstances during a public performance.

It is only through harmony that intimacy is possible. Conversely, it is only through intimacy that true harmony is possible. You achieve this creative resonance by surrendering to your scene partner. That means listening to them with all your being and allowing them to "see," change, and affect you while you do the same to them. For partners to harmonize, they need to vibrate with their whole beings, like two tuning forks on a glass table. It needs to be an expression of your human delight. Acting is nothing if not intimate.

Let's be clear. I am not talking about romantic intimacy. I am talking about artistic intimacy. As you well know from your own life, not all intimacy is romantic, and not all romance is intimate. Intimacy is the act of being close to someone or allowing them, in one way or another, to get close to you. This closeness vibrates our entire humanity; it possesses many forms, senses, and states. It is arguably the state in which we feel most alive as humans, even if it is not always the most comfortable. The greatest joys and gifts in life arise from intimacy. Romantic love, platonic friendships, birth, and parenting are all intimate experiences, just like grief, loss, and sorrow are also intimate. A myriad of examples abound. In acting, understand that this level of affinity requires being in full and harmonious synchronicity with your scene partner. Playing action is an intimate act. The space between, *ma*, and the beautiful game of acting only come to life when this deeply personal connection is alive in you and your scene partner.

Intimacy calls for listening with your entire being, kinesthetically as well as aurally. You must be deeply curious about your scene partner, giving them the gift of your attention, and receive them as fully as possible. They must be your target: outside you at a measurable distance, there before you need them, active and always changing, your source of action. Your relationship with the target must be open and available if your acting is to have any depth. Otherwise, your work will remain just that—work—and heavy lifting at that. Without intimacy, there will be no joyous, risk-filled play in the dance of your acting, and the space between will remain dormant. Of course, the catch is that all this must cost you something.

The Cost

True heroism is remarkably sober, very undramatic. It is not the urge to surpass all others at whatever cost but the urge to serve others at whatever cost.

—Arthur Ashe

Every time you get up and act, it must cost you something—every time. Not in the abstract, but in the real-life, flesh-and-bones costs: costs in your heart, in your soul, in your mind, in your imagination, and in your entire being. You must have artistic skin in the game if you want your work to be compelling. If you are just running lines, doing the bare minimum, playing it safe, marking it, easing into it, sketching it out, saving it for later, just getting by, self-generating, playing the language or a quality or for laughs, demonstrating, delivering the minimum, showing, showing off, waiting for opening night, saving it for your close-up, pretending, or worst of all phoning it in, then you are not committed enough and not working at an artistic level.

And here's the catch: Everyone knows it. The audience knows it. Certainly the camera, the world's best BS detector, knows it. But most of all, deep down, you know it, too. Even if you can't face the truth and won't admit it to yourself, you know it. You feel it in your gut, and it doesn't feel good. It feels disingenuous.

Here's the truth of it: If you are skating by somehow, which includes procrastinating, not fully preparing to the best of your ability, slacking off, waiting and wishing for ideal conditions (which will never arrive), blaming others, and arriving habitually late, then it's because you're scared: of getting it wrong, of not knowing what to do or even how to do it, of not getting it right, of forgetting your lines, of looking foolish, of your scene partner being better than you, or of being told you have no talent. You are frightened of being fired, terrified of plain old sucking, which means you're really scared that if you commit as fully as possible and then are told your best is not good enough, you will be found the fraud that you fear yourself to be. And that will be the end—not only of this particular job, but also of your entire career. Scared, scared, scared. So, to play it safe, you never bring your A game. That's your constant excuse. And your analytical mind has built a fortress of reason around all this. It rationalizes all your excuses, baking them into your identity: "It's just who I am."

Remember: Excuses are like assholes; everyone has one.

But what I really believe people are afraid of, deep down, is success. If you are successful, then you will have to show up and take responsibility for your own work and face massive amounts of public judgment and critical response, time and time again. You will have to deliver the proverbial mail, rain or shine, just like the US Postal Service. Success is a no-excuses zone, where your feet are held to the artistic and financial fire. It is a blazingly hot public domain, where all your choices play out on the big screen, the wide-open stage, and television sets across the planet, a zone where you will be taken apart by critics under a microscope in scathing reviews on thousands of websites from here to Timbuktu. It is a space where you might be skewered with ridicule, humiliation, and psychological destruction.

However, if you're not successful, you don't have to face any of that. It's easier to make excuses and not do your best work, easier to be unsuccessful. And deep down in the pit of your humanity, you know it. Not bringing the best version of yourself to your work slowly eats away at you. Success is what really scares people because when you *are* successful, you must be responsible. There is no one else to blame.

None of these fears are really true, of course, unless you let them be. But the inner critic is mighty and can play terrible tricks on your performance practice. It loves to exaggerate and amplify catastrophic scenarios, negative stories that work their way into the ongoing newsreel in your mind. This is why you not only need technique, but you also need to commit to your acting with your entire life. This is why you need to become proficient at playing action.

When you know what to do, precisely, concretely, and repeatedly, you are not afraid. You will access your confidence through your vulnerability, and you will want to bring your A game every time. You will be excited because you don't know how it's going to go (which is the whole fun of the thing), but you are not *worried*. Nervous, perhaps. Intimidated, no. Fear is a mercurial beast that eats away at all performers, no matter the arena. It bears repeating: For the actor, fear is nothing but your ego. Fear is ego.

Acting is an art form in which you are in service; service costs you something. Art forms do not merely require discipline, sacrifice, and total commitment; they demand all three, all the time. Acting is called a discipline for this very reason. Just as being in the military, being a musician, being a chef, being in a religious order, or being on an athletic team requires disciplined suppliance to a worthy cause, acting, too, must cost you something each time you do it.

You are in the service of the script, the story, the ensemble, and the director's vision. However, the good news is, like with anything of value, the higher the cost, the more generous the reward. You will get out of your acting, as will your audience, exactly what you put into it. The cost to you in your work must be deeply personal and intimate. It takes 100 percent pure, unadulterated bravery. To release your full potential as an actor, you must surrender your ego. To do that, you will need buckets of *courage*.

I believe that our modern society has a problem with intimacy. True, honest, raw, unfiltered intimacy scares people. Consequently, people aren't as connected with one another as they could be, leading to higher rates of depression, loneliness, obesity, addiction, and even suicide. This lack of human connection is only getting worse, as more and more people spend more and more time with cold, inanimate smartphones and not with other living, breathing, fallible, unpredictable, often unreliable, and delightfully spontaneous human beings.

It takes courage to be truly close with someone. Fear is the genesis of disconnection and keeps people from truly opening up to one another. People often build psychological walls and even physical ones around themselves. They develop highly sophisticated and robust social masks, addictions, rigid defensive habits, and strong distancing rituals, even employing sarcasm and humor to keep safe and hold others at bay emotionally. Yet, that safety, that protection, costs more than the risk of affection itself. The cost of hiding from personal connection, which is what we are really talking about when we play it safe, is much greater; it costs you the fullness of your life. If you hide from it in your acting, it will cost you your artistic vitality, too.

Honest, raw, unfiltered intimacy is what we all truly desire deep down, even if it unnerves us. Often, we don't have healthy familial role models for it, yet we know in our bones that it is the only path to love; friendship; and, in our case, inspired acting. The art of acting is, in and of itself, a personal act, full stop. Love scenes are intimate; fistfights are intimate. Ask any boxer, martial arts practitioner, schoolhouse brawler, or bartender who has had to break up a fight. Fights are very intimate affairs. In fact, every scene you will ever play between fucking and fighting is intimate, too.

> As actors are professional human beings, acting requires the whole range of your humanity.
>
> —Earle Gister[2]

All well-written scenes are intimate in one fashion or another. They require skin in the game from the actor. You must put yourself out there and go for it, results be damned. There is no halfway. Just like a real-life relationship, it must cost you something up front to be worth something in the end. And here's the kicker: You may fail in the pursuit of it. You may get rejected. You may lose. Even when you put your best artistic foot forward, the scene may indeed go poorly. But it is also the only way to eventually succeed. The degree to which we may fail is the degree to which we may be victorious. If you want to reach unimaginable heights in your acting, you also must risk hitting humiliating lows.

Acting requires you share your imagination, energy, body, voice, intellect, desire, faith, ability, humanity, and sense of play. You alone chose to swim in the proverbial fishbowl of public performance. No one insisted you become an actor, of that I am sure. So why wouldn't you give all of yourself to the thing you decided you want to do with your life? If you believe in God, don't you think She would want you to trust yourself and realize the full potential that She gave you? To find your way into the radiance of the space between, you personally must commit as fully as possible. As the old saying goes, you reap what you sow. If it doesn't cost you anything to act, you are not going to get much out of it. Neither will the audience. They will demand their money back.

Ask yourself, "Would I pay good, hard-earned money to watch my own acting?" If not, it probably didn't cost you enough. Find a way to make it more important. Use your imagination. Dig deeper. That's what you are hired for. Dare to fuck it up—and largely. Not politely, but boldly. Paint with a big brush on a huge canvas. Spill some proverbial paint. Draw outside the lines, for God's sake—way out. The cost must be high for the stakes to be high and for the audience to want to watch you act. The artistic tightrope needs to be at 35,000 feet with no net. We go to the circus because the acrobats might actually fall, not because we know they are safe. Playing it safe is not compelling. Why do you think half of the world is obsessed with Formula 1 car racing? Because the cars might crash, at very high speeds. Even on your worst night in the theater, you won't actually die, so go for it.

An old actor joke seems appropriate here: How many actors does it take to screw in a lightbulb? The answer: One hundred. One to screw in the lightbulb and ninety-nine to say, "I can do that better." So, screw in your damn acting lightbulb like it's the only bulb of creative luminosity left on earth. Otherwise, every actor who sees your performance, as well as every wannabe actor in the audience, meaning every dentist, lawyer, banker, baker, and candlestick maker, will be saying, "I can do that better."

But, if you *do* take a risk (a *courageous* one at that); if you don't play it safe and your performance *costs* you something artistically intimate, creatively vulnerable, and boldly imaginative; and if you are in true harmony with your scene partner, listening with your entire being, radiating and receiving, releasing your energy outward, and the space between is crackling with energy—*then* the audience will want to tune into your artistic channel. *Then* they will gladly suffer all the financial and personal indignities thrust on the modern theatergoer. *Then* they will get their butts up off their plush couches, spend a small fortune, and squeeze into an inhuman torture device to watch you act. But only then.

Only if you change the air in the theater; cause molecules to rearrange themselves before their very eyes; ignite the space between; reach into their chests, grab their hearts, and shove them into their throats, reminding them that they are blessed to be alive. Only if you have prepared for your performance with every free moment; given your entire artistic energy to your fellow actors and imagination; left the stage emotionally spent, creatively exhausted, knowing that was the best you could do. Not until, or unless, you dig deep within yourself, dissolve your ego, and muster the courage to act in intimate harmony with your fellow castmates. Only if you summon *ma* and play the beautiful game of acting.

But, if you do all that, then the audience, recognizing you left everything on the field, will be your biggest champion. Then they will be on their feet at the end of the show, celebrating your courage. And so will I and every other actor watching you, for we recognize and appreciate the cost.

Artistic Love

> For one whose heart is large, a tiny room is as the space between heaven and earth.

What does it really mean to be intimate artistically? It means incorporating all the aspects of the technique of playing action that I have explained so far in this book. You must breathe fully, slowly, and with ease. You must let down, take off, and set aside your social masks. Your target of attention must be wholly outside yourself; you must source your scene partner with deep, genuine curiosity. You must listen and respond with your entire being while simultaneously releasing your energy onto your scene partner and allowing the connection to be fluid and potent. You must have faith in yourself and the depths of your imagination; you must trust your scene partner and allow them to affect you. You must play with childlike abandon and joy.

In essence, you must fall in love with your scene partner artistically. Let me be clear: I don't mean fall in love with them romantically, fraternally, familiarly, or literally in any way, shape, or form. I mean you must use all the mechanisms that are at play when you are in love, but you must use those same technical mechanisms for creative, fictional aims. You do this through the power of your own imagination, creativity, and vulnerability. There is no love without vulnerability. There is no intimate harmony without vulnerability. There is no inspired acting without vulnerability. Vulnerability, paradoxically, is one of your greatest artistic strengths. It leads you to an artistic love.

Courage

> Courage starts with showing up and letting ourselves be seen. . . . Vulnerability is the birthplace of love, belonging, joy, courage, empathy, and creativity. It is the source of hope, empathy, accountability, and authenticity.
>
> —Brene Brown[3]

To create something that ignites the space between, calls forth *ma*, and whistles the beautiful game of acting into action takes courage. Anything exciting worth doing takes courage. You know this from your own personal experiences on this planet. Yet, courage is often misunderstood. It does not mean being heroic, all powerful, or without fear. It means just the opposite. It means playing with sober vulnerability and opening your heart fully in your acting.

The Latin root of the word *courage* is *cor*, meaning "heart." The original meaning of the word *courage* is to "tell all of one's mind by opening all of one's heart." We associate the word *courage* today with acts of bravery. Yet, this is a deviation from the original and true sense of the word *courage*. Bravery takes heart. Intimacy takes heart. Acting takes heart. This is not debatable. There is no end run around this little nugget. You must open your heart and imagination together, simultaneously, if you want to play freely in intimate harmony with your scene partner and reach a level of excellence in your craft. Everything else operates at the level of mediocrity and mendacity. Getting to this level of excellence and honesty in your art certainly will cost you something. However, the only way to love, or act, is to open your heart.

Unless you are a soulless automaton, a cyborg, or a sociopath, there is no such thing as fearlessness. There is no technique or secret sauce or magical pill that will free you from fear. There is, however, courage. Open your heart, and you will discover just how much of it you possess. Opening your heart means you must surrender your ego. When you open your heart, you can love more. When you love more, your ego retreats. Then, when your ego releases its fierce grip, you can engage more fully in the moment and play freely in the now with childlike abandon. You will become present. Your acting will open up and fully release your entire performance potential. When you do this, fear flies away like a feather in the wind, and the space between is charged with energy.

You must open your heart and act from your unprotected self. This takes true courage. Actor training means being in the courage business. Working with an open heart must be part of your ethos; it must be who you are if you want to act with any human dimension and texture. Everyone wants to see in an actor their ability to open their heart in the work, breathe, listen, be fully present as they bring their authentic self into the room, engage their imaginations facilely, and play with courage from their unprotected self—the ability to work from their unprotected self under imaginary circumstances. Actors must learn to do all this and then do it under high pressure, publicly.

> Acting is playing freely, like you did as a child, because you will always be protected by the playwright.

> —Earle Gister[4]

In the current generational climate of safe spaces, trigger warnings, and the like, this level of excellence in training is unfortunately becoming more and more challenging to achieve, but it remains imperative. Young actors must learn that acting is anathema to safe spaces and that actors are, in fact, if nothing else, professional "trigger-ors." We trigger ourselves willfully and joyfully under imaginary circumstances. That's who we are and what we do. This work is not for the faint of heart or the safe-space crowd. Actor training that results in excellence demands training for adversity, not safe spaces.

Of course, the training space must be free from actual physical, mental, or psychological harm. This goes without saying yet should not be taken for granted. All acting teachers and directors must be professional, responsible, and respectful and insist on creating encouraging environments filled with permission and trust. But concept creep around the word *safety* has unfortunately led certain students to naïvely wish for spaces where they can be emotionally safe and, even worse, believe they are intellectually safe. Art's entire purpose is to challenge and confront established norms, beliefs, limits, policies, and modalities of thinking as it rearticulates the experience of being human. Art's very purpose is confrontational.

The English word *obscene* derives from the ancient Greek theater word *obskene* (pronounced "ob-skeen-ey"), which literally means "off-stage," or that which was not appropriate to be seen onstage. Yet, the purpose of theater is to bring the truth of life, no matter how difficult, challenging, or radical, onstage. The best theater has a revolutionary streak in it. There is no revolution without challenge to the status quo. Actors must be able to go to those challenging and confrontational behavioral places under imaginary circumstances in order to tell those stories.

In actor training, teachers have a choice: either "prepare the student for the road" or "prepare the road for the student." I advise the former; the latter is selling rainbows. Acting may be therapeutic, but it is not therapy. If you have deep psychological issues or personal trauma from your past that hasn't yet healed, you need to seek professional medical help before wading into the acting waters. Actors need to be fully present, awake, available, and accessible across all arenas of mental, physical, and emotional health. If you don't think you can trigger yourself into high-stakes imaginary circumstances without releasing your inner demons, then wait and get professional mental help before you act.

Your acting teacher is not a therapist. They are not trained in the tools needed to deal with your trauma, nor should they be put in the position of having to divine your own issues, past or present. They are there to facilitate your acquisition of the art of acting. As a student of this art form, you must accept full adult agency in the training process and seek out the necessary assistance to put you on solid mental, physical, and psychological ground. Acting demands the best version of you in all these arenas because the art form will ask you to work with courage.

This concept creep around safety is anathema to acting and, I believe, all art. Acting requires that you go to a brave space and engage your courage. The business of acting is certainly not fair. You are going to experience heaps of rejection, disappointment, and criticism. If you can't take the artistic heat, then I humbly and kindly advise you to get out of the creative kitchen. Acting, at least not professional acting, may not be for you.

Not everyone gets a trophy in acting. You don't get to be on the team just because you want to be on the team, even if you believe in your soul you deserve to be on the team and your mother tells you how great you are. You have to earn a spot on that team. Your ability has to meet the needs of the team and the level of play of everyone else. You have to rise to the level demanded by excellence and prove yourself. You have to earn the respect of your coaches and your fellow players. They don't owe you anything, except the chance to prove yourself. Some people just aren't cut from this cloth. Some get cut from the team. That's the reality of life in sports, acting, politics, finance, law, music, medicine, haute cuisine, and any other high-stakes endeavor worth pursuing in life.

Your acting needs to be engaging, dynamic, and worth watching. It must come from the core of you. This means you must always work from your unprotected self, artistically and imaginatively, because that is your most human place. That is what everyone wants to see: your raw, sacral humanity, filtered through the mask of a character.

And you have to love doing all this. Love is the antidote to fear. If you don't absolutely love acting more than anything else, then the work won't emit from a genuinely joyful place, the same place you played from when you were a child. In fact, you don't need a safe space because you love it so much you would do it if there were no extrinsic rewards. The intrinsic value of simply doing it is, in fact, the true value of it.

And realize: You will always be protected by the playwright. You will always be wearing the mask of the character, so you're covered, literally and figuratively. The playwright has you, so go for it. We go to a performance to watch the cracks in the armor, not the armor itself. Bring the cracks in your armor, which is your vulnerability, intimacy, imagination, and ability to empathize with what the character is going through, and then trigger yourself to believe it's *as if* it's happening to you, and the world will sit up and pay attention. Then you will be doing the actor's work. You may actually earn a spot on the team.

Landscapes of Paradox

> There are what appear to be many paradoxes. Courses of action, which in a common sense would lead to one result, turn out in fact, to lead to an opposite result.
>
> —Alan Watts[5]

The landscape of actor training is littered with paradoxes. What is true for one aspect of the work is not for another. In fact, the exact opposite may be true in the next moment, and rightfully so. Acting is complicated, paradoxical, and irrational at times. Do yourself a favor and don't make it more so trying to analyze. Paradoxes abound in actor training. Accept this premise, and do the work.

In the case of intimacy, vulnerability and surrender are essential elements. Paradoxically, it is only through this intimacy, through vulnerability and surrender, that you will discover confidence and power in your acting. True confidence arises from faith: in yourself, your abilities, your imagination, your experience, and in your scene partner. The greater your ability to let your guard down, to let go of the desire for control (sorry, but control is an illusion anyway) and surrender to what is happening in the moment, the greater levels of confidence you will experience. Faith is the path to liberation in performance.

The Latin word for *confidence* is *con-fides*, which translates as "with faith" or "with trust." Confidence is born from faith—not religious faith, although that may help you, too, depending on your own personal spiritual orientation, but for our work as actors, this means faith in self. True confidence is having faith in your human ability to accomplish the acting task at hand. This means you need a lot of trust: in your technique, your imagination, your humanity, and your fellow actors.

> If you are human, you have done 90 percent of the work. The other 10 percent is cops and robbers.
>
> —Earle Gister[6]

I advise you watch Brene Brown's TEDxHouston talk of 2010 entitled "The Power of Vulnerability." It is highly illuminating. If you have already watched it, watch it again. It merits multiple viewings. I examine confidence more thoroughly in a later section, but for now, if you want to be able to play action fully, if you want to electrify the space between, you need to surrender, trust, have faith, and work with courage and the joy of intimate harmony.

Perception

> Nobody sees a flower really; it is so small. We haven't time, and to see takes time—like to have a friend takes time.
>
> —Georgia O'Keeffe

What you *see* determines what you *do*. The old cliché about the glass being half full or half empty applies here. Are you someone who generally approaches life as a glass half full or half empty? How you see the world around you determines how you operate in it. If you see the world as a glass half full, you will act accordingly. If you view it as half empty, you will also act accordingly.

Action follows perception. This is perhaps the most underappreciated part of playing action. Sure, you need to know what it is and how to do it, but you must also realize that action is born out of perception. What you see, your point of view, ultimately determines what you do and how you do it. As the seminal American landscape painter Georgia O'Keeffe states in the earlier quote, you need to have time to see like an artist. That is your job.

As an actor you need to see the world, life, people, and human behavior more clearly than Joe Q. Citizen. You need to be able to see into the space between, peer into negative space. Like a Japanese landscape architect designing a Zen garden, you need to see *ma*. You need to see what others fail to recognize. To see with this heightened clarity, to perceive the world at a higher pitch, you need a different relationship to time. You need to train yourself to slow down—way down. And breathe. Only then can you really begin to see.

The original word for *theater* in Greek is *Teatron*. In ancient Greece, *Teatron* literally meant the "seeing place," derived from the Greek word *theáomai*, meaning "I view." The ancient Greeks believed that the theater had nurturing qualities. This is why they built all their acoustically perfect amphitheaters in spa towns, locations they believed had healing properties. The theater had, and still has, the power to heal. But we first must see before we can be healed. We must see together, in one room, and move through a collective cathartic experience to move our own lives and our society forward.

The Greeks understood the power of public performance. They understood it was not simply entertainment but a dynamic, important, and progressive act of democracy. The theater and its participants were, as Eleanora Duse said, the original shamans of any community. Called to a higher purpose, these shamans, or actors, allowed their imaginations to take over their bodies and transform them in the act of storytelling for the benefit of the greater good. This still holds true today. However, your ability to transform yourself under fictional circumstances, to surrender to your imagination, all depends on your ability to see not only more clearly but also more deeply and carefully than the average human being, to truly perceive what is actually happening in front of you—not an *idea* of what you want to happen but what is really, concretely happening in front of you.

> I'm curious about other people. That's the essence of my acting. I'm interested in what it would be like to be you.
>
> —Meryl Streep

When asked why she loves acting, Meryl Streep once said she was curious about other people. There's the word *curious* again, the glue that holds your attention to the target. Meryl Streep didn't say she was interested in performing or interested in herself or her abilities, awards, money, or fame, although I'm sure she enjoys those aspects of acting, as well. Meryl Streep, arguably one of the most accomplished and gifted actresses of our time, said, "I am *curious* about *other people*." And to be curious, you not only have to target your attention outside yourself, but you also have to spend quality time observing and paying attention to what you are perceiving.

Let me repeat: *Action is born of perception.* And your powers of observation drive that perception. What do you notice as you move through your day? Are you truly paying attention to the world around you? Or are you caught up in negative, sharp, quick, egocentric thoughts focused on the past or future? Or are you fully engaging your curiosity by observing and perceiving the world around you in the moment? Perhaps more importantly, what do you perceive in your scene partner when you act? Are you really noticing what they are doing? What are they doing differently from the last time you did the scene? Are you able to perceive the difference and react accordingly? Are you releasing your energy onto them in equal proportion to what they are giving you?

> All the technique in the world doesn't compensate for the inability to notice.
>
> —Elliott Erwitt

Listening and seeing are fundamental to the art of acting. If you're busy acting (and by that, I mean self-generating), then you aren't listening, and if you're not listening, then you're not in the moment. After observing literally thousands of actors over the past thirty years, both in performance and in the training studio, I feel that there is always more room for astute observation and perception in the work. Literally, if everyone would simply stop what they're doing, slow down, breathe more fully, have faith in themselves, trust their preparation, listen, and react, then their acting would improve tenfold.

For the actor, powers of perception can be put into two categories: (1) what you perceive in life and (2) what you perceive in performance. You need to develop your ability to do both, to listen to the world around you and listen to your scene partner; and then to react accordingly to both, more fully, more alertly.

However, most people are so busy with their own ego thoughts in life and so busy "acting" in performance (i.e., their attention is on themselves in both cases) that they are missing what is right in front of them, and they are holding their breaths while they do both. This is a chicken-and-egg situation. If you start to hold your breath, your attention disengages from the target and flies back onto yourself. Conversely, if your attention flies back to you from the target, you will begin to hold your breath. No matter the genesis, as soon as you begin to hold your breath, your imagination starts to falter, as imagery begins to fade when you hold your breath and tension creeps into your body.

Ease flies out the door as self-consciousness and fear raise their ugly heads. Game over. The space between evaporates back into the ether.

> You must see the world from the character's point of view. See as if through their eyes. There will you find the world of the play.
>
> —Earle Gister[7]

Again, to alleviate self-consciousness and interference, slow down, part your lips ever so slightly, breathe, redirect your attention to a target outside yourself, and get genuinely curious about what you observe. See more clearly. See more fully. See more carefully and with joy and gratefulness. And you need to love doing all this. Artistic love is the key to unlocking your powers of observation.

Reception

> The degree to which I make myself available to my scene partner is the degree to which I can play action onto them.
>
> —MacKenzie Meehan

A former student of mine, MacKenzie Meehan, who plays Taylor Rentzel on CBS's hit show *Bull*, stopped in her tracks one day in class and blurted out, "Oh, I get it! The degree to which I make myself available to my scene partner is the degree to which I can play action onto them." The penny dropped for her. At that moment she got playing action. But she had to make herself available to her scene partner to do so. She had to not simply listen to them but truly receive what they were sending to her. To do that, she had to decide to allow herself to be changed by her scene partner. She had to give herself permission to truly receive what they were doing and then let that change her. Only then could she fully send her action back onto her scene partner.

Acting is a gesture of *giving* and *receiving* in equal measure. You can only give what you receive and vice versa. This means that you have to be as fully available to your scene partner as is humanly possible and in alignment with your character and the given circumstances in which they find themselves. But the character is relying on you to be available. That means, if you want to be able to play action, then you must allow the other actor to play action onto you, to allow them to change you. Both have to happen.

You will need to first give yourself permission to fully receive your partner's energy. This can be very powerful and sometimes scary, so dropping your social masks and crossing the threshold from your daily self to your artistic self is mandatory for a healthy acting practice. However, if you are as sensitive and receptive as a brick, so, too, will be the effect you have on your scene partner. This is why vulnerability and surrender are so important to the craft of playing action. You need to *allow* (the allowing again) the other actor to vibrate you, to play you. You are your instrument.

You need to play as wide a range of notes as is humanly possible and let yourself be changed by your scene partner. If you don't, someone else will, and then they will get the job and not you. As a prime example, I encourage you to watch Rachel McAdams's audition for *The Notebook* in the extras of the DVD, and you will see what you are up against. Her attention rarely waivers from her reader, the actor Ryan Gosling, who is off-camera. She listens with her whole being, breathes and radiates her energy back to him, making him feel something, for sure. Even though it's only an audition, she brings her A game and performs it as if it is really happening, for the first time. You can see in her eyes the connection between her and Gosling. Notice her relaxed jaw, parted lips, full and easy breath. McAdams is listening and responding under imaginary circumstances, alive, spontaneous, vulnerable, allowing herself to be seen. The scene is intimate, and she allows herself to go there, even in the audition. In fact, it is precisely because she allowed herself to go there that she got the part. She allows Gosling to change her while sending her energy out to him. Even though we can't see the other actor in the audition tape, you can sense the space between them is alive, full of energy. There is clearly a connection between them. They have, as we say, chemistry. And lore has it that McAdams only got the script the night before the audition. Yet, she's completely off book, totally memorized, no hesitation about the words at all. Now, that's a pro. That's what you're up against. Watch it (you can also find it on YouTube). Learn from it. It's intimate harmony in action.

> Let everything happen to you. Beauty and terror. Just keep going. No feeling is final.
>
> —Rainer Maria Rilke

The degree to which you are available or playable is the range of notes you will be able to play. Playing action is not just sending energy; it is the exchange of energy; it is both the sending and receiving of energy *simultaneously*. You must be as receptive as possible. Your ability to receive what is coming at you and allow it to affect your humanity, vibrate your nervous system, and trigger your entire body determines the range of accompanying circumstances you can bring to your performance. It also determines the strength, power, and effectiveness of the action you play back onto your scene partner. Notice how McAdams manages to accomplish all this and with a sense of ease, *as if* it's really happening to her.

The minimum requirement as an actor is to deliver what Stanislavski called the leading circumstance. You play action throughout the entire scene to make the event of the scene happen in pursuit of your character's need in service of the play. The measure of your maximum ability as an actor is how many accompanying circumstances, colors, nuances, notes, shades, and levels and the range of humanity you can bring to how you play that action. This is the true evaluation of an actor's ability. In her audition, McAdams doesn't simply play her action onto Gosling with one note; she allows for a symphony of changes to accompany her action, shape the "how" of it, each coming as a *reaction* to what she gets from Gosling. More on this in part II of this book.

However, if you have a huge damper placed over your instrument, which usually comes in the form of daily, personal, and idiosyncratic defensive habits (which are all different manifestations of fear), no one will be able to play you, and no notes will come out of you. It's like trying to play the piano with your foot on the damper pedal. Your work will sound dull. Sure, you can act that way, play the same notes over and over again, often based on your daily self or personality, and even book professional work. But it won't vibrate as fully and richly as possible, and ultimately, it won't be artistically rewarding. It will feel hollow inside because it didn't cost you something. For your work to cost you something, you must take your foot off your own personal damper pedal and let the world play you. When you fully receive someone is when, as Duse said, the Grace appears, *ma* makes itself visible, and the space between comes to life. That is a divine artistic gift.

> Listening is technical; receiving is spiritual.
>
> —Alexandra Billings

As the brilliant actress, singer, acting teacher, and activist Alexandra Billings says, you can't simply listen as an actor; you must also receive your scene partner. This is part of your artistic self and manifests as a metaphysical energy, what Michael Chekhov calls the higher self. This is where the cost of your performance meets perception, when you fully receive another human being. You will be changed by them, and you won't be able to create an intellectualized buffer zone between what they do to you and the experience you have, but it is also the gift. And every gift costs something.

As Billings says, the gift is nothing less than a truly, artistically spiritual experience. It is a larger communal energy cocreated between two artists that appears in the space between them. It is the "vortex" to which Nina refers in *The Seagull*. If you want to achieve excellence in your acting, and by excellence I very specifically mean *performing at your highest potential with the least amount of interference*, then you must allow your scene partner, and the imaginary circumstances of the script, to *disturb your entire being*. There is a not so small part of every true actor who desires to be disturbed and triggered artistically, to ultimately transform themselves. It's why we do it and the purpose of theater itself.

> We don't let ourselves become upset or disturbed. We continue to do revivals because we think ourselves immune to the disturbance of a Tennessee Williams. A new play doesn't allow us to go in with a shield armored against disturbance. The Greek root of the word *obscene, ob-skene*, literally means "off-stage." Yet, the purpose of theater is to bring into public that which is kept off-stage.
>
> —Paula Vogel

Paula Vogel, one of our finest contemporary playwrights, refers to plays in this quote, but the same holds true for acting, the theater overall, and artful television and feature film. You need to allow yourself to be artistically and creatively disturbed by the script you are in. And you can only do this if your instrument is open and tuned and ready (and willing) to be played. You can only be played from a place of the unprotected, vulnerable self, coupled with your imagination. And this takes courage.

A very clinical way to think of this is that you need to tighten up your ratio of impulse to expression. For example, when you receive an impulse from your scene partner—when they trigger you, affect you, change you, play action onto you—your response, the expression that comes from you, directly correlates to that impulse. Your reaction to that impulse needs to be free of interference. Yet quite often, self-consciousness, fear, and doubt raise their ugly heads, creating mental and emotional interference that loosen the ratio of impulse to expression. You must train your instrument to arrive at a 1:1 impulse-to-reaction ratio. We go to the theater to watch people's reactions. Everything is in the reaction.

Exercises

Have I Ever Acted?

This exercise was first developed by Lloyd Richards as an experiential answer to the oft-asked question, How do I know if I have played action? Fundamentally, it is an endowment exercise, as the two partners endow each other with prompted qualities. However, Richards geared it toward igniting the space between by nurturing a strong exchange of energy between the two actors, resulting in the experience of played action. Over the nearly twenty years I have used this exercise, I have added a number of additional prompts of my own. What follows is a hybrid of the two versions.

"Have I Ever Acted?" is one of the most important exercises I use with my students. It should be treated as a precious talisman by actor and teacher alike. Normally I only do it toward the end of the semester, when the class has coalesced into a true ensemble and they are ready to have a mature, supportive, and vulnerable encounter with each other under imaginary circumstances. It works most efficaciously after my students have done a first pass on their scene work. They have already gotten up on their feet once with me in class and have begun to get the given circumstances into their bodies in a meaningful way.

The second pass in my class is focused on playing action, and this exercise provides the experience of playing action in the students' bodies in an organic, playful, and immediate way to help them move into their second pass. Also, on the day, I only do it after the students have crossed the threshold, stepped out of their daily selves and into their artistic selves, as well as done a vigorous physical warmup, one that engages the imagination and the ability to surrender to their partners. Otherwise, why bother trying to go deep? Actors in this exercise must be working from their unprotected selves for it to deliver its true potency, resonance, and repeatability.

It would be ideal to have an acting teacher, a director, or even another actor in your class read these prompts aloud while you do the exercise rather than try to do them alone with your scene partner. Alternatively, you could record these prompts yourself ahead of time and play them back during the exercise. No matter which method you use, you certainly want to ensure quality time to do this, as the entire sequence takes between thirty and forty-five minutes to complete at a minimum, not including your warmup. And you will want substantive quiet time to process it when it's all over. How you frame this exercise has as much to do with its success as the exercise itself.

A note to the person reading the prompts: Allow for enough quality human interaction between each prompt. Do not simply read and jump to the next one. That said, don't take too much time, either. This exercise shouldn't be indulgent. But the actors need to have time to process the prompts and then experience the exchange with their partners. In order to strike the right balance, you need to sensitively read the room, paying close attention to what happens between the actors. As Hamlet says, "Let discretion be your tutor."

Prompts:

Stand about three feet from your partner. Find a comfortable standing, neutral position. Let your attention come to your lips. If they are closed, let them fall gently apart and notice what happens to both you and your partner when you do. Now look at your partner. Really *see* them. Really *take them in.* Ask yourself silently,

- "What does it mean to really see someone?"
- "Am I really seeing them, or am I just looking at them?"

Now, find *five* new things about this person that you never noticed before. Realize they are doing the same thing for you. Take your time. Don't rush. Once you have found five new things, raise your hand briefly so the facilitator knows you're done with that task.

Now, allow yourself to *wonder* what it must be like to be your partner? Wonder what it is like to see the world through their eyes. Ask yourself silently,

- "Do I really know this human being in front of me?"
- "What do I really know about them?"

Realize that your partner is wondering the same thing about you. Now, ask yourself silently,

- "Am I really letting them *see me?*" If not, notice your lips again, allow them to part slightly, and let yourself breathe in a little more vulnerability, permitting your social mask to drop.
- "Can I allow myself to be even more available to the human being in front of me?"

Now, direct the target of your attention to the image of your heart. When you have found a connection to your heart space, ask yourself silently,

- "Can I open my heart more fully to this human in front of me, more than I am already?"

- "Can I enlarge the image of my heart for them?"
- "Can I send my heart to them?"

Realize your partner is doing the same. Notice what is now happening between you.

Then, think the following thought—without speaking—as you source your partner: "There is something about the human being in front of me that I *like*." (It can be anything real or imagined.) Realize they are thinking the same thing about you. There is something about you that they like. Notice.

When you have identified at least one thing about this person that you like, raise your hand so your partner knows. When you both have raised your hands, move toward each other, touch one point on your partner's body, and say out loud, "There is something about you that I like." When you are both done, step back to your original positions. Notice that your relationship has changed. It is not the same as it was at the beginning of the exercise. It is becoming more dimensional, more alive, more immediate, more present.

Now, if we are honest with ourselves, often, even with the people we are the closest to, there are things about them we want to change. There are, accordingly, things about them we *don't like*. So, now, think the following thought—without speaking—as you source your partner: "There is something about the human being in front of me that I don't like." (Important: It can be anything real or imagined, yet it must be specific. This is why the actors must have already crossed the threshold. They need to be in an artistic space and not worry about the social pressure to be nice or polite. This is not personal. It is part of the authentic game of acting under imaginary circumstances.) Realize your partner is thinking the same thing about you. There is something about you that they don't like.

When you have identified something about your partner that you don't like, raise your hand so your partner knows. When you both have raised your hands, move toward each other, touch one point on your partner's body, and say out loud, "There is something about you that I don't like." When both of you have completed this, step back to your original positions, three feet apart. Notice, again, that your relationship has changed even more. It is now more complicated, more real, more honest, more truthful, more human.

Now, source the human being in front of you and think to yourself without saying anything, "There is something I find *ridiculous* about the human being in front of me." Realize they are thinking the same thing about you. There is something about you that they find ridiculous. When you have identified that ridiculous thing, raise your hand so your partner knows.

Now, before you do or say anything, when prompted, run to another person who is *not* your partner and tell them what you found ridiculous about your partner. Once you have told that person what you find ridiculous about your partner and they have done the same for you, return to your original spot.

Now face your partner and realize that—*you have just betrayed them*, and they just betrayed you. You both are capable of betraying one another. You are looking into the face of betrayal; so are they. That's life. Look it in the eye. Notice, again, that your relationship has gotten even more rich and nuanced. There are things about each other you like, things you don't like, and things you find ridiculous about each other, and you both are capable of betraying one another.

Now, source your partner, and think to yourself without saying anything, "There is something about the human being in front of me that I *admire*." Realize they are thinking the same thing about you. There is something about you that they admire. Raise your hand when you've found what it is that you admire. Step toward them, touch one point on your partner's body, and say out loud, "There is something about you that I admire." Once you have both completed this, step back to your positions. Notice, again, that your relationship has gotten even more layered, more resonant, more meaningful. Breathe with one another.

If we again are brutally honest with ourselves, we must admit we are envious of other people in our lives, so now source your partner and think to yourself without saying anything, "There is something about the human being in front of me that I *envy*." Realize they are thinking the same thing about you. There is something about you that they envy. Raise your hand when you have identified what it is that you envy. Step toward them, touch one point on your partner's body, and say out loud, "There is something about you that I envy." Once you have both completed this, step back to your positions. Notice, again, that your relationship has gotten even more textured, real, and lifelike.

Now, source your partner and see them as a human being who has hopes and dreams. As sure as they are standing in front of you, they are filled from head to toe with hopes and dreams for their future. Now, think to yourself without saying anything, "This person in front of me has *hopes and dreams*." Realize they are thinking the same thing about you. They see you, too, as someone filled with hopes and dreams for your own future. Step toward them, touch one point on your partner's body, and say out loud, "I believe in you." Once you have both completed this, step back to your position. Notice, again, that your relationship has gotten even more layered and resonant, more filled with all that is our human existence on this planet.

Now, life is not fair, but in service of our art, we must be truthful, so source your partner, and think to yourself without saying anything, "This person in front of me will *fail* at their hopes and dreams." Realize they are thinking the same thing about you. The truthful reality is that you, too, may not succeed in life. You and they may never see your dreams realized. You both see each other that way now. When you feel the impulse, step toward them, touch one point on your partner's body, and say out loud, "I'm sorry." Once you have both completed this, step back to your position. Notice, again, that your relationship has gotten even more layered, real, resonant, and connected.

Now, step away from your partner. Go to another spot in the room where you can be more or less by yourself (depending on the size of the room). Once you are settled in your own space, notice all the energy moving through your body. Notice what you have experienced so far, what you have received from your partner, and what you have sent to them. Allow yourself to visualize the image of your partner's face, their presence, their smile, their eyes, their laughter. Source their image, and receive their energy from that image. Realize that this energy is your relationship to them.

Then, once you have done that, honestly ask yourself, "What is the one secret you keep to yourself?" or "What is that thing you did in your life that you would undo if you could?" Answer this silently and honestly. If the word *secret* doesn't have resonance for you, try perhaps *regret, guilt,* or *shame.* This should be from your real life.

Now, once you have settled on your secret, you have a decision to make: whether you would tell your partner this secret or not. Visualize your partner. Source their image, receive their presence and their energy, and decide whether you can share this secret with them. There is nothing malevolent about this. No one will make you reveal your secret if you don't want to. You are in total control of this decision. The choice is all yours. But you do need to *wrestle* with this decision. Also realize that your partner is doing the same thing. They, too, are deciding if they can tell you their secret. Once you have identified your secret and made your decision, raise your hand, and then go back to your original spot in the room.

Now, as you walk back to your standing spot, wait for your partner to join you and receive them in person. Source them. Breathe with them. Allow them to see you and receive you. Know that they, too, have a secret. Know that they, too, are seeing you as someone with a secret. You *both* have secrets. And you both have made decisions about whether to share your secret. What will you do if your partner has decided to share their secret with you but you have not, or vice versa? Will you change your mind and do something different from what you planned? What's going to happen?

Now, before you say or do anything, *imagine that you are standing at an airport departure gate* and now see the human being in front of you as if this is the *last moment* you will ever set eyes on them. This is it. It's as if you will never see them again. Memorize their face, their presence, their voice, their essence, their smell, their eyes, their smile, and so on. Take a psychophysical photograph of their energy with your mind's eye. Remember them as they are in this very moment. This is them. And realize that they are doing the same thing for you.

Now move toward them and touch them gently in one place silently. Breathe with lips apart. Now, say out loud *as if* it's forever, "Goodbye." Then, after both of you have said goodbye, walk away from each other, go off, and be by yourself in the same spot where you contemplated your secret, knowing that you will never see your partner again.

In your mind's eye, see your partner. Visualize the image of their face, their smile, their presence; hear their voice, their laughter. Feel their touch on your body as a sense memory. Source the time you spent together today, and breathe in thankfulness for it.

Now, imagine that twenty years have passed; you are heading to a home-town reunion and now find yourself in the same airport where you said goodbye to your partner. You look up from where you are sitting and see your partner from across the terminal. Jump up, run to them, and reunite with your friend as if after twenty years! Give them a hug! Experience this human being again as if after a long time. Say out loud, "It's so good to see you!" End of exercise.

Now that the exercise is over, share your experiences. Try to contextualize it against what we need to learn how to "do" as actors. Acting is doing. What did you *do* precisely and specifically that you can learn to repeat as a professional actor?

In this exercise, you have

- acted;
- played action (exchanged, radiated/received energy);
- functioned interactively by targeting your partner with your attention;
- made your scene partner feel emotions;
- felt emotions yourself without trying;
- responded to imaginary prompts (a.k.a., took direction);
- took the direction you were given and used it to change your partner;
- interacted with another human being in a specific imaginary situation;
- *permitted* the impulse (you didn't *force* it);
- *allowed* the work to happen *between* the two of you; and
- *created* the space between.

You worked on

- intimate harmony,
- artistic intimacy,
- permission,
- vulnerability,
- surrender,
- courage,
- artistic love,
- cost,
- release,
- perceiving,
- receiving,
- imagination (*as if*),
- availability,
- action,
- energy,
- emotion,
- direction,
- justification of an act or person,
- the secret,
- suggestions (from others and for ourselves), and
- breathing in the other person and letting it affect you.

You built a complex, multidimensional, authentic, compelling, and dynamic human *relationship* based on a series of given circumstances (prompts) in less than forty-five minutes. This is what every scene you act should be composed of: this much detailed human connection. You discovered that actors don't so much make things happen as *allow* things to happen. Your imagination does the work. Your humanity provides the raw material. These are all the things we do as actors. *Dran* is drama. Drama is doing. Doing is action. Acting is action. You played action. You acted.

Summary

- Inspired acting requires joyful play in intimate harmony. You must arrive at artistic intimacy with your scene partner to play action fully.
- Acting must cost you something every time. To cost you something, you must leave everything out on the artistic field.

- There are many paradoxes in actor training. Your vulnerability is a strength in acting. Confidence is born out of your vulnerability. Confidence literally means having faith in yourself.
- Action is born of perception. What you perceive determines what you do. Actors must have two heightened powers of perception: (1) perception in life and (2) perception in performance. You must perceive the world like an artist.
- Actors are professional human beings; acting requires the whole range of your human experience, not just the parts with which you are comfortable. You have already done 90 percent of the actor's work by being human; the other 10 percent is playing in your imagination.
- Acting requires playing with childlike abandon under imaginary circumstances from your unprotected self.
- Fear is ego.
- You will always be protected by the playwright.
- All the technique in the world doesn't compensate for the inability to notice. You must see your scene partner as clearly as possible. To see more fully and clearly, you must slow down and breathe with lips apart.
- You must see from your character's point of view, see out as if from their eyes. Really see your partner; they are your source. Only there will you find the world of the play.
- You must be as fully available to your scene partner as possible and in alignment with your character and the given circumstances in which they find themselves. You must let your entire nervous system and imagination be disturbed by your scene partner. The degree to which you make yourself available to your scene partner is the degree to which you can play action onto them.
- The minimum requirement as an actor is to deliver what Stanislavski calls the leading circumstance. You play action throughout the entire scene to make the event of the scene happen in pursuit of your character's objective and in service of the play.
- The measure of your ability as an actor is how many accompanying circumstances, colors, nuances, range of humanity, you can bring to your action.
- We go to the theater to watch people's reactions. You need to develop a 1:1 impulse-to-reaction ratio.

End of Part I

The preceding pages have provided you with a high vantage point from where to look out over the landscape of playing action. Now it's time to do a deep dive and get the craft in your body. Again, you can learn *about* acting from reading a book, but you cannot learn *how* to act. To learn how to play action and ignite the space between, you will need to get on your feet, as all questions in acting are answered in the doing. To that end, please turn to part II, "Practice."

PART II

PRACTICE

CHAPTER SEVEN

Invisible Action

Cognitive Analysis

You're only as confident as you are prepared.

Reading the Script (or, Becoming Event Detectives)

To evaluate the facts means finding a key to the secrets of the character's spiritual life hidden under the facts and the text.

—Konstantin Stanislavski[1]

As discussed in part I, at the most fundamental level, you need to be able to read a play for its dramatic action, as playing action is what you will eventually do in performance. More specifically, as action is embedded in events, you need to read the play for the specific event in each scene. Therefore, you need to become an "event detective," actively investigating and discovering clues for how to discover the events that you will eventually act in performance. Action is at the heart of every event, so when you identify the events of any script, you also reveal its dramatic action. Or, if you prefer, think of a script as a blueprint of action; the playwright as the architect; and you, the actor, as the builder. You don't just start hammering away without knowing what you're building; you need to have the requisite tools to read the blueprint before you construct your performance.

The Prompt Book

The first thing you will need to do is create a prompt book for yourself. Procure a black-and-white composition book (or any notebook of your preference), as they are sturdy and can take a beating. You can simply use the film or television script itself if you like and write on the blank opposite pages. Just know that the script will get dog-eared quickly if you don't use a separate hard-bound notebook or a three-ring binder.

Photocopy all the scenes from the play. Paste the photocopied pages, one by one, onto one side of the composition book, leaving the opposite side blank. You will use the blank pages of the book for writing and capturing your own preparation notes. If you are pressed for time, you can paste only the scene in which your character appears into your prompt book. You will, of course, read and reference the entire script, not just the scenes in which your character appears.

The body of the prompt book will consist of distinct sections that include your ideas about the story, your character, imagery, personal connections, musings, drawings, inspirations, and discoveries. It will also house all rehearsal notes, direction, blocking, dramaturgical research, and answers to the "Five Questions."

The Three Reads

Before beginning work on your role, you must read the play a minimum of three times, uninterrupted.

> Creative feeling is guided along the pathways prepared by mental analysis. The actor should observe this sequence during Active Analysis.
>
> —Maria Osipovna Knebel[2]

The First Read

Focus of the first read: overall impressions.

First impressions are very important in life. The same holds true for first encounters with a script. The first read is a vital step in your creative process as an actor and not one to be treated lightly. When you read a script for the first time, you want to create an environment for yourself where you can best receive all its gifts. The way in which you meet the material will have a lasting effect on your relationship with it. Let's go through a step-by-step reading process.

The first time you read any script, you want to make sure you set aside quality time to read it, ideally without any distractions. I suggest you read it in the following manner.

The Preread

Find a place where you can read undisturbed. Make sure you have quality time to read it all the way through without interruption. Make yourself a cup of your favorite coffee, tea, or other beverage. Turn off your phones, computers, iPads, televisions, and so on. Have your prompt book or any notebook and pen at your side to take notes. Do yourself a favor, and use the bathroom before you start. Make sure your dog is fed and your cat has plenty of treats. I'm serious.

In order to give yourself an artistic framework, before you begin to read, be mindful that you are about to enter an imaginary world. Notice that you are about to cross a threshold into someone else's imagination, the author's. You are also about to begin something important, your own artistic process. This is not to be taken for granted. Nor is it arbitrary or haphazard. This moment has purpose and meaning, not only for the production, but also for your artistic life. It should be important to you. The seriousness with which you approach reading the script for the first time should reflect not only the depth of the performance you want to deliver but also the seriousness of your career. Be aware that this is the vital intersection of where your imagination and humanity meet and merge with the author's imagination and humanity for the first time. This experience is precious and not to be squandered by laziness, carelessness, cynicism, or unprofessionalism.

Practice the ninety-second artistic threshold transition:

- Acknowledge that you are about to enter another arena in your life, your artistic arena, and are taking ninety seconds to do so.
- Breathe slowly and easily as you become aware that you are leaving your daily self and beginning work on your creative process. Even though you are reading and not acting, you are still crossing the threshold into your artistic self. The artistic side of you needs to read the script, undistracted by everyday chatter.
- Allow yourself to slow down and transform into a more receptive state of being, a creative one. Take a moment to be conscious of the fact that you are holding a gift in your hands. That gift is the script. Breathe in a little gratefulness for the gift you are about to receive.

Ninety seconds is enough time to allow for this simple yet important transition. But take as much time as you need to become focused and present in a state of artistic receptivity.

The Read

Acknowledging your artistic side, read the script like you would if you were experiencing it in the theater or cinema: If it is a theatrical play, read the entire first half of the script all the way through, uninterrupted. Take a fifteen-minute break like you would during an intermission at the theater. Then read the second half of the script all the way through, uninterrupted. If it is a film script, read it all the way through like you would experience it in the cinema, roughly 90 minutes for a comedy and 120 minutes for a drama.

As you read, feel free to take some notes, perhaps at the end of each scene or act, but don't get bogged down in writing. You don't want the writing process to put you in your head as you read. You want to receive the story as an actor does: experientially, imaginatively, and psychophysically.

The Postread

Once you have read the play for the first time, ask yourself, "What moments stand out? What images remain with me? What does it make me feel? What does it make me want to do? What inspires me about the story? What aspects of the story, character, or imagery awaken my desire to act? What does it make me reflect on?"

Note any major plot points that jump out at you, any events or moments that made a clear or bold impression. How were you moved by them? Note the overall atmosphere of the play. What did it do to you? What is the tone of the style of the writing? How did it affect you? What do you believe the theme is?

Capture for yourself the story elements that resonate with you and any other strong reactions you had. Don't worry about writing well, editing, or being grammatically correct. Just write, even if it is a total stream of consciousness. Get your thoughts, images, impulses, emotions, gestures, sounds, and what have you down on paper. Or if writing doesn't inspire you, draw pictures or paint on the blank pages of your prompt book. Or get up and move, sing, dance.

The important part here is to notice and take stock of how the story moves you. Remember: You are an instrument. You are the vehicle through which this story is going to be told. You need to allow the story to play you. So, how does it play you? This is the important part: noticing how you are struck by it as you meet it for the first time. There is no one way to do this.

And your first encounter with a new script may move you in a different way, hopefully, than the last script you read. This new script may alter your process slightly. Allow for that change.

Give yourself some time to ruminate and reflect on what you just read. Try not to rush off into the next thing you're doing in your day. Give your brain some free time and space to allow the images, the characters, and the story to absorb into your being. Allow yourself some artistic time to breathe in the creative gift you just received for the first time. You will never get another first time to be provoked by the story without preconceived ideas, images, or experiences.

Begin to visualize yourself playing your part. Envision yourself in scenes from the script. Allow these images to inspire you, move you, and affect you, and notice any sensations these reactions stir in your body, your psyche, your soul. Ultimately, you want to allow yourself to get *excited* by the possibility of playing this part. How does your character excite you? Scare you? Motivate you? How does it speak to you creatively?

Perhaps you are so moved by the story or your character or the images from the script that you literally get to your feet and while standing make a full-bodied, archetypal gesture that is a physical manifestation of how the story provoked you. Perhaps you voice a sound while you make that gesture or say a word out loud that is inspired by the story. This is the beginning of creating for your character what Michael Chekhov calls the psychological gesture for your character (more on this later). The whole process of acting involves transforming ink on a page into human behavior, to get it in the body, so don't wait; start that process immediately. Get on your feet, and explore movement in relation to the images you just received. Get it in the body, get it in the body, get it in the body.

The important aspect of all this is to try to capture the essence of how the story moved you, how it affected you. And each one of us processes story differently. I encourage you to examine, explore, and allow for a variety of responses, which will lead to a practice of reading a script to extract maximum artistic nutrients from it and inspire your acting. There is no right way. Follow your impulses and natural inclinations in how to process what you just read.

I also encourage you to *not* simply read the script and immediately begin to memorize your lines. That's like walking into the Louvre in Paris, seeing only the *Mona Lisa*, and then saying, "I saw the Louvre." Okay, yes, literally that's what you did. Sure, you saw a part of the Louvre and its most famous painting. But you didn't really experience the heart of the museum, not really, not with any quality, integrity, or thoroughness. You have no idea the depth and breadth of art, talent, beauty, joy, history, craft, spirit, human expression, pain, pathos, laughter, light, sensuality, composition, lust, power, war, ambition, technique, ease, blood, sweat, and tears, not to mention inspiration and divine intervention, you missed by going so quickly. That way leads to superficiality and lack of dimension.

The only way to experience the Louvre with any quality is to give it time and, here's the key point, to *get lost in it*. I mean *really lost*. I suspect if you are reading this book, you want to go deeper into your craft. Just like the bowels of the Louvre, you need to go deeper into the architecture of the script and get lost in it. You need to walk down blind alleys, try to open locked doors, discover things you didn't know you were looking for, walk into strange and atmospheric rooms, allow yourself to be surprised, feel the temperature changes from one space to the next, get off the grid, notice how the light plays across the architecture, follow your curiosity, tear up the map, realize you are insecure and unsure about where you are going, but notice that that same uneasy feeling is exciting to you and is telling you that you are alive.

It is exciting to get lost. A prepackaged, antiseptic, Saran-wrapped bus tour is no way to get to know a city, a museum, or anything really, to truly discover something intimately. The same holds true for a script. You've got to wander around in a script, get lost in it, if you want to know it intimately. If you want intimate harmony to arrive in your performance, you need to start by getting intimate with your script. It's where the artistic excitement lives, as well as creative quality.

So, before moving on with the next thing you have to do in your day, give this first read a moment of qualitative, meaningful artistic closure. Create in a moment of gratefulness or appreciation for the story, the characters, and the images you just received. Give a moment of thanks to the unseen playwright, the author who toiled, perhaps for years in solitude, to bring this work of art into the world and bequeathed you the role you are about to inhabit and the world you will enter. Each script is truly a gift. Treat your script accordingly, and you will be rewarded artistically.

Lastly, be aware that fear will try to manifest as cynicism and talk very loudly via your jaded, caustic, adult inner critic, which is your ego-self. It will belittle this process and make fun of it, perhaps loudly. Resistance will rear its ugly and persistent head and tell you that you have many other more important and immediate things to do with your day right now: start to clean your garage with a toothbrush, iron your underwear, check social media, bake Greek sugar cookies for the first time, binge-watch a new hit show, change your car's oil, shop online, or smoke a little weed, "just one hit." No matter how your own personal fear-habit manifests, it will because you're human and it's your habit. Realize this is fear, and for the actor, fear is always ego. It is resistance and avoidance couched in cynicism and so-called jaded professionalism. And recall what Eleanora Duse said about the ego: To arrive at the Grace in our acting, we must dissolve the ego. Dissolve the ego. Get lost. Get intimate. Do the work.

Stay the artistic course; remain in the joy of your creative process, which means keeping the beginner's mind. Enjoy not knowing. Discover. Explore. Expand. Breathe. Take your time. I am sure the playwright, the architect of the story, spent quality time. So must you.

The Second Read

> Language and sound can do things for us physically and emotionally.
>
> —Lloyd Richards[3]

Focus of the second read: arc of action for all characters in the script, including the three essential events of the story.

The Preread

For the second read, you want to create an environment similar to the first. Make sure you have enough uninterrupted time and a quiet space in which to read the script. Again, if it is a theatrical script, take a break for intermission at the halfway mark. If it is a film or television script, read it all the way through in one sitting. Have your notebook and pen ready.

The Read: The Three Essential Events

According to Stanislavski, at a very minimum, there are always three major events that are necessary for any story to be told. A story may have more than three events but never less than three. The three major events that you need to identify as you read the script for a second time are the

1. initial event
2. central event
3. main event

> It is important to remember that each event generates a new action, which in turn generates a new event.
>
> —Maria Osipovna Knebel[4]

Remember Stanislavski's definition of an *event* from part I of this book: An event is the change of one action or the leading circumstance to a new action and hence a new event. It is the point of highest conflict between the characters in the scene. It is the result of the characters pursuing their needs and playing action. Once the event happens, the characters are changed forever. They immediately have new needs and actions and are thrust into the next event. The event usually happens right at the very end of the scene. It is always a noun: a seduction, confrontation, confession, kiss, fight, and so on. In a well-written script, there is only one event per scene.

The Initial Event: The initial event of any script sets the story's action in motion, gives it movement, and propels the plot forward. It is the springboard for all the subsequent action in the script. Without the initial event, the story would never take place. It is the event that develops the action of the story; it is the story's *impulse*; it pushes the story in a specific direction.

The initial event happens *before* act 1, scene 1, before the curtain rises or filmic images begin to cross the screen. When the curtain goes up on a theatrical production or the film starts rolling, the initial event is already in motion, thrusting the characters into the story. The audience never sees the initial event of the script, as it is always outside the visible action of the story.

The initial event of the story affects all the characters. They are already living it, dealing with it, processing it, reacting to it when the story begins onstage or on-screen. An initial event in a well-written play is the same for all the characters in the play. The initial event is the same for each character.

The event itself is objective. That said, each character perceives the event individually; therefore, their *reactions* to it are subjective. The initial event affects all the characters and is the closest to the beginning of the first scene, setting them into action with one another. There might be multiple events that affect all the characters before the story begins, but the initial event is the one that is closest to the start of the story that affects all the characters.

The initial event is always mentioned at some point in the story by one or more of the characters, so ask yourself, "What is driving all the characters when act 1, scene 1, begins? What must have happened before act 1, scene 1, for the rest of the story to take place? What is the flow of action that my character is involved in when the film starts or the curtain rises?"

The Central Event: The central event is the highest expression of dramatic conflict in the entire script. This conflict is a struggle of some sort that comes to a head in one heightened moment. Aristotle calls the central event the climax. When you find the highest peak of conflict for the whole script, it is the central event. All prior action in the story rises to this point. The central event is the "booster rocket" event that propels the final action of the story to the very end.

According to the golden ratio (golden rectangle, represented by the Greek letter Phi), the central event usually happens two-thirds of the way into the story or later. All well-constructed works of art obey this ratio. The more gifted the author, the later they push the central event in the story. But it never happens sooner than the two-third mark in the script. So ask yourself, "What is the highest point of conflict in the script?"

The Main Event: The main event is the last possible event in the script, after which no other event can happen. It is visible onstage or on-screen. The main event is an epiphany moment, the aha moment of the script, and it is ultimately why the author wrote the story. The main event reveals the story's theme. So ask yourself, "What is the very last event that takes place in the script that the audience will witness? Why is it in the script? What does it reveal?"

Again, as you read, feel free to take notes, perhaps at the end of each scene or act.

The Postread

Now that you have read the play a second time, what did it make you *feel* this time? What did it make you *think* about this time? What did it make you want to *do* this time? Were there any new *images* that appeared during this read-through?

The Third Read

> Let the power of suggestion work on you.
>
> Lloyd Richards[5]

Focus the third read: the arc of action for your character, the individual events in each scene in which your character appears, and your character's superobjective (hopes and dreams).

For the third read, you want to create an environment similar to the first two read-throughs. With the third read, you will become even more specific, intimate, and familiar with the story.

The Preread

Make sure you have enough uninterrupted time and a quiet space. For a theatrical script, take a break for intermission at the halfway mark. If it is a film or television script, read it all the way through in one sitting. Have your notebook and pen ready.

The Read

Next, you want to identify the event in each of the scenes in which your character appears, as well as your character's overall superobjective, what I call "hopes and dreams." I suggest reading the whole script through as you do this rather than simply reading only the scenes in which your character appears. This will give you what Michael Chekhov calls a "feeling of the whole" for the entire script and how your own character's arc of action dovetails with the rest of the story.

This particular read is ultimately focused on the individual event that carries the core meaning of each scene and how these all lead to your character's overall superobjective. The event is why the scene is in the script. Each scene has a raison d'être in the overall arc of action of the story; that reason is made manifest as an event. The event is the scene's purpose. Think about it this way: You can't get up and act the scene unless you know why the character is there. The event is the reason your character is there. It is what they are there to do and accomplish. Your job as an actor is, first and foremost, make that event happen.

Accordingly, the event of any scene is directly tied to the characters' need (or objective) in the scene. Whether the characters achieve their needs or not is irrelevant, as there is always an event. The event usually happens toward the very end of the scene, right before the scene ends, before we "cut to commercial." Once the event occurs, that particular scene has served its dramatic purpose in the overall story. The characters have either achieved their needs or they have not (per question 5 of the "Five Questions"); the event happens, and simultaneously new needs and, therefore, actions are born out of the event.

The only way an event can manifest is if all the characters are actively pursuing their goals and moving their lives forward by changing the *other* characters in the scene. This is an artistic obligation, and the only way it can be fulfilled is by going *through* or *changing the other actors*. The other characters in the scene are the agents, the source, by which your character will achieve what it needs or it won't. Playwrights put particular people together in scenes for very specific reasons: to watch them change each other in order to ignite the event of the scene. The visible process by which the actors change the other characters is called playing action.

The action begins to relieve the need, which in turn makes the event happen. No need, no action. No action, no event. No event, no scene. No scene, no story. Action is, therefore, inextricably tied to each need, event, hopes and dreams, and the story's arc of dramatic movement. Action ultimately originates in the event. When reading each scene, look for the point in the scene that is the highest point of dramatic conflict. This is the event. The clue for this is to look for the major change of your character's inner line of action. How does this moment change them and help move their life forward?

Events are a change of action for all the characters in the scene at the same time. In other words, the event happens simultaneously for all the characters in the scene. The change in inner line of action will often manifest as a change in *language*, or in how the character is speaking or what they are saying. But remember that the words are only an outer manifestation of the inner change of action. The change in inner line of action will often manifest as a change in *physical behavior*, or in how the character is moving, or what they are doing. But remember that the character's physical life is an outer manifestation of the inner change of action. In a well-written script, this change of inner action will happen toward the very end of the scene. The event arrives at the moment of highest dramatic action and is when the action will change. The event will always happen for all characters at the same time.

> Indeed, the events themselves are always greater than the words spoken by any of the characters involved in them.
>
> —Maria Osipovna Knebel[6]

For example, a confession of love is always an event. The whole scene may lead up to a kiss; in the moment of the kiss, the objective of both characters is satisfied. The character may or may not actually say, "I love you," but the kiss is a physical manifestation of the confession of love. It is in this very moment, the kiss, when the lives of these two characters are changed.

The inner action or movement of the character is in this case manifested by a physical activity: a kiss. But there are many events that happen without a physical manifestation of that inner line of action. It may be that one character literally says to the other, "I love you." The admission of verbal love, for example, is always an event. The kiss is the physical manifestation of that admission, and the words, the linguistic manifestation. Both represent the inner line of action for the characters, which manifests in an event called a "confession."

Remember:

- In a well-written scene, there is only one principal event.
- The event is always a noun.

- The event of every scene happens no sooner than two-thirds of the way into the scene, according to the golden ratio, and usually happens toward the very end of the scene.
- The event determines your character's visible actions, what they do in the scene.
- The event is the moment in which the characters change.
- You must play your action onto your scene partner (make them feel something) to make the event happen.

You will need to become an event detective and search for clues of how and where the event happens. If you have not worked with events before, this may take some time to develop, but it is necessary that you work to refine this skill. If you are serious about getting more specific and demanding in your work, then you must ask yourself, "If I haven't been acting to make the events of the scenes happen in my past performances, what exactly have I been doing?" No matter what your answer is to this question, it can't be as artistically responsible as making the event in each scene happen. You can go deeper.

Now, you must keep in mind that "all questions are answered in the doing." Therefore, you really won't "know" what the event is until you get up on your feet and play your action all the way through the scene. But at least you now have a concrete roadmap of what you are actually doing in each scene you act in.

> Stanislavski repeatedly stated that a true super-objective arises in the actor only when he manages to understand where the actions of his character lead. In other words, the actor moves towards the super-objective of the role by way of its through action. Action—this is what the actor needs to understand in his early approaches to understanding the play.
>
> —Maria Osipovna Knebel[7]

After reading the entire play identify what you believe to be your character's ultimate goal. Ask yourself, "Where are all actions leading them? What do they hope will happen in the end? What do they dream about as a future for themselves? What is pulling them forward in each scene of the script?" This is what Stanislavski called the superobjective. *For practical acting purposes, this needs to become an image of how the character sees themselves in the future.* This image, this desire, this hope, this dream, is what gets them out of bed in the morning.

You must, as the actor, turn the idea of an intellectual superobjective into an *image* that motivates and stimulates you to action in every scene. As discussed throughout this book, imagery is part of your *source material* as an actor. You draw something from it; like from an electrical source, you draw acting energy. Take time to actively imagine the character's superobjective. Perhaps draw it out in your prompt book or find an image in a magazine. The image of their hopes and dreams ultimately needs to be specific and clear to you. The clearer it is to you, the more precise your acting will be. It is where you are headed. It is the image pulling you forward in your role and helping move your character's life forward in each scene.

The Postread

Something to keep in mind is that what you identify as each of the events for the script on the third read-through may or may not be correct. They are your *initial attempts* at identifying them. Don't get hung up on whether they are ultimately right or wrong. You will solidify them on your feet in rehearsal via études as part of the physical analysis of the script. What is important here is that you begin to identify the map of action, the overall arc of action in the play and for your character. You begin to find your way.

This gives you a place to start so you don't head into rehearsal, blindly making choices. The blueprint begins to take shape and gives you solid ground from which to choose and play action. You are starting to sketch out the flow of both the overall story and your character's journey within it. You will keep refining these discoveries over your rehearsal process because ultimately all questions in acting are answered in the doing. The map of your performance will come more and more into focus the more work you do on the script, both at home and in rehearsal. After you have given the script a thorough reading a minimum of three times and have done this event analysis, you are ready to move onto the next step: answering the "Five Questions."

The Arc of Action

At this point, you are ready to sketch out your "Arc of Action." Figure 7.1 shows the major events of each of the scenes in which your character appears across the entire script. You can break it down by individual scenes, acts, or both. Feel free to adapt it as you see fit, but it fundamentally will look like this.

Sketch an arc across one full page of your prompt book using the landscape layout of the page, like a rainbow. The arc represents the timeline of

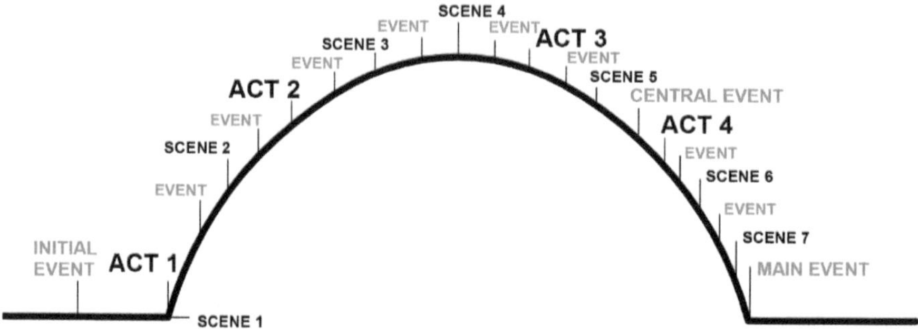

Figure 7.1. Arc of Action.
Courtesy of the author

action for your character. The left side represents the first scene of the script or even any significant event that affected your character before the play or film begins. Now, dissect the arc by drawing small, perpendicular lines across the arc to represent each scene that your character appears. You should also do the same for any significant event or action that your character experiences off-stage or off-screen and takes place between scenes. Then write in the corresponding event, objective and action for each corresponding section. When you are done, you should be able to look down at this arc and all at once see the journey your character takes across the span of this particular story.

For example, I once acted in a television miniseries where we filmed five two-hour episodes over eight months with two different directors and multiple film crews across four countries. The script for all the episodes was more than one thousand pages long. One day we would be at Pinewood Studios in London, filming an interior scene from episode 1, and the next, in Austria, filming a scene from episode 4 on an Alpine lake. My "Arc of Action" diagram kept me grounded in exactly where my character was on their journey, what scenes we had already shot, and in what order. I constructed an "Arc of Action" wall in the living room of my London apartment, with each scene represented by an individual piece of paper taped to the wall with the title of the scene, the moment before, the psychological gesture, the event, other significant plot points, and dialogue. I taped all forty or so scenes from all five episodes in an arc on the living room wall like one huge color-coded script rainbow. Once we had filmed a scene, I would slide its corresponding piece of paper below the others and draw a huge X through it. This way, I was able at all times to see the big picture of my character's journey and keep it all in my head in a manageable way. I knew where we had come from, where we were, and what still had to be filmed at all times. Feel free to adapt this diagram to suit the needs of your particular performance, and use it as you see fit.

The Five Questions

The Five Questions comprise the core of your solo preparation before you enter the rehearsal studio. They begin as part of your invisible work on the page and over time transform into your visible behavioral action in performance. After reading the script three times uninterrupted, now read *each scene* in which your character appears throughout the entire script and answer the "Five Questions" for each scene in your prompt book.

Some of the questions, like question 1, may remain more or less consistent for all the scenes in which your character appears, while your answers to questions 2–5 will most likely be different for each scene. You will need to read the individual scenes over and over again, dozens of times, in fact, to answer the questions with any meaning, specificity, and quality.

To give you a means by which to measure the depth and precision of your work, Sir Anthony Hopkins reportedly reads each scene in which his character appears a minimum of 250 times before he gets up to act. Would that every actor was this thorough. The work we witness would be that much more dimensional, human, powerful, and free of interference if always prepared with such rigor.

Now, of course, your answers to the "Five Questions" may change and evolve over the course of your rehearsal period. However, answering all five questions as specifically and carefully as possible will provide you with a solid and detailed framework from which to build your eventual performance. You won't be flailing in the wind, complaining, "I don't know what to do here." Remember: How you talk about your work is how your work will happen. This begins with answering the "Five Questions."

Question 1: Who Am I?

Part A: What Are My Character's Biographical Facts?

> Fundamentally, what my character likes and doesn't like. Get this deeply inside, and the rest of the play will take care of itself.
>
> —Earle Gister[8]

The first part of question 1 contains all the biographical information about your character given to you by the author, including *where* they were born, *when* they were born, parents and family, nationality, social status, economic status, marital status, race, age, education level, love life, self-identity, sexual preference, and so on. Fundamentally, it is all the concrete biographical facts from the character's past and current circumstances about themselves. Question 1 remains more or less consistent for your character across all scenes in the script, with slight changes from scene to scene, and helps shape their point of view on the world.

That said, for you, the actor, the development and discovery of the "Who am I?" of your character is always changing, continuously growing, developing, being revised and refined artistically from the first read all the way until closing night or the martini shot. Ultimately, the "Who am I?" is unknowable in its entirety. Like yourself, the character is always evolving. Can you even now fully say with exact precision and with complete comprehensiveness who you are in your own life? Of course not—not completely. Much of who we are and how we behave depends on the circumstances in which we find ourselves and the goals we pursue. The fictional characters you will play are no different. They, too, will be in a constant state of evolution, building on the facts from their past.

That said, question 1 will shape and color every action you play in the present moment of every scene. With question 1, you compile a list of circumstances that are always working on your character, shaping their behavior, and informing their worldview.

Part B: What Are My Character's Likes and Dislikes?

The next part of question 1 is your character's likes and dislikes. Draw a vertical line down one page of your prompt book. Label the top of one side "Likes" and the other side "Dislikes." Reread the play, and write down a comprehensive list of your character's likes and dislikes. Once you have completed this task, take a moment to look at the list and reflect on it. This is the spine of action for your character.

In life, the action we take is, at its core, driven by what we like and what we dislike. We pull things we like toward us, and we push things we dislike away from us. In other words, our likes and dislikes are the deep motivators of all our actions and provide a compass for us to orient ourselves in our own lives, as well as in our character's point of view. Question 1 helps us see the character's world through the lens of their own personal perspective and then act from that point of view accordingly.

Once you have this list completed, just take a moment to look down at the page. See what your character likes and what they dislike. This is how they see the world. These preferences shape their point of view and all the actions they take in their life. You are literally looking down at the spine of all their actions. This is hugely important. Once you have done this, move onto parts C and D of question 1.

Part C: How Is the Character Like Me?
    1. Thoughts
    2. Feelings
    3. Actions

Part D: How Is the Character Different from Me?
    1. Thoughts
    2. Feelings
    3. Actions

This part of question 1 is pretty straightforward but bears some explanation. Michael Chekhov suggests you answer the six subquestions of parts C and D for yourself as part of question 1: How is the character *like* me? And how is the character *different* from me? Answer both questions for thoughts, feelings, and actions. The ways in which the character is already like you (in thoughts, feelings, and actions) is work that is already in you, as you are similar to the character in those ways. The construction you need to do in creating your character lies in the areas of the character's thoughts, feelings, and actions that are *different* from you in real life.

Part E: What Are My Hopes and Dreams?
    This subquestion of question 1 is hugely important, as in life who we want to become and how we see ourselves in the future motivates much of our behavior. You need to ask yourself, "Who do I want to become?" We are literally pulled forward by the images of who we wish to develop into. In Stanislavski's terms, this is the superobjective. Again, for me personally, as both an actor and acting teacher, I have found the words *objective* and *superobjective* too analytical and intellectual for the actor. I prefer to use *hopes and dreams* in place of *superobjective*. I humbly suggest you do, too.

    You must ask yourself as part of question 1, "What are my hopes and dreams?" Hopes and dreams are what get us out of bed in the morning. The same holds true for the role you are playing. Now, this is important for a number of reasons: First, it provides an overall roadmap for where your character is headed in the script. You are able to line up all the individual scene needs in the script and orient them toward their larger hopes and dreams.

    Additionally, as hopes and dreams are images, you are able to source this imagery, which will activate you into your imagination and affect you physically, emotionally, and intuitively. These images help propel you into character as part of your preparation. We call this the "incorporation process," that is, incorporating the facts, images, and circumstances from your character's life into your body through your imagination.

Part F: What Is My Secret?

We all have secrets—all of us. Arguably, the more secrets a character has, the more interesting they are to play. It's not much fun to play a well-behaved character, unless they have a deep secret. Otherwise, where's the drama? Where's the conflict? What your character hides from the outside world is one of the interesting aspects of who they are and makes them dimensional and fun to play. So search for your character's secret.

What is it that they don't tell anybody? Why are they hiding it? From whom? And why? And what do they gain by keeping this fact a secret? Sometimes the author gives you this directly in the given circumstances, and sometimes they don't. If they don't give it to you, make one up. It's fun, playful, and imaginative and gets you excited to play the part.

From this knowledge, create the image (or images) of the secret. Give it a quality, a power, a color, a shape. Give it a location on the character's body. Imagine that the image of the secret lives in their heart or their mind or their pelvic region. Where do they carry it? How do they hold onto it? Do they think about it all the time but not talk about it? Do they hold the secret in their emotional heart space? Does it live in their will center and drive all their outward behavior? Incorporate the image somewhere into the body of the character. If you take a moment to reflect on it, you yourself know where your own secrets live in your body. Secrets are powerful and help define character. Use them.

Question 2: Where Am I?

Characters behave off of environment.

—Earle Gister[9]

Question 2 is composed of all elements of location and environment. Your answers to this question will be specific to each scene in the script and may or may not change. In other words, you may have different answers to question 2 for each scene.

What is the *physical location* and environment where the scene takes place? What is the year, period, or era in which the scene takes place? In what country does the scene take place? Is the scene set in an urban, suburban, or rural environment? What time of year is it? What season is it? Where exactly is the scene located? Is the location indoors or outdoors? What time of day is it? What is the temperature? What is the weather like? What is your character's subjective relationship to this location? Do they like it? Do they dislike it? Is the location public or private? Are the characters alone in the scene? Or are they being observed by others?

What is the *atmosphere* in which the scene takes place? This atmosphere is objective for all the characters in the scene. It is comprised of two parts: What is the literal *physical atmosphere*, as informed by the actual site where the scene takes place? A beach at sunset? A gothic cathedral? A prison? A music festival? A hospital cafeteria? A run-down, flea-bag, roadside hotel? Or a four-star Michelin Parisian restaurant? What is the *emotional atmosphere* of the scene? Love? Tension? Hatred? Eroticism? Frustration? Celebration? Revenge? Sensuality? Guilt? Joy? Grief? Regret? Freedom? Is it a "home" game for your character? Or is it an "away" game? Do they feel comfortable, open, and free in this location, or are they shut down and closed off by it?

Imagery, sensorial responses, endowments, and substitutions should be made for all these elements, from either fantasy, imagination, or personalization for question 2. You need to feel as if you are actually in the fictional space and develop reliable artistic and sensorial triggers for yourself to release into the sensation of really "being there." For a film, you might be on an actual location that realistically resembles the location in the script. However, you will also need to add the emotional atmosphere of the scene and how the location affects your character. In the theater, you might be on a bare stage and not have anything but your imagination to create the environment. In either case, the more you can allow your imagination to engage the "as if" of the location to play on your senses and nervous system, the more your actions will be colored by the particulars of the given circumstances of time and place.

Question 2 is the aspect in the preparation process that is most overlooked by actors. They underestimate the effect that location, atmosphere, and environment have on behavior. Yet in life, where we are has arguably the greatest effect on our behavior. We behave the way we do precisely because of *where we are*, combined with the event we are in and what we need in the moment. Pay close attention to question 2. Have fun using your imagination to create the "Where am I?"

Question 3: What Do I Need? (the Objective)

> The objective cannot be a thought; it must be a need. This will make it stronger, so when this is as strong as it can be, you will be able to drive right through the scene.
>
> —Earle Gister[10]

The Need

As discussed in part I of this book, question 3 is what Stanislavski calls the character's objective or goal; I call it the need. It is what your character absolutely needs in the scene that can only be gotten from the other character. Your character's action is driven by this need. The need must be more than just an idea. You have to use your imagination, energy, and physical life to translate the idea of the need into a palpable psychophysical human experience. To do that, you must create a precise image for the need and incorporate that into your body to create a corporeal and sensorial human predicament.

The need must help your character move their life forward. The need must be vital to your character. The need is immediate and must be pursued now. The need can only be gotten from the *other character* in the scene. The need must be represented by an image. You must visualize what victory looks like in the scene for your character if they get their need. The more specific the image, the more palpable and playable your action.

This human predicament must be dropped into your body as part of your moment-before preparation, for it ultimately drives your action in the scene. For example, if your character needs the other character to kiss them in the scene, then it is your professional responsibility to drop the desire to be kissed into your body *before the scene begins* because this is where your character is coming from as the scene begins. You can use Michael Chekhov's psychological gesture or Warren Robertson's psychophysical gestures to do this. More on how to do both types of gestures later this chapter in the section on "Coming from Someplace."

> Make your objectives relative to the other person in the scene.
>
> —Earle Gister[11]

The Event

> It is never enough to just feel; you must make the other feel something, too. Release onto the other. Our job is to make the event happen.
>
> —Earle Gister[12]

From the analysis work you did in the third read, write down what you believe the specific event of each scene to be. It can be answered by asking yourself, "What am I doing here?" or "*Why* am I doing what I do?"

Remember: The event is the moment in the scene where the character's inner line of action is changed to a new action.[13] It is the moment in the scene when the relationship with the other character is changed. In this moment, either your character achieves its need, or it does not. Usually this moment happens toward the very end of the scene, and there can be corresponding changes in physical behavior and shifts in what the character is saying. These changes are symbolic of a change of action, indicating the event.

Question 4: What Do I Do to Get What I Need?

> An action is what I do to make my fellow actor feel something in order to get what I need.
>
> —Earle Gister[14]

Question 4 is your character's visible playable action in the scene. This is what you want to make the other actor feel to get what you need. It should be stated in the form of an emotion and is the action you play in the scene.

The Visible Action

This is what you want to make the other actor feel: "I want to make the other actor, my scene partner, feel scared (or loved or special or guilty or sexually excited or small, proud, stupid, etc.)." If your need is to be kissed, then perhaps you would want to make the other actor feel desired or excited sexually or sensual or warm or beautiful, depending on the relationship between the two characters and other variables in the set of given circumstances. Pick only one, and play it in rehearsal. Then pick another, and try that one. You should try at least a half-dozen or so to see which activates the scene the most and gets you excited to act the role.

If you need your partner to confess something to you, perhaps you would make them feel guilty or wrong or small. The important thing here is not whether you actually achieve this state of being in your partner but that you affect them. You need to see the change in them. Only they will know exactly what they feel. They may never feel that way, and you may never know for sure. But you work incessantly toward it, trusting that what you are doing is working, and see that something is happening to them, even if you can't put a word to it. Ultimately, you should be able to see the effect of your action on your scene partner. You need to see that you are changing them.

If I am doing my job as a professional actor, then the audience will want to watch my scene partner more than me. Remember from part I: People go to the theater to watch reactions. If I am doing my job, then the audience will want to see how my partner is going to react to what I am doing to them. "What will they do next?" Ideally, my scene partner is doing the same thing to me, which brings us back to chapter 1, when the space between comes alive. It's like watching a tennis match. They don't know who to watch, but they do know that the space is electrified by what the two players are doing to each other.

> Find an action choice that you can connect to. Don't worry about the right word. Find the language that you can relate to: "make him feel loved" or "make her feel soft."
>
> —Earle Gister[15]

Positive and Negative Actions

Actions fundamentally fall into one of two categories: positive or negative. In other words, you are trying to make your scene partner feel, in one fashion or another, a positive or negative emotion. Start here by simply asking yourself, "Am I making the other person feel positive or negative in the scene?"

- **Positive Actions:** "I want to make the other actor in the scene feel: loved, special, cared for, warm, excited, funny, tickled, sexy, proud, big, turned on, seen, smart, kind, open, important, beautiful, hot, happy, cheered up, alive, safe, and so on." Even colors work: "I want to make them feel: yellow, pink, sky blue."
- **Negative Actions:** "I want to make the other actor in the scene feel: scared, guilty, small, wrong, dumb, ugly, sad (blue), envious (green), cold (black), silly, invisible, shamed, shut down, alone, ignored, unwelcome, regretful, bullied, anxious, worried, obliterated, dead, and so on."

Pick one and send it. Release your energy onto your partner to make them feel that emotion. That is what you are there to do.

Opposites

> Always look for the polarity in the scene. Where do the characters start, and where do they end up? What is the distance they travel? What is the journey? The arc?
>
> —Earle Gister[16]

Always explore opposite choices. It is always a good idea in rehearsal to explore the exact opposite of what you initially believe your action to be. For example, if the event of your scene is a confession of love, and you need (your objective) to have the other character kiss you, then to do that you may believe that making the other actor feel loved (your action) makes sense. So, in the first run-through of your scene, you might indeed make the other person feel loved like a lover, but then, in the next run-through, you might make them feel wrong and see how that works. Oddly, you discover that making them feel wrong works better than making them feel loved.

When you play the opposite choice, the scene often comes to life and takes on a dynamic quality that actually plays against the characters' dialogue. You realize on your feet that, in fact, the other character doesn't actually believe you really love them. And by making them feel wrong (about that fact), they come around to believing you. It is only then, by making them feel they are indeed wrong, that they confess their love and kiss you:

Actor A: I love you.

Actor B: You don't really love me.

Actor A: Yes, I do.

They kiss.

That, curiously perhaps, is what makes the event happen—the exact opposite of what you originally thought. Paradoxically (there's that word again), what you thought was going to work at home working on your prompt book didn't work as well as the opposite choice when you got on your feet in rehearsal. The lesson here is to stay open, fluid, and experimental in your exploration phase. Sometimes it is the exact opposite choice from what you intellectually thought when you first read the scene that actually works on your feet.

A good rule of thumb is not to get married to one idea of your action. Try many. Play one action at a time in each run-through, but try many over many run-throughs. See what works in rehearsal. That's what rehearsal is for: exploration, experimentation, and daring to mess it up. Play loose; get messy. Give your rehearsals the seriousness you give to a performance but stay experimental. Continue to feed yourself permission to try new actions and freedom to fail. But be precise in each individual choice.

All questions about acting are answered in the doing.

—Earle Gister[17]

It is important to remember that all questions for the actor are answered in the doing, so the initial word you choose here is only a tool to get you up and doing something specific. This is where "how you talk about your work is how your work will happen" becomes super precise. The more specific you are in the words you choose here, the more specific you can be when you get up to act. In other words, each time you run your scene, you need to do something specific to the other actor. That precise word may actually change from time to time as you explore, but each time, the choice should be specific to that run-through. For example, "I need the other actor in the scene to confess to me (my objective). To get that, I am going to make her feel guilty (action)." This is clear; straight to the point; and, most importantly, *actable*. This is an actor who is ready to get up and act. They are talking from the first person ("I"), and they know exactly what they *need* from the other character in the scene and what they are going to *do* to satisfy that need.

> Treat every rehearsal as if it were a performance and every performance as if it were a rehearsal.

Actors shouldn't ramble on for five minutes, ruminating on thematic threads in the play that might be appropriate for a literature class but are completely absent of actable choices, such as "Huh, that's a good question. Who am I? Hmm, well, I think, having read the play a few times, that my character, Joe, is going through a crisis of consciousness, and the theme of 'self-doubt' is apparent throughout. Therefore, I want to conquer that crisis and discover love in my life so I can be happy with Sally." This actor is distancing themselves from their role by speaking about a character in the third person ("they/Joe" instead of "me/I") that is distant from them while intellectualizing broad thematic strokes in the script. All these things may be true factually, but they are unactable. You can't act themes or general ideas. You can act actions.

> How you talk about your work is how your work will happen.

> —Earle Gister[18]

The "How" of Visible Action

How you actually play your action is determined by at least two factors: the adverb and the reaction.

> The "how" qualifies the action.

> —Earle Gister[19]

The Adverb

How I play my action is stated as an *adverb*. For example, there are lots of ways to make someone feel loved: tenderly, roughly, gently, romantically, directly, shyly, sensitively, boldly, like a lover, like a niece, like a sibling, like a child, and so on. You need to be specific about exactly *how* you make them feel loved. This can also be stated in the form of "like": loved *like* a friend, *like* a lover, *like* a nephew, *like* a daughter, and so on. This *adverb* or *like* is determined, of course, by the relationship between the two characters. This is also sometimes called the tactic. Whether adverb or tactic, they both are *how* you play your action.

The Reaction

As stated throughout this book, acting is fundamentally listening and responding to external stimuli, targeting your attention outside yourself. As your scene partner is the primary source of all your behavior (you react to what they do to you), much of *how* you play your action is determined by them. This is unknowable ahead of time. Just as a soccer player can't know where the other team is going to pass the ball in any one moment, neither can you predict *how* you will react to what your scene partner does to you. So, *how* you release your energy onto them, *how* you send your action, is only made apparent in the moment of playing. This is ultimately the fun part. You want to both be surprised by your scene partner and surprise them with what you send back to them and how you do it. Each moment should be a sneak attack of sorts onto your scene partner.

The precise actor also knows exactly what to do technically in the moment. Accordingly, they talk about their work with clarity and authority:

> To send my action, I must give my scene partner all of my attention (where my attention goes, my energy flows). I play my action by releasing my energy onto her. How I do this depends on what she does to me. I must simultaneously release my action onto her and receive what she sends. I do this by breathing fully and deeply (lips slightly parted), targeting my attention on my partner (she is my source), listening, receiving, and reacting in the moment to what she does. And I do all this from a place of vulnerability and intimacy. I let them play me as I change them in real time so the space between can come alive and crackle with energy.

Beat Changes

> The given circumstances are by definition given to you by the playwright; you cannot play them; they will shape the "how" of question 4.
>
> —Earle Gister[20]

Be aware: Changes in *how* you play your action, what are known as beat changes, *are not changes in action.* Use them, follow them, flow with them, but don't be led astray by them. They are vital to the extent that they affect *how* you play your action. But beat changes are not changes in action itself. They are changes in *how* you play your action. You will only have a change in action if you have a new event, for the definition of an event is the change of one action (or leading circumstance) to a new action. So, unless there are ten events in your scene (which there won't be, unless the script is poorly written), you don't have ten actions; you have one action. What changes throughout the entire scene is *how you play the action.*

Recall the analogy of the river of action from part I of this book. You only get a new action when you arrive at the terminus of the river and find yourself in a new river. Then you are in new action. Remember from part I, the action is part of your "what" of the given circumstances. It is the "how" that is always changing.

Many young actors (and unfortunately directors and acting teachers) mistake beat changes for changes in action. Beat changes can be represented in a multitude of ways. Usually they come in the form of changes in the character's language or dialogue; the direction you are given at a specific moment in the scene by your director; or, most often, what you get from your scene partner in the moment of performance. Beat changes represent the shifts in *how* you play your action, which is always an improvisation, otherwise you are trying to play your idea of the scene instead of reacting in the moment to what is happening in real time. Recall from part I, the "what" stays the same, and the "how" is always changing.

You only have a new action when you have a new need, objective, or event. Every change, nuance, color, shift, and adjustment up to the event is a change in *how* you play your action. This change in how you play your action is a beat change.

Beat changes can be written into the dialogue of the script, or they can come off of what you are getting in the "pinch and ouch," moment-to-moment exchange with your scene partner, or they can come from the director's direction. But unless you have a new event, the character's action remains constant. Only *how* you play it changes. One of the traps is over-marking your script, or what is sometimes called "actioning your script," with multiple actions and multiple beat changes on each line of text. Doing this will put you in your head during performance. You will try to act your plan instead of listening and responding in the moment to what is really happening between you and your scene partner. You can't possibly play different actions on each line of text, or every other line for that matter, and remain present with your scene partner.

Yes, there are beat changes in each scene. Some of them are triggered by the text; some, by what happens physically; some, by the direction you have been given; but mostly they are changes in how you play your action, or changes in the beat of the scene, which will come from your scene partner. You can't possibly know ahead of time how you are going to react until you have some stimulus to respond to. Beat changes, the changes in how you play your action, will come from how you and your scene partner react to one another. And if you are in your head, trying to do what you wrote down in your script, you won't be listening and responding to what is actually happening in the moment with your scene partner.

In baseball, the swing of the bat depends on the pitch coming at it. You have to swing in real time at what is moving toward you. The same is true for an action you are playing in your scene. *How* you play your action, *how* you swing your bat, depends on what is coming at you. You must always react in the present moment to the pitch that is coming at you, not try to act your idea of how your scene partner should have thrown the ball. That only ends badly for the batter, and you. Beat changes provide spontaneous variety and flavors to the action of any scene. Enjoy them and flow with them; just don't confuse them for new actions!

Question 5: What Do I Do If I Get or Don't Get What I Want?

> If I don't get what I want, the author will tell me what to do. Change of objective is usually the result.
>
> —Earle Gister[21]

This question lays out the *consequences* for your character in the scene and determines what is at stake for them. These are the stakes in the scene. Question 5 should be represented by two specific *images*.

The Image of Success

This is a specific image of what success in the scene looks like for your character: obtaining, achieving, or realizing their immediate need. This might be the image of you with a huge smile on your face, radiating joy as you kiss the other character. Or it might be of you standing proud in a confident, open gesture.

The Image of Failure

This is an image of what failure in the scene looks like if you do not obtain your immediate need. This might be the image of you sitting alone, depressed in your dark, small apartment. Or it might be of you curled up in a ball, hiding from the world. Or the image might be you, standing alone at a picnic, surrounded by happily married couples.

It is your job as the actor playing the role to empathize with the predicament in which your fictional human finds themselves. You internalize these images and make them as meaningful to you, as if they were from your own life. These facts may or may not have been provided to you by the author, so it may be up to you to imagine what their life would be like if they *do* get what they need *and* if they *don't* get what they need. These are two very different images. Both images motivate you and drive your action.

This essential step in the process will begin to inform the psychophysical predicament that your character finds themselves in as they enter the scene. It is humanly where they are coming from. Internalizing and incorporating these images are part of your invisible work, your preparation, and must be dropped into the body via your imagination during the moment before. Ultimately, it is these two images together that are working on your character and driving their behavior in the moment-to-moment work of the scene. This is true for all of us in life. We are driven by what we desire, as well as possible failure, the fear of not getting it.

You should ask yourself,

- "What is at stake for my character in this scene?"
- "Is the outcome literally life or death?"
- "If I don't satisfy my need, what will happen to me?"
- "Will I be homeless? Lose my job? End my marriage? Fall in love for the first time? Save a family member from destitution?"

The higher the stakes, the deeper the need, the stronger and more immediate the action you will play in the scene.

The Five Questions: Prompt Book Template

1. Who Am I?
1. Biographical facts
2. Likes and dislikes

How is the character like me in

- Thoughts?
- Feelings?
- Actions?

How is the character different from me in

- Thoughts?
- Feelings?
- Actions?

1. Hopes and dreams (superobjective)
2. Secret

2. Where Am I?
1. Location, time, etc.
2. Atmosphere
3. Relationship to place

3. What Do I Need? (the Objective)
1. The need
2. The event

4. What Do I Do to Get What I Need? (the Action)
1. Visible action
2. How I play my action (adverb and reaction)

5. What Do I Do If I Get or Don't Get What I Want? (the Stakes)
1. Image of success
2. Image of failure

Coming from Someplace

You must always be coming from someplace as the character to do something that is immediate and important and moves your life forward.

—Lloyd Richards[22]

Now that you have launched your invisible work, read your script multiple times, began your prompt book, started answering the Five Questions, worked on your event analysis, and sketched out your arc of action, you will want to, simultaneously, get all this imagery into your body. Ultimately that is what the work of the actor is all about, transforming your daily self into an imaginary role. That means incorporating as many of the given circumstances as humanly possible into your own body, mind, voice, energy, and imagination. It is never too early to begin this process.

> All plays begin off-stage, and it is the actor's responsibility to bring the off-stage life, onstage.
>
> —Earle Gister[23]

It is your artistic responsibility to align your instrument with as many of the given circumstances from the script as you enter each scene. This part of the actor's preparation process starts as the invisible work and then transforms into visible action in performance. "Coming from someplace" is colloquially referred to in the business as the "moment before." In other words, it is the moment before your character enters the scene; it is where they are coming from in their life.

This doesn't just mean where they are physically coming from, although that is certainly part of it. What is meant by this is more human in context: where your character is coming from psychologically, mentally, and emotionally, as well as physically—what is actually living in them as they enter the scene. Your character has lived an entire life before they enter, and it is incumbent on you to incorporate as many of the leading and accompanying circumstances as possible from that life to create the sense that your character is coming from someplace and that you aren't just entering the scene cold. The trap for many actors is that they are inadequately prepared to start the scene and actually use the beginning of the scene to warm up into it. This is a huge mistake. You must enter with the state of being of the character before the scene begins.

There are many effective ways to do this. The Meisner Technique suggests engaging your imagination through daydreaming or active fantasizing. Lee Strasberg and the Actor's Studio approach prefers actors to use sense memory, substitutions, or personalization to get themselves into the moment before. I have found both these approaches useful, depending on the role, scene, script, and medium in which I am working. However, the more experienced I became, the less I relied on personalization, and the more I found psychophysical approaches powerful and efficacious. Those techniques that engage the body and imagination simultaneously without engaging my analytical mind proved more useful and liberating. To that end, I propose the following two psychophysical techniques to use in your moment-before preparation.

The first is Michael Chekhov's psychological gesture. The second is the suite of psychophysical gestures developed by twentieth-century New York–based acting teacher Warren Robertson. As with any acting technique, you must practice them over time and develop your own working relationship with them. But you can start working on them immediately after reading the script and long before you enter the rehearsal room or sound stage. In fact, the sooner you start working with them, the deeper the work will be in your body when you get to the performance.

> The actor must figure out what is the appropriate state of being. A good playwright will do this for the actor with an early or preceding scene. You cannot play this, but it must be present in the actor's life when they play their action.
>
> —Earle Gister[24]

The Psychological Gesture

Michael Chekhov developed what he called the psychological gesture (PG) as a means to engage the entire actor's instrument while circumventing the analytical mind. He called the PG a "charcoal sketch of the character."[25] Chekhov developed the PG as a key to unlock the actor's will. As the need of any character resides in their will center, by making a PG, you awaken your own will in service of the character. Gesture is movement, and movement creates energy, so when you make a PG, you fill your body with the necessary energy to play action. The PG loads your proverbial artistic gun, so you can go into the scene and fire it.

Fundamentally, the PG is a way to drop your character's need into your body without thinking too much about it. It is an essential and reliable tool to activate you in any genre of work in any medium. To do a PG, you simply make a full-bodied gesture inspired by the given circumstances that engages your entire being and activates your desire to play the part. Because it is a "sketch" of the role and not meant to be the finished product, you can start working on it immediately after reading the script and develop it across your entire rehearsal process. In fact, the sooner you start using it in your process, the more effective and reliable it will be for you.

Although it is physical in nature, the PG is more than just an exercise. It is a way to stimulate your instrument artistically into the entire psychophysical nature of your character, to tangibly awaken the psychology of the fictional role via your own humanity. By using a PG, you are able to translate ink on a page into real-time sensations in your body, *sensations* that align with the predicament in which your character finds themselves at any moment in the script, and it allows you to do so without intellectualizing the moment. The PG is not an idea of a moment; it is a live, dynamic experience that energizes your desire to act. When done fully and creatively, the PG will awaken the character's soul for you and fill you with the desire to play out their life.

A psychological gesture can be used in many ways. It can be used as a tool to connect to your character overall or more specifically to their hopes and dreams or to help create the psychophysical state of being of the moment before a scene. It can be used as a tool to discover the character's need and action; it can be used to explore individual moments in the script, lines, words, images, or even the event itself. You might develop one PG for the entire script, altering it slightly before each scene as the story evolves and your character changes. Or you might develop entirely different PGs for your character for each scene they are in. Really, it is up to you. But it is always there to help you get the work in your body. The PG will never let you down in this regard.

> You can always make a gesture, and it will always create a sensation in your body.

For the purpose of this book and playing action in particular, I focus on how to use a PG to drop the character's need into your body, creating the energy you will send out onto your scene partner as action. Like a tuning fork, the PG strikes your instrument artistically; it gets you in tune with your role, creating palpable vibrations in your body that simulate your character's need. Done as part of your preparation process, the energy generated by the PG is carried into the actual acting of the scene and then *released* onto your scene partner.

Remember: You always *have* a state of being, and you *play* an action. You cannot play a state of being. Trying to play a state of being in performance is self-generating; it means your attention is on yourself during the scene. Recall the discussion from part I: No one in life is going around, trying to feel anything. Feelings come along in the living. Feelings follow actions; they come as reactions to stimuli. But a PG can create in you the state of being that the character has when they enter the scene. It creates a real psycho-physical need in your body, manifested as energy, that you will then send as action onto the other actor in the scene. The PG aligns your being with where your character is coming from.

With the PG, you are not looking to create an emotion; rather, you are making a large, bold, strong, specific, full-bodied archetypal gesture to create a *sensation* in the body. By adding a quality of movement to it, *how* you make the gesture, you can arrive at a wide variety of sensations. Emotions will either follow, or they won't. But the PG will always alter the landscape of sensation in your body.

The objective of the PG is to create psychophysical *sensations* in your body that closely resemble where your character is coming from in the scene. The PG will always move you from your daily self into your artistic self and, ideally, into the state of being the moment before. This is hugely reassuring to the actor. It will reliably shift your energy closer to that of the character, closer to the imaginary state of being of the role. And, perhaps most impor-tantly, it is not an *idea* of a moment before; it actually kick-starts an active and dynamic *energy* flow in your own actor's body, one that is vibrating in you when you enter the scene. It is real, palpable, imaginative, and human.

> There are no rules telling us how to discover the Psychological Gesture; it must be discovered intuitively.
>
> —Michael Chekhov[26]

Although there are no rules per se to the psychological gesture, Michael Chekhov gives us some helpful guidelines for creating an effective one. You need to practice these so that doing PGs becomes second nature to you and part of your invisible prep.

Making a Psychological Gesture

A consistent recipe for PGs involves the following ingredients: The PG is always made off-stage or as part of your rehearsal prep; it is never made on-stage during performance. The PG is made *standing* on your feet and involves your whole body. Both feet are planted on the ground. You may make one step, if need be, but the PG should not be done while walking or moving around the room. It is a gesture, not a dance movement.

Michael Chekhov suggests starting by asking yourself, "What is the main desire of my character?" For our purposes here, you can either do this for your character's overall hopes and dreams (superobjective) or for their need (objective) in the scene. You don't have to have a concrete answer to this to begin exploring. The important thing is to start exploring, experimenting, and playing. Even if you have only an inkling, begin moving.

A PG is one *strong*, specific gesture with a precise beginning, middle, and end. It is the strength of the movement that awakens your will center. A PG must be *simple*. It is not a series of movements. A PG is *not* an exploration of complex postmodern dance movements. It must have a specific *form*. It should eventually be precise and repeatable. The movement is not sloppy or random. Explore your PG until you find a precise form for it. By the end of your exploration process, you should know exactly where it starts, where the sweet spot is in the middle, and how it finishes.

The PG should be an *archetypal* movement. By archetype, Chekhov means a gesture that is universally recognizable and involves the entire body. The archetype speaks directly to your will center. It is decidedly not a daily gesture, like waving goodbye or hello. If you are making the gesture to push, for example, make the most basic, fundamental, full-bodied, archetypal push you can. Anywhere in the world, someone should be able to recognize that you are pushing by watching you. When you start to push the air around you with your whole body, it awakens a deep, corporeal understanding of what it means to push. Lots of characters are pushing up against things in their lives. From your own life, your body knows what it is like to have to push. The PG will stir that corporeal knowledge. The archetype taps into primal body memory and releases a strong and powerful flow of energy. Keep the gestures obvious and archetypal. Your PGs will be more effective and reliable that way.

The movement of a PG should align archetypally with a *verb*, such as to open, to expand, to close, to contract, to push, to pull, to lift, to smash, to penetrate, to gather, to reach, to tear, and to wring.

The PG needs a specific *tempo*. Play around with different speeds along the tempo spectrum until you find one that speaks to you kinesthetically and ignites your desire to play the part. The tempo of your PG will have a direct and immediate effect on the sensations you experience in your body. Different tempos will create different sensations.

You don't need to have an idea of what you are actually pushing when you make the gesture of pushing. Simply push and see what happens to you. Push and notice what the gesture stirs in you. Start pushing the air around you with your whole being, and you will find that images come to you. You don't need an image of what you are pushing to begin—quite the opposite, in fact. You will find the more you use the PG, the more the gestures themselves generate imagery.

By engaging the *entire body*, the PG wakes up the *will center*, the lower chakra in the pelvic girdle. It will stir in you the will to act. Archetypal movements provoke us on a primordial level. Thanks to sacral knowledge of millions of years of evolution, our bodies have a deep-seated memory of what it means to fully open, push, pull, smash, tear, lift, reach, and so on.

The PG always involves a *shift of weight*, a *level change*, or *one step*. This movement will activate the will center. If you don't engage the will center, the PG is less powerful.

The PG is activated in three steps:

1. **Preparation:** Take a moment to prepare yourself to do the PG. Don't just bang it out. Before you actually push, say to yourself silently or out loud, "I desire to push." Allow the desire to push to actually build up in you before you make the gesture physically.
2. **Action:** When you build your inner desire to a place where you must push, then follow that impulse to push, and make the actual gesture; push with your whole body.
3. **Radiating or Sustaining:** During this step, you *listen kinesthetically* to the gesture, allowing it to play on you. You notice how it provokes you, triggers you, and changes you corporeally, emotionally, energetically, and psychologically. Remember: This is the whole point of doing the gesture. You are using the PG to provoke yourself into the given circumstances. Chekhov suggests *sustaining* the end position of the PG for ten to fifteen seconds to allow its power to fill you to the brim. This vibration created by the PG is the energy that you will *radiate* outward as you enter the scene. Then, you radiate the energy created by the PG out onto your scene partner.

The "dish" is good, but the "gravy" is the pleasure. This sustaining is the "gravy."

—Michael Chekhov[27]

Quality of Movements

A PG always has a quality of movement to it. *How* you perform the gesture is also deeply important. Like tempo, the quality of movement with which you execute the gesture determines the feelings it stirs up in you. A quality of movement is *how* you move your body physically. Chekhov suggests four fundamental qualities of movement to start: molding (image of clay), floating (image of water), flying (image of air), and radiating (image of fire). Before you work on a gesture itself, simply practice moving your body with these four different qualities. "I *mold* the space around me" (imagine yourself surrounded by thick, slightly moist clay); "My arm *floats* through space" (imagine your body buoyed by water); "I *fly* across the room" (imagine strong currents of air are lifting your body from all around you); "My walk is filled with the movement of *fire*" (imagine your body filled with flames as you move effortlessly yet powerfully like a fire across a valley).

The possibilities for qualities of movement are virtually endless, including emotional states, as well as tempo and rhythm. For example, pushing quickly will stimulate you differently than pushing lethargically. Pushing as if you are surrounded by clay creates a radically different experience in your body than pushing with the quality of movement of fire. You can also push with emotional qualities of movement, such as rage, care, or joy. Even though your body performed the same exact archetypal gesture of pushing with the different qualities of movement, you get completely different experiences in your body. Here are some possible qualities of movements:

- **Tempo and Rhythm:** staccato or legato, quickly or slowly
- **Images:** molding (earth), floating (water), flying (air), radiating (fire)
- **Emotions:** joy, anger, care, tenderness, power, confidence, fear, panic, caution, surprise, sensuality, release, sexuality, desire, revenge, guilt, regret, anticipation, mischief, silliness.

Feel free to mix and match. Explore *opposites*. If you think the PG might be to smash, also try to lift. Keep your options open, and listen to your body. When it feels right, you will know it, as you will be filled with the desire to act the scene.

Radiating

The third stage of the PG is radiating. Radiating is the act of sending something out. For the actor, it means sending their energy beyond the body, or what is commonly known as "presence." It is the energy that emanates from someone and what we receive from them the instant they walk into a room. To create this radiating, Chekhov suggests sustaining the end position of the PG for ten to fifteen seconds after you have reached the physical limit. Imagine your body continuing to make the gesture, even though your body has stopped moving.

So, we may say that the *strength* of the movement stirs our will *power* in general, the *kind* of movement awakens in us a definite corresponding *desire*, and the *quality* of the same movement conjures up our *feelings*.

—Michael Chekhov[28]

A Few Words of Caution

Refrain from touching the floor or any other object with any part of your body except your two feet; otherwise, the energy that is generated by the PG will exit your body and dissipate into whatever you are touching.

Don't try to hang onto the state of being in the scene. You *have* the state of being created by the PG as you enter the scene, and then you *release* the energy by *radiating* it to your scene partner. In essence, the PG creates the energy that you will release onto your source.

Practice stepping *forward into* the experience of the PG. After you have done your PG, step forward, and take the experience with you in your body. Taking a step backward after you perform the PG seems to drop some of its power. It's not as effective when you step back after it. Even after "pulling," take a step forward *into* the sensation you just created. Step *into* the experience, not out of it, and take it with you.

Exercise: Expanding and Contracting

Expanding

Before you explore a PG with a character, first try this fundamental, archetypal exercise to see how performing a PG changes your psychology. Standing on both feet, bend slightly over, and place your right hand on your left kneecap and your left hand on your right kneecap. This starting point is a slight contraction of your body, where your arms are crossed in front of you, touching the opposite knee, like an X.

Now, say to yourself, "I desire to expand." Allow the desire to expand to build up in you. Then, expand your body as fully as you can, opening your entire body while one foot steps out to the side; your arms and eyes reach up to the sky at a forty-five-degree angle. When fully expanded, your body should resemble the letter X, taking up as much space as is physically possible. Sustain this position for ten to fifteen seconds, allowing the image of the gesture to continue to expand you. Now, allow your arms to float down by your side, and *allow the inner sensation of expanding to continue*, even as your arms come down. *Step forward* into the experience, *sustaining* this sensation, and allow your attention to move to another person or objects around the room. Walk around the room, radiating this energy outward.

Repeat this sequence but with different qualities of movements. Try expanding with the quality of movements of molding, floating, flying, radiating, staccato, legato, confidence, joy, release, power, and so on.

Contracting

Standing on both feet, say to yourself, "I desire to contract." Allow the desire to contract to build up in you. While remaining on both feet, begin to collapse your body as fully as you can, drop your center down, and become as small as physically possible. Keep your knees off the ground. Tuck your chin and shoulders in as tightly as you can. Even after your body has become as small as it can while remaining on two feet, imagine that you are still contracting. Sustain this position for ten to fifteen seconds, allowing it to continue to make you smaller and smaller in your mind's eye. Allow yourself to feel that you are inwardly collapsing, becoming smaller to the point of disappearing. Then, slowly stand back up, and *allow the sensation of contracting to continue.*

Step forward into the experience, *sustaining* this sensation, and allow your attention to move to another person or objects around the room. Walk around the room, radiating this sensation outward. Repeat this sequence but with different qualities of movement. Contract with the quality of movement of molding, floating, flying, radiating, staccato, legato, confidence, release, grief, sensuality, defeat, and fear.

Play with the range of expanding and contracting, noticing how the landscape of sensations in your body changes as you move from one end of the spectrum (fully open) to the other end (fully closed). Even though you are not working on a character yet, you will begin to understand kinesthetically how making a full-bodied gesture and then adding a quality to it can instantaneously change your psychology and state of being. This experience is decidedly not intellectual; it is psychophysical.

> Movement plus a quality equals a sensation in the body.
>
> —Michael Chekhov[29]

Exercise: PG Applied to a Scene

Now let's experiment with the PG in relation to a character in a scene. Let's say you are playing Vershinin in Anton Chekhov's play *The Three Sisters*. You are working on the scene in act 2 with Masha, when they decide to have an affair. You have read the play a minimum of three times and the scene dozens of times and believe that your need is to get Masha to commit to the affair now. To achieve this need, you want to make the actress with whom you are working feel *loved respectfully*. So, before the scene, you must drop into your body Vershinin's psychophysical predicament, where he is coming from as the two enter. To do this, you might experiment with a variety of different PGs. Let's use "to lift" as an example. If you can lift Masha's heart, perhaps she will acquiesce to the affair. Most importantly, your choice must be supported by the text, for which, in this case, *lift* works.

Standing on both feet, with one foot slightly forward, bend down into a crouched position with your arms straight out, parallel to the floor, and your palms facing up. This is your starting position. Now say to yourself, "I desire to lift." Allow the desire to lift to build up in you. Then, with your entire body, lift as simply as you can, with one foot stepping forward and your arms and eyes reaching up to the sky at a forty-five-degree angle. The movement should be so obvious that anywhere in the world, someone watching would say, "That person is lifting something." Sustain this archetypal position for ten to fifteen seconds, allowing it to continue to lift you. Then, allow your arms to float down by your side as you *allow the inner sensation of lifting to continue*.

Step forward into the experience, *sustaining* this sensation, and allow your attention to move to another person or objects around the room. Walk around the room, *radiating* this *lift energy* outward. As Vershinin is deeply attracted to Masha physically, emotionally, and intellectually, repeat this sequence but with different qualities of movement. Try lifting with the *quality of movement* of sensuality, love, desire, joy, care, tenderness, warmth, legato, flying, and caressing. Remember that movement plus a quality equals a sensation in the body that can then be radiated outward. By changing the quality of movement, you will necessarily change the sensation generated in your body.

Then, explore opposite choices. Try the PG "to lift" with the quality of movement of frustration, anger, staccato, and molding. Sometimes, the exact opposite of what you think provides the answer. You may discover that when you drop in this *opposite* energy and make Masha feel *wrong lovingly*, the scene is activated more dynamically. Also try an opposite PG. Try "to smash" or "to tear," and see what energy that creates in you as Vershinin before you enter the scene. You never know until you try, as all questions are answered in the doing.

Some Possible Archetypal Gestures

1. Expand/Open
2. Contract/Close

3. Push
4. Pull
5. Smash
6. Lift
7. Tear
8. Wring
9. Gather
10. Penetrate

Some Possible Qualities of Movement
1. Molding, floating, flying, radiating
2. Staccato, legato
3. For *positive* actions: love, joy, release, power, confidence, sensuality, sexuality, desire, support, kindness, tenderness, surprise, anticipation, silliness, mischief
4. For *negative* actions: anger, fear, panic, caution, regret, sadness, remorse, grief, loss, frustration, guilt, revenge

It [the PG] is right if it satisfies you as an artist.

—Michael Chekhov[30]

Ultimately, you will need to experiment, explore, and try many different gestures to find the one that speaks to your actor's intuition. More detailed information on Michael Chekhov's psychological gesture can be found in his book *To the Actor*. Filmic demonstrations of actors performing PGs can be found on the MICHA DVD series *Master Classes in the Michael Chekhov Technique* available through Routledge, as well as online at www.michaelchekhov.org.

Psychophysical Gestures

Similar to Michael Chekhov, twentieth-century American acting teacher Warren Robertson developed a set of psychophysical gestures to circumvent the analytical mind and avoid the need to do any personalization or affective memory (emotion memory) exercises, which he found were both unreliable and potentially psychologically unhealthy.[31] As Robertson himself was a psychologist, he developed the following suite of katas to engage the actor in the moment before and connect their entire being to where their character is coming from.

They all take more or less the same format: Stand with your feet about shoulder width apart. You want to feel connected to your will center. Look slightly up at an angle, as if staring at a movie screen, perhaps onto the back wall of your rehearsal studio or theater if you are onstage. This will become the screen for any imagery that comes from your mind's eye during the exercise. You will simultaneously make a series of gestures while saying an accompanying text out loud.

Repeat the gesture, and say the text over and over again, until you begin to discover some imagery on the screen in your mind's eye. If and when an image appears, make the gesture, and say the text to that image. Release out onto the image. If the imagery changes while you do the exercise, simply respond each time with your movement and text to each new image. If no imagery appears in your mind's eye, don't worry. Simply keep making the gestures and saying the text. This combo package will work on you.

Suite of Psychophysical Gestures

I Take Mine.

Stand with your hands touching your chest and say out loud, "I." Really feel connected to yourself as you speak. Reach your arms straight out, parallel to the floor, and make a grabbing/taking gesture with your hands as you simultaneously say, "Take." Pull your arms back, as if you are pulling something toward your body, as you say, "Mine." Repeat this sequence until images begin to appear. When an image appears, say the words as if you are talking to that image. If images change, let them, and respond to the new imagery.

Leave Me Alone.

Stand with your hands by your side and say, "Leave." Then place your hands on your chest and say, "Me." Really feel connected to yourself as you say, "me." Then, push your arms forward, as if you were shoving someone away, as you say, "alone." Repeat this sequence until images begin to appear. When an image appears, say the words as if you are talking to that image. If images change, let them, and respond to the new imagery.

Goodbye.

Start standing with your hands by your side. Raise one hand as if you are waving goodbye to someone while simultaneously saying, "Goodbye," out loud. Alternatively, hold both hands facing outward, as if to reach for someone, and slowly wave goodbye with your fingers while saying, "Goodbye."

Repeat this sequence until images begin to appear. When an image appears, say the words as if you are talking to that image. If images change, let them, and respond to the new imagery.

I Need, I Want.

Stand with your hands touching your chest and say, "I." Really feel connected to yourself as you say, "I." Reach your arms out slightly, with your palms opening forward, and say, "Need." Place your hands back on your breast as you say, "I." Open your arms out again with your palms facing forward, and say, "Want." Try switching the order: "I want, I need." Repeat this sequence until images begin to appear. When an image appears, say the words as if you are talking to that image. If images change, let them, and respond to the new imagery.

I Love You.

Stand with your hands touching your chest and say, "I." Open your arms out slightly, with your palms opening forward, and say, "Love." Extend them a little further, as if to reach for someone, as you say, "You." Repeat this sequence until images begin to appear. When an image appears, say the words as if you are talking to that image. If images change, let them, and respond to the new imagery.

I Give Yours.

Stand with your hands touching your chest and say, "I." Open your arms out, as if to hand someone a gift, and say, "Give." Pull your arms back to your side as you say, "Yours." Repeat this sequence until images begin to appear. When an image appears, say the words as if you are talking to that image. If images change, let them, and respond to the new imagery.

You will begin to see that many of these psychophysical gestures line up with events in scenes. There are lots of scenes when characters say goodbye or want to be left alone or confess their love and so on. They are in essence goodbye scenes or love scenes or desire scenes. Play around with different combinations, and see which one activates you the most into the scene. Other possible gestures include "Come back"; "Don't leave me"; and "Let me go." Also, feel free to experiment and make up your own psychophysical gestures. Find what works for you. The point is to get your voice, body, and imagery lined up in your instrument so you can approximate, as best you can, where the character is coming from as they enter the scene.

A word of caution: Don't expect to have the same experience each time you do the gestures. Each day will bring different results. Just repeat the movements and say the text, and see what happens. If imagery doesn't come immediately while you're doing the gestures, don't worry; keep repeating the movements with the text. The act of doing this alone will stir in you a new psychophysical experience. Conversely, if any imagery emerges that is too personally powerful, avoid using it. Sourcing recent trauma is not acting and is to be avoided at all costs.

As with the PGs, don't try to hang onto the state of being created by these gestures in the scene. You *have* the state of being created by the psychophysical gesture as you enter the scene, and then you *release* the energy by *sending* it to your scene partner. Your state of being will immediately or slowly or eventually be changed by the action your scene partner plays onto you.

Once you have fully completed the first part of active analysis, the cognitive analysis for invisible action, then and only then, are you ready to move onto the second part of the rehearsal process, physical analysis for visible action, which you will do with your scene partner on your feet. After you have done all this preparation work, you are ready to head into rehearsals with your scene partner. Let's go there!

CHAPTER EIGHT

Visible Action

Physical Analysis

The innovative value of Stanislavski's late discoveries is that while still considering action as the basis of the actor's creative process, he also thought about the series of activators that could lead to mastery of a scene by way of its action.

—Maria Osipovna Knebel[1]

The Approach of Physical Analysis

You will find yourself in a myriad of different rehearsal situations as a professional actor. There is no "one size fits all" approach to rehearsal for all occasions. However, the rehearsal process presented here, what Stanislavski called physical analysis, is adaptable to many different circumstances. It is ideally suited for the student actor or the professional actor in a scene study class who needs to prepare a scene without the aid of a director. If you have a director who is open-minded enough, you can ask them to work this way, as well. The benefits will be bountiful. Feel free to adapt it as you see fit to suit your immediate rehearsal situation, but also try to follow the outlined steps as closely as possible. With patience, this process will bear concrete results, namely a deep psychophysical connection to your role and playable action in performance.

The important aspect of this approach is that it works on the entire human mind-body connection from the very first rehearsal, finding a unity between the two. Right out of the gates, you get the scene into your body and work from a holistic psychophysical perspective. The work you will now do on your feet must be grounded in the text work you have already done on your own as part of the cognitive analysis.

Quite often, actors read the script one or two times and then immediately begin to memorize their lines. What they are doing, in essence, is only working on a mental level. They show up at rehearsal with all the words memorized but have no true human or imaginative connection to the role or how the human being they are playing is moving their life forward. They have failed to drop the human point of view of the role into their acting instrument. They have memorized the lines, but they have no true, profound, heartfelt understanding of where that person is coming from in their life. As actors, we need to memorize the role, not simply the words.

We know from our own lives, however, that the words we say are born out of what we are doing and the circumstances in which we find ourselves. To address this mental-physical gap, the physical analysis works on the entire human level, so in effect, you are "memorizing" the role and "learning" the human being, their life, their point of view, their perspective, their desires, their imagery, their feelings, and their sensations, not just the words they say. You are learning a *life*, albeit a fictional one, not lines. Ultimately, you are learning the *action* that gives rise to the language. Perhaps, most importantly, you are learning all this through your entire being, not just your mind.

Very simply, you will alternate between reading the scripted scene and then improvising the scene in your own words. You will discuss major points (action, counteraction, event) after each; then, you will repeat the process a minimum of twenty times. Fundamentally, that is it. I walk you through a more detailed explanation later. Basically, you are completing the following phases of work:

1. Read the scene together from the script.
2. Discuss discoveries or thoughts on action and the event.
3. Improvise the scene in your own contemporary words.
4. Discuss discoveries.
5. Repeat the entire process a minimum of twenty times.

Me in the Circumstances

Stanislavski saw the purpose of Active Analysis not to conclude with a characterization emerging in finished form, but to put into operation not only the brain but also the entire organism, the entire being of the actor immediately from the outset, and to help him feel himself in the role and the role in himself more quickly.

—Maria Osipovna Knebel[2]

Remember: I encourage you to use the word *role* instead of *character*. Stan-islavski does so, as well, for a very good reason. A character is something distant from you. A role is something you can play. When you say, "I am playing a role," your performance will feel more grounded in you. You are indeed playing the role after all, not someone else. You can only use yourself and your imagination for your performance. If I sit in the audience, read the play program, and see your name next to the name Lady Macbeth, as far as I'm concerned, as soon as you walk out onstage, you *are* Lady Macbeth, even if you aren't "playing a character," even if you haven't made a characteriza-tion choice. You don't have to do the audience's work for them. They have an imagination, too. Let them use it. From the moment you are visible in real space and time onstage, you are already Lady M. Then, from that point, the audience waits to see what you are going to *do* and *how* you are going to do it.

As you, the actor, are a human being, you have done 90 percent of the work just by being you. The other 10 percent is your imagination and action. Remember: Human beings haven't changed all that much over time. Neither has the world around us. We like to think it has, but deep down, the daily fundamental human experiences of life haven't evolved all that much in thousands of years. We love; we fight; we work; we play; we give; we steal; we make dinner; we eat; we have sex; we break up; we sleep; we relax; we con-fess; we lie; we teach; we get married; we have children; we learn; we cheat; we do heroic things; we commit cowardly acts; we win games; we lose games; we rise; we fall; we live; we die—every day, all of us, since time immemorial. We experience the agony and the ecstasy of life, as well as everything in between, today much as people have done since the beginning of humanity.

We still sit in chairs, a Grecian invention that dates to the seventh century BC. Even the forms of chairs we sit in today date to the sixteenth century. We still eat our meals with forks, which date to the fourth century AD and the Eastern Roman Empire of Byzantium. We still drink wine, which has been around since 7000 BC, when fermentation was invented in China. The cheese we eat with our wine has been processed in more or less the same fashion for almost eight thousand years. Being human hasn't really changed all that much over time; only the accoutrements have become a bit more refined and modernized. All this to say: *You are enough.* As you are a human being, you already have everything inside you that you need to live the role. You simply need to harness your humanity via your imagination within the fictional given circumstances and trust yourself.

In the acting world, there are at least two schools of thought about this. You either "lose yourself in the role," or you "find yourself in the role." I hap-pen to believe that both are true and that they are not mutually exclusive.

It has been my experience as an actor and an acting teacher that you must find the "me in the circumstances" or "find yourself in the role" if you want your work to be believable and grounded in your humanity. You are playing the role; someone else isn't playing it. You got hired because you are you. You are not playing someone else's idea of the role; you are inhabiting your vision of the role. The producers want *you* to do it. The director hired you from a wide range of casting possibilities. It is your creation, and you are the raw material. You must use yourself and tap into your instincts, your sensibilities, your impulses, and your interpretation of the role. Technique can be taught; interpretation can't. Remember from chapter 5: Actors are sculptors of energy under imaginary circumstances. How are you going to sculpt your life force to shape this role?

Once you have identified all the ways in which the role is like you (in facts, thoughts, feelings, and actions) and you have tapped into your own personal interpretation of the role, then via the process of creative transformation, you begin to leave your personal associations behind; you move imaginatively away from your daily self as you "lose yourself in the role." You step out of your lower self and into your artistic self via the role you play as you identify all the ways in which the character is different from you (in facts, thoughts, feelings, and actions). So, at this point, in this sense, you lose your daily self. Both maxims are valid, and both are essential in the art of transforming yourself into the role you are playing. You are the vehicle; you must drive to get you where you're going. You're not driving someone else's vehicle. But you're also not staying home. You're going to an imaginary destination that is different from your personal life.

The process of physical analysis will help you find the "me in the circumstances." If you found yourself in the same fictional circumstances, how would you act? How would you react to things? What would you do? This way of working grounds you; your choices; and your own body, mind, and imagination in the circumstances in which the character you are playing finds themselves.

The work is coming from you, filtered, of course, through your imagination via the eyes of the fictional human being you are playing. You will see out *as if* through their eyes, as you have oriented your perspective via question 1. You will see the world as they see the world. You will align all the parts of you that are similar to the role in thoughts, feelings, and actions (find yourself in the role), and you will discover all the parts of you that are unlike the role in thoughts, feelings, and emotions (lose yourself in the role).

Responsibility of the Actor

Working this way also grounds the responsibility for playing your role in you, the actor.[3] You are not waiting for a director to tell you how they want you to play the part. You are the primary agent of action and creation. Employing this process, you will develop a sense of ownership over the role, that it is indeed yours, not someone else's idea of how it should be performed.

Stanislavski wanted to empower his actors to have ownership over their roles. He understood that when actors are given permission, time, and freedom to discover what their characters are doing in any scene, their performances are more fully realized and multidimensional. The question then becomes, How do I arrive at ownership of my performance?

Performance Defined

> We've been doing this since we were kids. Teaching acting is an attempt to counter all the blocks that have gotten in the way since we were kids. We're just cleaning out the crap most of the time.
>
> —Lloyd Richards[4]

Performance is the act of doing something, carrying out a task or function, or accomplishing an action, where the outcome matters to the agent. There are stakes and consequences involved in the acting of it. If the results don't matter to you, then it isn't a performance. Performance is a high-pressure environment where there is a cost to engaging in it.

Accordingly, the brain perceives the performance space as a threat, which is why we get an adrenaline rush from performing. It does this to prepare our bodies for perceived danger.[5] Even after millions of years of evolution, our brains don't realize we won't really get hurt, at least not physically, that we won't be eaten by the performance. The high-pressure environment of performance triggers this chemical rush, which changes our bodies. The sensation of nerves in the abdominal region, known colloquially as "butterflies" is nothing more than blood rushing away from the digestive system and to major muscle groups and the brain. The body says to itself, "We can digest the rest of that burrito later, but for now, let's get more oxygen to the legs and brain so we can run faster and see more clearly." It does this to get us out of danger, as it senses there is something to either win or lose.[6]

A global, metadefinition is, "performance equals potential minus interference." Understood this way, performance can be boiled down to this equation:

$$\text{Performance} = \text{Potential} - \text{Interference}$$

Potential means the full ability of the actor to perform what is asked in the here and now. *Interference* means anything that impedes that ability. A healthy performance process, such as Stanislavski's active analysis, is one that strengthens and liberates the former (potential) while also minimizing, if not eliminating altogether, the latter (interference). Stanislavski understood that you, the actor, need a creative process that simultaneously empowers your ability, while reducing any interference you might have.

Paradoxically, one of the great causes of interference is the actor's relationship to their text. How and when that text is introduced to the actor's process has a direct effect on whether it enhances the actor's potential or becomes a source of interference. This is why the process of études must begin *before memorization*, so you can have the fullest possible release of your potential under the high-pressure environment of professional acting, resulting in a sense of ownership over your creation.

Études

To create an *étude* about an event from the play and to find the sequences of actions for each character, it is necessary to undertake serious preparatory work.

—Maria Osipovna Knebel[7]

You will enter the rehearsal process with your scene partner having completed the cognitive analysis. Part 2 of active analysis, the physical analysis, is comprised itself of two steps: (1) brief table work, a read-through of the script, to arrive at an agreement on the fundamental given circumstances of the scene—the event, the action, and the counteraction—followed by (2) an on-your-feet exploration of that scene, called an étude.

The étude is an organic creative process by which you will discover your playable actions in the doing. The word *étude* means the study of a subject and is commonly associated in English with instrumental music compositions. In the Stanislavskian context, études are fundamentally improvised explorations of the text for the actor. They take place in the studio *before you have memorized your lines*. You have explored the overall text for invisible action, events, and other evidentiary given circumstances but have not yet committed the text to memorization.

After each improvisation, you will reread the scene, discussing your discoveries, and then improvise the scene or event again. This process is repeated until the architecture of the visible action is clear to both you and your scene partner, and it is clear which character is the driving action and which has the counteraction. An ancillary benefit of working this way is that you will organically commit your lines to memorization in a psychophysical manner that connects the text to the scene's actions and event.

Action and Counteraction

Choose an action; see how long it can be played and what, if anything, changes it.

—Earle Gister[8]

For dramatic conflict to occur, any scene needs at a very minimum two competing forces pushing against one another. Those forces are the actions that each actor plays onto the other. Therefore, in a scene with two characters, there are two independent playable actions, one for each character. Stanislavski calls the first of the independent forces the action, and the second, counteraction.[9] It is the energy of the action against the counteraction that creates the conflict, which results in an event.[10] The action drives the scene, and the counteraction determines, more or less, how the scene will go and how long it will last.

a. The Action
b. The Counteraction

Every action meets with a reaction which in turn intensifies the first. In every play, beside the main action we find its opposite counteraction.

—Konstantin Stanislavski[11]

Using the previous event of the confession of love via the kiss, it might be that the two characters are making each other feel loved and wrong, respectively. But it is character A who drives the scene and has the principal action, as they are trying to convince the other that they really do love them, that the other is wrong to believe they don't. And character B has the counteraction, as they are the one pushing back and saying, "I don't believe you."

It is only when character B, the counteraction, gives in and says, "I believe you," that the event happens, and the two characters kiss.

Coming into the rehearsal room, you need only have an idea of who has the action and who has the counteraction based on your cognitive analysis. You will discover and confirm them in the doing. Initially, you might not even know who has the action and who has the counteraction, just that there are two actions. That's fine. All questions will be answered in the doing. This brings us to the obstacle.

The Obstacle

Always check in with your partner to see if they got what you were trying to send to them, to do to them.

—Earle Gister[12]

Each character in every scene has an obstacle. The obstacle is what keeps your character from getting what they need. As it is a noun, you can't *play* an obstacle, but you *have* an obstacle, and you play action to get by it. Like a wall blocking your path, the obstacle is something you need to get around, go through, burrow under, climb over, drill a hole through, or blow up. You must navigate your obstacle with your action. And the higher the wall, the more interesting and creative and dynamic you must be in the action you take. Good playwrights make the obstacle something directly between the two characters and, in a well-written scene, shouldn't be too hard to identify. The more it interferes with the two characters getting what they need, the more dynamic and high-stakes the scene will be.

An obvious and common obstacle in many love scenes is that one of the characters is married to someone else. This fact stands in the way of the two declaring their love for each other and eventually kissing. Continuing with our two would-be lovers, character B might not believe character A because character A is married, hence the hesitancy to give into their proclamations. This fact, this obstacle, stands between both characters and presents the dramatic friction necessary for both actors to play their action strongly onto one another.

The obstacle is your friend as an actor. It strengthens your action choices, making them more interesting and compelling. The greater the obstacle, the greater the need to get around it, and the stronger the action required to negotiate it. Again, you don't need to know for sure what the obstacle is before you begin rehearsals; you simply need to have an initial idea. Like with your action, the answer to this is found in the doing. This brings us into the rehearsal studio.

The Rehearsal Process

Step 1

Location

Secure a place to rehearse. Ideally, it is in a theatrical space of some kind, an acting studio or dance studio or the like. It should be as clean and private as possible, somewhere you are free to explore choices, improvise, and play.

Set

You will need to set the stage as best you can with furniture and the like that reflect the given circumstances from question 2 in the script, Where am I? The set can include chairs, tables, a doorway, a bench, a couch, and so on.

Props

You will need all properties that are handled or referred to by the characters in the scene: glasses, plates, cigar, newspaper, broom, money, photo, knife, and so on.

Costumes

You will need at a very minimum a pair of shoes that resemble the shoes your character wears as closely as possible. Shoes are a key component to getting into the role. If you are going to walk in someone else's shoes, then it helps to have as close an approximation of their shoes. You will also want to wear rehearsal clothes that are similar to what your character wears. A military commander from the end of the nineteenth century wouldn't be wearing sneakers. A lady from the 1920s isn't wearing flip-flops. Appropriate rehearsal costumes are obligatory if you are serious about your acting.

Agreements

Before you work, you and your scene partner must come to verbal agreements on how you will work:

- You both are clear on the rehearsal structure of physical analysis.
- You agree on any physical touching, combat, and intimacy that occurs in the scene. You are not free to simply use the other actor as you wish without their permission or consent. If there is physical contact or

intimacy of any kind in the scene, you must obtain consent from your partner to engage in those activities beforehand.

Each one of you has the right to say no to anything you aren't comfortable doing. It is even a good idea to practice saying no to each other before rehearsal. This may seem unnecessary or even awkward but is in fact vital to ensure a safe and productive rehearsal process. You should rehearse saying no with your scene partner before you begin rehearsals. Use this template to practice:

- Stand facing each other, and decide who is A and who is B.

  Actor A should make a move to touch actor B on the shoulder using the following script:

  ACTOR A: "May I touch you?"

  ACTOR B: "No."

  ACTOR A: "Thank you."

Then reverse roles. Repeat this miniscript multiple times, until you are both comfortable saying no. It may seem easy or silly, but saying no can be very difficult for some people.

Let me state again: Drawing clear and respectful boundaries in rehearsal is vital to a safe and productive rehearsal process, yet it is not readily apparent nor always easy to do. The more transparent, vocal, and precise you are about these issues up front, the more freedom you will actually have during the on-your-feet work, as you both know exactly where the limits are.

Social Chatter

Keep any social chatting to an absolute minimum. You can go to a café together later if you want and socialize over a coffee. You are here to work. Keep any talking you do about the work, and then get to work. How you talk about your work is how your work will happen. Just do it.

Step 2

The Reading

Sit in two chairs, facing one another, knees almost touching, and read the scene all the way through. Take your time. Don't feel the need to give a performance or say the words in any particular way. This is an *exploration* of the material in the presence of your scene partner. Use it as such. Give your attention to the line of text you are about to say; then, once you have the line in your head, come up with your eyes and direct your attention to your scene partner; then say the line. Try not to speak the lines of dialogue into the script itself. Have your attention on your scene partner when you say your lines.

From the outset, make sure to monitor your breathing. With your lips slightly parted, breathe fully and slowly. Don't rush this process. Take your time. Remember: When you have very little time, go very slowly. Practice releasing your energy as you speak out onto your partner. Conversely, when they are speaking, breathe in and receive what they are sending you; do this as openly and vulnerably as you can. You are building communion with the other actor and working toward creating an artistic bond of intimate harmony. Make sure not to have your eyes down on the script when they speak and release to you. Receive them fully. Read through the entire scene this way. You are in essence learning the scene in the presence of your scene partner. You are receiving both the author's energy and your scene partner's energy when you work this way. The two are becoming one in you.

The Discussion

After you have finished reading, discuss what you both believe to be are the essential elements of the scene:

- What do you believe is the event of the scene?
- Who has the action? Who is driving the scene?
- Who has the counteraction? Who is pushing back?
- What are you here to do?
- What are the key physical activities in the scene? Are there any entrances or exits or other important moments that involve physical contact?

It is important here that you also acknowledge what is confusing to you, what you are struggling with, and what you don't understand. Work together to find common solutions.

Step 3

The Étude

Now it's time to get up on your feet. Using the framework of the written text as a guide, you will improvise the entire scene using your own contemporary language. You will act out the scene from the moment before, all the way through to the event and the final moment.

Before you begin, say to one another, "We are only doing an étude!" This gives you ultimate freedom to explore and discover. Your creative objective here is to explore your action choices and see if you can make the event of the scene happen. You will use set, props, and costume pieces. You will enter and exit as the characters do in the scene. You will behave physically in accordance with how the characters do in the scripted scene. If, for example, the script says, "Johnny downs a shot of whiskey," then you will do so (with water, of course). Complete as many of the bits of physical business as possible.

Feel free to speak as you would in your everyday life. Even if the text is written in heightened language, such as Shakespeare, improvise using your own language. This is the whole point of the exercise. Don't try to say the lines from the script at all. Give yourself a healthy dose of permission to follow your creative impulses and explore as freely as possible. Dare to mess it all up. Fail better.

That said, the improvisation here is not random. It is an on-your-feet exploration of the precise given circumstances of the written scene using your own words and body. You are still attempting to make the event happen but are getting there using your own words and movement. You pursue the need from question 3 using your own words and actions. You work to make the other actor in the scene *feel* what you wrote down for question 4. You do not need to tell the other actor your action. In fact, I advise keeping this a secret. It will have more power that way and keep your scene partner on their toes.

Your scene partner is the source of your behavior. Make them your target of attention. This does not mean, however, that you have to be looking directly at them all the time. If, for example, you *need* them to *leave*, you might choose to make them *feel small* or *ignored*. You do not need to look at them to do this. Quite the contrary, in fact. You might look away and give them your back. In this case, you would radiate your energy to them via your back space, as people do in life when they are ignoring someone.

During this étude process, place yourself in conditions where you are forced to articulate in your own words what your character is trying to communicate. You must find a way to express the author's thoughts and intentions yourself. This way, you understand in your own being the struggle of the role you are inhabiting. It forces you to grapple with finding your own words, your own way to get what you need, and make the event happen. Your character's struggle immediately becomes real and relatable.

The Discussion

After you have finished improvising, discuss what you discovered:

- Do you still think the event is what you previously thought? If not, rename it.
- Were you able to make the event happen? If so, how? If not, why not?
- Were you able to play your action?
- Who do you now believe has the primary action? Who drives the scene?
- Who has the counteraction? Who pushes back?
- What are you here to do?
- What worked overall?
- What didn't work?
- What did you struggle with?
- What is clear?
- What is still confusing?

It is very important here that you also acknowledge what didn't work, what you struggled with, what weren't able to do. Don't hide these things from each other; share them. They are as equally important as what you were able to do well and what worked. The struggles and failures are perhaps even more important than what worked, as you will discover the work you still need to do and what you still don't understand.

Step 4

Repetition

Repeat the first three steps nineteen more times. What you will notice as you work is that at the very beginning, it may be quite difficult to find your own words for the improvisation. This is actually a good thing—because it not only gets your character's struggle in your body but also, and perhaps most importantly, *creates a genuine, organic desire within you to say the author's words.* After the improvisation, when you return to the reading phase, the words on the script will mean much more to you. You will be delighted to have these now delicious and precise words at your beck and call and will ultimately speak them. The actual dialogue from script will no longer simply be words on a page but carry much more meaning, specificity, and importance for you.

> In the improvisation you should reach the "seed" of the author's main thought, the thought that led him to write this piece of text.
>
> —Maria Osipovna Knebel[13]

Stanislavski never precisely stated how long this process should last. Maria Osipovna Knebel suggests in her writing that he had his actors work this way until they felt solid about both the given circumstances and the text, until they had uncovered what he called the "seed" of the scene, which is the author's main intention or thoughts in writing the scene, the purpose of the scene in the overall story. By the twentieth time through this process, both you and your scene partner will have a desire to only speak the scripted dialogue and also have discovered what the seed of the scene actually is.

An ancillary benefit of rehearsing this way is that you will probably be more or less off-book without having to actually sit down and memorize your lines in a rote fashion. You will have organically, dynamically, and methodically embodied the meaning of the scene, your need, your action, and the event and learned the lines as a holistic mind-body process. The more secure you feel in what you are doing in the scene, the more you have embodied it, and the more you can focus on playing your action. Over time, the focus shifts from discovery to refining how you play your action onto your scene partner to get what you need and make the event happen.

At this point, you will be ready to share your work with either a director or an acting teacher for objective input. This is when my students come into the studio to do their first pass in front of the class for feedback.

Once You Are Off-Book

Once you are off-book, you should continue to employ this rehearsal technique. At any juncture in your rehearsal process, feel free to go back and completely improvise the scene. Or, if there is a small section of the scene where you feel stuck or unsure, simply improvise this portion of the scene and see what you discover.

The Mechanics of Playing Action

Let's review from part I of this book what playing action is and what you do to play action.

> Playing action is the exchange of energy, purposefully directed, to make the other actor feel something in pursuit of a need, to make the event of the scene happen, in service of your character's hopes and dreams.

Your scene partner is the most important person in the scene. To achieve your character's need in the scene, you must change your scene partner.

To do that, you must make your scene partner the target of your attention. Where your attention goes, your energy flows. Playing action is the exchange of energy to make the other actor feel something in pursuit of a need. It then follows that to play an action, you

1. direct the target of your attention onto your scene partner (or an image) outside yourself;
2. separate your lips slightly, breathe, and source your scene partner or target;
3. *send* or *release* your energy onto your partner or target to make them feel an emotion;
4. listen and respond in the moment to everything your partner does; and
5. simultaneously receive your partner's energy and react accordingly.

As energy is action, like an electrical conduit, you *allow* the energy to flow between yourself and your source, your scene partner. This creates the give and take of energy, the releasing and receiving of action. The playing of action is really a sense of allowing it to happen to you as you simultaneously affect your partner, just like life. Then, you will find yourself in a deep and powerful exchange of energy, one that ignites the space between you and your scene partner. This takes faith, in yourself and in your partner. But it is the only way to live believability under imaginary circumstances with precise repeatability and complete spontaneity.

The Two Sources of Action

As I discuss in part I of this book, sourcing is a key part of playing action. The script is obviously the original source material, for it is the source of the invisible action of the story. However, there are two other principal sources from which we get our visible actions in the performance: (1) our scene partner and (2) imagery.

Again, a source is something you draw from. In French, *une source* means a well, which is, of course, a source of water. Electrical outlets are sources of electricity, into which we plug appliances. Similarly, as actors, we must plug our attention into either our scene partner or, if we are alone in the scene, imagery. It is from one of these two sources that we draw energy for our actions, as playing action is an "exchange of energy to make the other actor feel something." Your attention is the tool you use to "plug" into the other actor.

Scene Partner as Source

The primary source of your visible action most of the time will be your scene partner. Truly paying attention to them will provide you with what you need to do. What you need to do can only be in *reaction* to what they are already doing. Like a river, the action of a scene is already taking place when you step into its current. Accordingly, an essential element of playing action is learning to source your scene partner.

Technically, what you do in order to source your partner is pretty straightforward. You make your scene partner the target of your attention by redirecting your attention off yourself and onto them. Once you have connected your attention to them, then you simply receive what they are sending you, let it affect you, then react and respond to what they are doing within the boundaries of the script. The more you remain curious about your partner, the easier it will be to continue to pay attention to them. The more you have faith, the more your source will provide all that you need in the scene. You will then receive your performance from your source, your partner.

When the target of your attention is outside yourself, when your breath is slow, and when your curiosity is high, then you will simply receive your performance from your source; they will make you act the part, and you will discover liberation, ease, and freedom in your work. You will know what to do by watching them with an eagle eye and responding according to what they do to you. When you arrive at the moment in your work where you are able to do all this without thinking about it, you are ready to release your energy fully back onto them.

If they are not the source of your behavior, then you are self-generating your acting. You don't have faith in this case, as you are trying to control how the scene will go and play your idea of the scene instead of the moment of action. This leads to mechanical, wooden, and uninspired acting. Avoid it. As Declan Donnellan writes in *The Actor and the Target*, you can either have faith in performance or certainty; you can't have both.[14] You will have to choose. Choose faith. It's where inspired acting lives.

Imagery as a Source

Images can also be sources of energy for you in performance. However, there is really only one instance when imagery will be your primary source of action, and that is when the character you are portraying is left alone and talking to themselves, in what is colloquially known as a monologue. But the word *monologue* is actually a misnomer. It is true that the character is alone onstage and speaking to themselves, so in that sense it is a *monologue*. But from that character's perspective and from inside their experience, they are in a *dia*logue with an image. They are sourcing an image.

You know this from life. For example, quite often, we are in our cars or somewhere where we are alone and undisturbed, and we find ourselves disparaging out loud that toxic colleague who drives us crazy at work. We talk to them *as if* they are present, even though they are not. As we know the "as if" triggers the imagination. We have the image of this person in our mind's eye; we are sourcing them, responding and releasing our energy accordingly. Another common and obvious example is when you fantasize about someone to whom you are sexually attracted. When you source their image, you are aroused by them—enough said.

A well-known example is Yelena's monologue in act 3 of Anton Chekhov's *Uncle Vanya*, after Sonya leaves and before Astrov enters with his maps. Chekhov strategically leaves Yelena alone, speaking to herself, so we get to hear her inner monologue. However, there are three very specific images that the actress playing Yelena must source in order to react and speak her lines. The first is the image of Sonya, who has just left: "I understand this girl. She'd make a wonderful wife for a country doctor." This changes into the image of Doctor Astrov: "From time to time he comes upon the scene." And then it changes again into the image of Yelena as a married woman who finds herself attracted to a man who is not her husband. She doesn't like what she likes: "Vanya says I have mermaid's blood in my veins."

In order to perform this monologue, the actress playing Yelena has to source, at a very minimum, these three images and then play action onto each of those images as if they were her scene partner. That is technically and mechanically what the actor must do onstage in performance of this part of the role of Yelena. Otherwise, if the actor is not sourcing imagery, then they are self-generating their performance, and the acting will be stilted.

The Door of Empathy

Your job is to find the door of empathy between your life and the character's life and then walk through that door in your imagination. No matter how vile the character, your professional and artistic job is to empathize with the human being you are portraying. Most people have a positive view of themselves, so even if you would never do in your everyday life what the character does in the script, you must find a positive reason that character behaves the way they do. They clearly feel the need to do those things and have positive reasons for doing so. You've got to figure out where they are coming from in their life and how you can get behind them creatively. We are all human;

if a human being commits an act in a script, no matter how repulsive to you personally, you, as a fellow human being, are capable of doing the same thing, whether you like admitting that it or not.

How can you identify with the role you are playing? How can you relate to that human being? How can you turn their struggle into your imaginary struggle? How can you engage your imagination to move their life forward? What circumstances in life would cause you do to do what they do?

The mistake many actors make is to judge the character they are playing: "Oh, I would never do that," blah, blah, blah. Of course you wouldn't, but the character is not you. The fun part of acting is playing roles that are decidedly *not* like your personal life, but you have fun arguing their cause in the courtroom of your imagination under fictional circumstances nonetheless. And the way to do that is by *empathizing* with them. Remember: As an actor, you are a *professional empathizer*. Find the door of empathy, the way into their perspective, and fight for them. They are counting on you to do it to the fullest of your ability. This empathic portal must not remain an idea in your head. It must become a sensation that you drop into your body. You can do this via imagery or a psychophysical gesture or a psychological gesture.

Memorizing the Other Actor's Lines

Most actors memorize their own lines. The smart actor first learns to pay attention to the other person's lines. Why? Because that is what *you are reacting to.* If you are to learn any lines first, it is the other person's lines. How can you know what to say unless you know what you are responding to? As you read through the script with your scene partner, and as you improvise, pay more attention to what your scene partner is saying than you might normally do.

A quick and fun exercise you can do to work on this is to repeat your scene partner's previous line as a question (out loud) before you say your own line:

ACTOR A: You didn't take out the garbage today.

ACTOR B: *I didn't take out the garbage today?* [repeated line] Yes, I certainly did. [scripted line]

ACTOR A: *Yes, you certainly did?* [repeated line] No, you didn't. I just did. [scripted line]

ACTOR B: *You just did?* [repeated line] You're hallucinating. [scripted line]

ACTOR A: *I'm hallucinating?* [repeated line] I think we both know who's hallucinating. [scripted line]

In effect, their last line becomes your new first line, only said as a question. You then use the rest of your line as written to answer that question, which is what your character is, in fact, doing, responding to what came directly before. Practicing this exercise allows you to become keen rhetorical hook detectives. You learn what it is exactly in the previous line that you are hooking onto and reacting to.

Playing Action in Performance

In a sense, this whole book has been leading up to this point, for this is what you actually do in performance: play action. If you have fully followed this comprehensive preparation process, then you should be in good stead to take the next step, which is to trust your rehearsal process, trust that repetition is the growing power, trust that you have incorporated all the fictional given circumstances, trust that you know what to do, and embody the role you are playing. Now is the time to let go of all the invisible work and trust that you know how to play your visible action.

At a certain point you have to return to the word *confidence*, which, again, in Latin means "with faith." Like riding a bike, at a certain moment, you need to take off the training wheels and have faith that your body has learned what to do and give it permission to do it in performance. Your imagination takes over, and you act *as if* you are the role you are playing. You let go of working things out with technique and play in your imagination. You surrender to the role as well as your scene partner; you allow yourself to be vulnerable enough to be played by your imagery and the fictional given circumstances that you work in intimate harmony with your fellow actors. You keep your lips slightly parted, breathe fully, target your attention onto your source, and release your energy onto them in order to make them feel something in pursuit of your need. And you do all this while listening with your entire being and simultaneously responding to what they are sending to you. When this happens, the space between comes alive, and both you and the audience are transported.

CHAPTER NINE

~

Advice from the Front

A centipede was happy—quite!
Until a toad in fun
Said, "Pray, which leg comes after which?"
Which threw her mind in such a pitch,
She laid bewildered in the ditch
Considering how to run.

—Alan Watts[1]

Unconscious Competence (or Forgetting Technique)

Michael Chekhov writes of technique, "First we must know, then we must forget."[2] What he means by this is that we are never working to develop any technique for its own sake. We learn a technique so that it may serve our creative ends. It is a means by which to create something. We must begin with a conscious development of technique, which is repeated and practiced over time, as "repetition is the growing power," and then we must integrate it into our psychophysical being.[3] We must literally move our creative work from the prefrontal cortex of the brain to the subconscious regions.

If I ask you now, "What is 2 + 2?" without even thinking about it, you can answer it. Without engaging the prefrontal cortex region of the brain, you can come up with the answer. This is because you didn't actually need to do the calculation. You had memorized it and already knew the answer; it was stored in the subconscious region of the brain, and the calculation immediately came to you via your mental retrieval process.

There was, however, a time, way back when, when you actually had to learn the calculation and how to perform it. During that first stage of knowledge acquisition, you had to indeed think about how to add digits of numerical value. You had to learn what numbers represented and what their respective and relative values mean and then how to calculate them. Even if what you are learning is completely physical, like swimming, or psychophysical, like acting, there is a stage in learning any technique where you need to actively think about what you are doing. The catch is that you will not want to remain in this stage any longer than is necessary for the acquisition of said technique. I now ask you to complete the following calculation:

What is 79 divided by 3?

Please actually do this calculation in your head right now, and don't read on until you have completed it.

To perform this numeric task, you needed to engage your prefrontal cortex. I use the word *perform* here precisely and strategically because doing a mathematical computation is a type of performance. Obviously, acting is also a performance. In learning any performance task, at some point the prefrontal cortex must be involved.

The prefrontal cortex is the area in the brain used for active thought. The storage area of the prefrontal cortex, or rather the staging area in the brain for active thought, is rather small. You can't do more than one or two calculations simultaneously by engaging the prefrontal cortex. For example, try counting out loud sequentially from one to one hundred while simultaneously saying all the letters in the alphabet backward out loud, starting with Z and ending with A. Try it—and good luck. You can't do both, at least not simultaneously. The brain is capable of toggling back and forth between the two tasks, but even this, without extreme repetition and lots of practice, is incredibly difficult, time-consuming, frustrating, and virtually useless.

What we want to do as actors is, over time, move our acquisition of technique from the prefrontal cortex region of the brain (conscious learning) to the subconscious region of the brain (unconscious competence). You no longer have to think about adding 2 + 2. It just comes to you (at least I hope it does!), but from where does it actually come? Of course, the answer is, it comes from your subconscious. The same holds true for your acting. You will want to practice your technique so thoroughly that you don't have to think about it and the answers to your acting problems; they will just come to you. This is why developing a practice, a deliberate practice, where repetition is plentiful, is essential in actor training. We in our work want to go from $79 \div 3 = 26.333$ in the prefrontal cortex to $2 + 2 = 4$ in the subconscious mind.

If the storage area of the prefrontal cortex can be represented by the size of one cubic foot, then the size of the subconscious region of the brain is represented by the size of the Milky Way galaxy.[4] Get your acting out of the house and take it for a journey, like Le Petit Prince, around your mental solar system. You have much more room to operate in the subconscious and the storage area, and possibilities are seemingly endless. We as actors must arrive at "Through conscious means we reach the subconscious."[5]

The Four Stages of Acquisition[6]

The acquisition of any technique has four distinct stages:

1. Unconscious Incompetence
2. Conscious Incompetence
3. Conscious Competence
4. Unconscious Competence

Stage 1: Unconscious Incompetence

Stage 1, "Unconscious Incompetence" is where most beginners start in the acquisition of any technique. They don't know what they don't know. Paradoxically, but perhaps not surprisingly, this is a stage when beginning actors are the freest. They are not aware of what they can or can't do yet, so their naïve yet beautiful lack of awareness permits near-total liberty. They are in effect unconscious, or unaware, of what they have and have not learned yet. And this ignorance is freedom. It is the freedom, however, of the amateur, not the professional.

This is not to say that at this stage of development they are globally incompetent in their abilities. They may possess the ability and potential to do what is necessary and are headed toward eventual competence but have yet to master the craft necessary to arrive at total professional and artistic competence. Only time will tell. But they are in fact missing something, and that is a fully formed technique. Actors in this stage are not fully formed in their ability; therefore, they are incompetent to one degree or another, in the true sense of the word that they are not yet fully competent. They may be able to live believably but not with any precision or repeatability. They might not even be aware of what it is they are doing when they act or what a comprehensive acting technique involves. What they are missing is everything they are yet to learn about the craft, technique, or art form. They have very little experience from which to draw consistency over time. In fact, at this stage, they are not even aware that they are missing something. They are unconscious of it all, which is blissful.

This is the stage where we usually meet our first-year university actors. They have just finished high school, where much of the performing they did was in musicals (which we love). And, for the most part, they have not had any formal actor training, or if they have, it's been cursory at best. Due to both of these factors, they quite often associate acting with indicating, representation, or generalized demonstrative behavior, what one might call colloquially overacting. They are usually completely unaware of the myriad of established, time-tested concrete acting techniques, nor have they practiced them, never mind employed them in performance. They enter our program with all the vigor, enthusiasm, and joy that their high school drama club instilled in them, which is absolutely wonderful and represents the word *amateur* at its best: someone who does something for the love of it. Yet in auditions at the beginning of their first year, they tend to overact, indicate, and demonstrate mechanical, rigid, or set performative choices. They are, for the most part, self-generating, locked into their choices, and are unaware of their incompetence, which is completely natural for this phase of their learning.

Coincidentally, much of the acting we see in the studio at this stage comes from the actor's conscious region of the brain, their prefrontal cortex. In other words, the actor is thinking about their acting as they act. They tend to be very self-conscious while working. Again, this is completely normal for a beginning actor in stage 1 of technique acquisition. It is, however, unacceptable for a professional. The professional actor must move beyond this stage. Your job in your own training is to advance your work from stage 1 to stage 4. However, you must first pass through the often-painful stage 2 to get there.

Stage 2: Conscious Incompetence

Stage 2 is where the neophyte student who is on the long road of mastery from amateur to professional becomes aware of their lack of technique, as well as their overall level of ability. Through the first year or two of training, the development of self-awareness becomes one of the core components of the daily work. It pulls, pushes, and prods their habits, kicking and screaming into the bright light of day. This causes a spike, by design, in self-awareness and, therefore, consciousness of how they are working. Self-awareness is a healthy version of self-consciousness. They are now aware of their incompetence. This brings the beginning actor fully into stage 2, "Conscious Incompetence," which, again, is a natural stage for the acquisition of technique.

Now, it has been my experience that this stage is the proverbial "shit or get off the pot" period for the young actor. It is somewhere in stage 2 where students look down the long road of actor training; the profession; a life as a professional actor; and their own ability, ambition, and personal work habits and decide "This is for me," or, quite often, "This is not for me." They are now conscious of where they stand relative to others in their field who are at a similar stage of development, as well as what professional actor training actually entails.

Now, if you are like me, you will realize at this moment, "This is exactly what I want to do." I loved this stage when I was in it, although admittedly, I found it extremely frustrating, even humiliating at times. I talk more in the next section about "loving the plateau," and stage 2 is where that love must begin. For me, this stage happened in graduate school, in the Professional Actor Training Program at the University of Washington. My own developing self-awareness was brutal at times, beyond humbling, and enormously challenging but ultimately deeply rewarding. Even when I was getting the proverbial shit kicked out of me, there was a sense of satisfaction that I was on a meaningful road and that someday it, too, would pass.

However, if you are driven by your ego or other extrinsic motivators, this stage will beat you down and cut you off at the knees. This is the stage where students' resistance rears its ugly head and roars loudly; they start blaming others and their circumstances for their inability to accomplish what is being asked of them. Their ego takes a brutal pounding, so they start to point fingers at others and make excuses for their own work. The conditions are never right for this type of actor during this stage. The teacher doesn't know what they are talking about. The director's vision of the production is poor. They didn't have enough time. Their classmates are idiots, blah, blah, blah. All this nonsense is one thing: fear. Fear deep down that they don't have what it takes. And, remember, fear is ego.

To avoid this, you must love the process of learning itself, the practice, the development, the setbacks, and of course the craft. When you do, when you *intrinsically* discover you love the craft of acting, even when you are sitting in glaring consciousness of your own incompetence, the whole beautiful world of acting opens up, for you are doing it on your own terms. This is truly a glorious thing to behold. The bruising will be real and sustained during stage 2, but if you want to grow and move toward professional execution in your performances, you must work from a place of intrinsic motivation, dissolve your ego, and stay the course, lumps and all.

Stage 3: Conscious Competence

This brings us to stage 3, "Conscious Competence," which is where "loving the plateau" is de rigueur and the pitfall of ego rears its ugly head. When you begin to become conscious of your own growth and development, there is a genuine sense of satisfaction. You begin to see that your work is paying off. You naturally feel good about this, rewarded, and happy. This is indeed a positive thing. You are becoming conscious of your competence as your training deepens and your ability expands accordingly. This stage is a true confidence builder. And, if you are like me, it will feel like a personal booster rocket, and you will fall in love with acting all over again.

Stages 1 and 2 can be very challenging, both in the actual doing and for your ego. Stage 3, however, is a bit of a reprieve, a reward for surviving the first two stages. It is here where you become aware of your acquisition of technique and the competence that you are building in using it. You begin to feel the work in your body without thinking about it, to feel, "I've got this."

However, it is here that you must remain on the path of humility, discipline, and dedication. The more you let it stoke your ego, the more attached you become to the need to be told you are good or are proficient at it. Don't take the ego-bait. Truly, this stage is a double-edged sword. Pay careful attention in stage 3. Enjoy demonstrating your ability without the desire for praise. Enjoy the sensations of getting the work into your body and having it drop down into your subconscious, yet stay alert. If you don't, there is a huge trap waiting for you to fall into it. Don't fall prey to your ego-mind. Keep doing the work for the work's sake. Stay on the road to mastery, and love the plateau. More on that in a bit. But for now, simply be aware that awareness of your competence does indeed bring its own reward, but like anything in life, too much of a good thing ruins it. Beware the ego. Ego is fear waiting to rear its ugly head further down the road when you least expect it. Keep it about the work.

Stage 4: Unconscious Competence

This is the stage you are ultimately working toward. This is where you will unpack your bags and set up an artistic camp. In terms of training, you will need to log about 10,000 hours of "deliberate practice" out of your comfort zone before you get here.[7] It is here where 79 ÷ 3 becomes 2 + 2. It is at this point in the journey that you are no longer actively thinking about the technique when you exercise it. You have memorized your technique and absorbed it via your mind-body connection. The knowledge has moved from the prefrontal cortex back to the subconscious regions of your brain.

This frees up your attention to focus on the life of your character, as you don't need to use any mental energy on technique or what you are going to actually do in performance. You now know what to do and how to do it without thinking about it. The target of your attention is free to focus fully on your scene partner, your imagery, and the life of your character, to live believably under imaginary circumstances with precise repeatability and complete spontaneity. This is true artistic freedom. It is the freedom of the professional actor, not that of the amateur who lives in unconscious incompetence. Seek me out when you are in this stage, and I will say to you, "Welcome, colleague!"

Loving the Plateau

> If you are doing it for a result in the future, you are not really doing it.
>
> —Alan Watts[8]

Throughout parts I and II of this book, I use the term *loving the plateau*.[9] This simply means that you need to love the doing for the doing's sake and not for some reward that comes with any potential future growth. You need to be *intrinsically* (inwardly: pure, genuine self-desire, internal rewards) motivated, not *extrinsically* (outwardly: grades, money, fame, approval) motivated. No one has to tell Lionel Messi to go out and play football each and every day. He loves football more than anything else in his life (wife and children excluded) and would play the game if he were on FC Barcelona or some small, unknown, semiprofessional club team back in Argentina and had never become "Messi."

> Money is not a motivating factor. My motivation comes from playing the game I love. If I wasn't paid to be a professional footballer, I would willingly play for nothing.
>
> —Lionel Messi

As Alan Watts clearly states, "If you are doing it for a result in the future, you are not really doing it." Enough said. You need to tap into your intrinsic desire, your inner satisfaction of acting, and stay in the now every time you act if you want to play the long game. This brings us to the plateau.

In his seminal book from the human potential movement, *Mastery*, George Leonard explains via the Japanese martial art aikido that the road to mastery is a long one but bears the most rewarding fruit. It involves many short stages of upward growth, followed by longer plateaus of no growth (see figure 9.1).

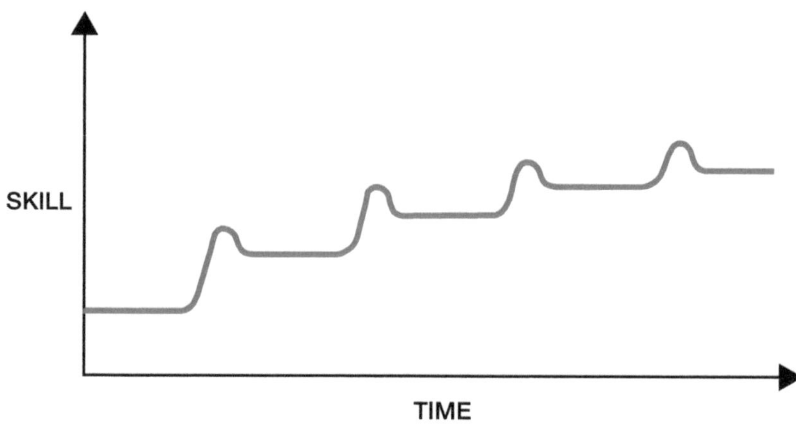

Figure 9.1. The Mastery Curve

For most of our training, we live on plateaus. From time to time, we experience short growth spurts, immediately followed by small dips back downward, only to arrive at a new plateau that is, normally, somewhat higher than the previous one. When looked at from a distance, it is clear that over time, someone on this curve is growing and moving toward eventual stage 4 of acquisition, "Unconscious Competence," and eventual mastery. However, at any given moment along the journey, it may feel to the participant as if they are not growing. And if their attention is focused on the need for growth or to be told they are good, then they will be deeply frustrated, unsatisfied, and disappointed and most likely will end up quitting. Yet, if you truly love doing what you are doing, in our case acting, then you are happy to remain on the plateau as long as is necessary to arrive at the next stage of growth, whenever that might happen, which we can never know. This is the mind-set you want to eventually arrive at mastery.

The person on the road to mastery will need to stay the course over time and not drop off. Now, for many reasons, some people will fall off. These people are what Leonard calls the dabblers, the hackers, and the obsessive types who don't really love the work for the work itself.[10] They love the idea of the work, or they love themselves in the work (their ego), but don't really love the work—not really, not deep down.

The person truly on the road to mastery simply loves doing the work for the work's sake, period, full stop. They do not do it for some result in the future. They do it for the joy in the now. As the prescient Nike slogan brilliantly claims, "Just do it."

The Beginner's Mind (or, Remaining an Eternal Student)

As I state throughout this book, the landscape of actor training is filled with paradoxes. Mastery is no different. The paradox of mastery is that to achieve it, you need to always work from the beginner's mind. A master doesn't believe they are a master; ask any sensei, and they will tell you they are an eternal student of their craft. They are simply someone who has "gone before." Becoming a master is like following the dao or wu wei. There is, in fact, no way. The way is found in the absence of the thing itself, yet one can arrive there.

To achieve mastery, it is essential to work from the beginner's mind. You won't be satisfied over the long term in any field of study or practice unless you possess this mind-set. It is the elixir of any creative and fulfilling life. As soon as you think you've arrived or got it or have mastered it, you're in trouble. Dissatisfaction is right around the corner. This way of thinking is a dead end and represents nothing but your ego satisfaction. And remember: Ego is fear. Thinking, "I've mastered this," in fact, is your fear speaking through a sideways door.

We live in a world where there is pressure on us to always have the right answer, to know what we are doing and never be wrong. Ask any student in any class anywhere. The pressure is real. It is also debilitating. Having the answer is not always the answer. Being *able to arrive* at the answer, a way of working, is actually what we are seeking: a *process*, a path, a method, a craft. If we are only interested in the answer or the rewards and benefits that the answer brings with us, we lose track of the joy of the work itself.

The beginner's mind is what psychology calls a growth mind-set.[11] This is a point of view fueled by ongoing exploration, curiosity, and wonder, one that remains active and dynamic, always looking to go deeper. Recall from chapter 5 that curiosity is the glue that keeps your attention attached to the target. It is the beginner's mind filled with curiosity, in fact, that keeps us in flow, in the moment, in the zone. If we already know, then there is no need to engage. But if we remain continuously open and seek the possibility of new discoveries, new realizations, new perspectives, new levels of awareness and ability, and ever-changing skills in our processes, then the engagement itself will remain robust and rewarding, no matter the outcome.

This is good news for you as an actor, as each job is a new adventure. The learning is endless, as you will never do the same job twice. Even if you are cast in the same role more than once, each experience will be different and exciting. The director might be different or bringing a fresh, new vision to the piece. The cast probably won't be the same, and you will be older and wiser than the last time you played the part. You will have a new take on it simply due to the laws of physics. It would be impossible to go back in time and actually do what you did before. The work itself is filled with the beginner's mind. It is baked into our art form.

I once watched a television interview with the renowned Indian musician Zakir Hussain, considered the best tabla drummer in the world and by all accounts a master of the drum. Yet when speaking about his drumming, he pushed back against this and said,

> No matter what you learn, just remember ultimately, you're a student. Just try to be a good student, and you'll get by just fine; don't even consider trying to be a master. That is something that I try to follow. Everybody else thinks I'm a master. I know that I am a student. I'm always learning. I haven't played well enough to quit yet. Hindsight always tells you that there is stuff you could have done better.[12]

That pretty much sums it up. This point of view is not only healthy and requisite for longevity in our career, but it also keeps the work fun, fresh, and spontaneous; it is, paradoxically, the point of view of mastery. If you work with the beginner's mind and remain an eternal student of acting, the rewards will be intrinsic and bountiful.

Confidence and Antifragility

Confidence is a confidence game.

Confidence is a fickle friend. Beware of it. Playing with confidence is like juggling razors. I wish I could give you some magic pill to make you feel permanently confident, but I can't. No one can. Deep down, you know that. Only you can develop your own *relationship* with confidence. But like any relationship, it is in a constant state of flow, development, reevaluation, and ups and downs. Your relationship with confidence is fluid. As you are human, it will certainly ebb and flow.

Truth be told, I would never want to actually give you that pill or a silver bullet to eliminate fear because many of the great joys in acting arise from overcoming adversity. I wouldn't want to deny you that. You shouldn't either. If you were to feel confident all the time (which you won't, so don't worry about it), where would the victory come from? Where's the battle? Where's the inner sense of accomplishment? The intrinsic satisfaction? Half the joy and sense of satisfaction in acting comes from being totally scared shitless about the possibility of utter failure and then rolling up your sleeves, getting to work, breathing deeply, and conquering both the task at hand and, circuitously, your fear. More on failure and your relationship with that tasty morsel in the next section.

The desire to feel confident actually has the opposite effect of confidence itself: It creates fragility in the performer. What you are subconsciously saying to yourself is "I need to feel this way (confident) in order to act." You are tilting at windmills. What if you don't feel that way one day? What do you do then? Do you *not* go out onstage and do your job? I don't advise this way of thinking, as it perpetuates a fragile state of mind in the actor and begins to play games with your mental relationship with acting itself. It is impossible to feel confident all the time anyway, so don't waste time and energy worrying about it. What I do know for certain is that there are going to be long stretches of your career where you won't feel confident at all, far from it. Better to accept that fact now and begin to build a healthy practice for how to work, a practice built on what behavioral economist and mathematical statistician Nassim Taleb calls antifragility.[13]

Antifragility plays out at the intersection of technique and experience. The more you practice, the more antifragile you become. Antifragility implies developing a keen diagnostic eye for what is required of you in performance, then assessing your arsenal and aligning your inventory of skills to solve the problem at hand. So, when you don't feel confident, rather than worrying about whether you are actually confident, you can call on a reliable game plan grounded in your skill set (the abilities you actually possess) to deal with this interference. You execute your plan, stick to it, and accomplish the task professionally, whether you feel confident about it or not. You do the work with what you have. Antifragility is trusting in your ability to do this.

What I can confidently say about confidence is that it *comes along in the doing.* It is not a state of being. In other words, you can't have it. If you are looking to feel confident, you are looking for trouble. A common misconception about confidence is that it is something someone possesses or owns. It is not. At best, it is something you can rent out, something someone lends you or, surprisingly, you find all by yourself in the moment of engagement because you have it until the second that you don't. And then it's gone, like a fart in a hurricane.

Confidence is a by-product of your love of the work. It emerges from having a serious practice, loving the plateau, and working with the beginner's mind. Actors whom other people call confident don't spend time trying to develop their confidence per se; they simply love to act, do the work, repeat it over time, and leave the qualifying of their work to other people. They know deep down that their disciplined work ethic will provide fertile soil for confidence to take root and appear in the doing.

Confidence is born of your work ethic and comes along in the doing.

Confidence comes from knowing what to do, plus preparation, multiplied by experience. In this context, knowing what to do means developing a reliable technique. Preparation means engaging as fully as possible in all the invisible work before your actual performance. Experience means racking up a minimum of 10,000 hours of deliberate performance practice out of your comfort zones and beyond. Therefore, confidence can be codified in the following equation:

$$\text{Confidence} = (\text{Technique} + \text{Preparation}) \times (\text{Experience})$$

But don't be fooled. Confidence is like a cat. It comes and goes of its own accord. If you call it, most likely it will not come, for confidence is not a dog. It is definitely feline in nature. You have no control over confidence. Sure, it lives in your house, but it has its own mind, behavior, patterns, and predilections and ultimately is out of your control. One moment you may feel confident, and then the next moment, you may not. And that, my fellow actors, is life as a performer. You have no control over that, so you better make peace with this little tidbit if you want to have a meaningful career and avoid a perpetual state of fragility. The more you desire to be confident, the greater your susceptibility to having it slip away, and the more fragile you will be in performance.

Whether you feel confident or not can change in a fleeting instant due to the detrimental effect of one seemingly inconsequential thought. You know this from your own experience. A sudden change in the situation or a passing critical comment can destroy your confidence in a heartbeat. In the quickest of instants and for the slightest of reasons, confidence can run out the door, never to be seen again. Remember chapter 5 and the power of one thought. If that negative stimulus happens right before you are about to walk onstage or as you enter an audition room or as the camera rolls, what are you going to do then? If you are beholden to confidence in order to do your work, then what are you going to do on the day when you are *not* confident? Not work? That is unacceptable.

One thing I know for sure is that that day is going to arrive. It always does, even to the best. But what separates a professional from an amateur is that when confidence slips away like a greased eel on an iceberg, the professional knows what to do about it. They know how to still accomplish the task at hand and "deliver the mail." They are able to perform under all conditions, favorable or adverse, and say, "Neither snow nor rain nor heat nor gloom of night shall stay me from the swift completion of my appointed rounds."[14] If you can work this way, you, too, will be antifragile. What you need is catnip to invite the confidence cat to come out and play. That catnip is your deliberate practice, your work ethic, your discipline. It is not sexy. It is not easy. But it is faithful and is the only way to move down the path of mastery with any confidence.

This is because what you can control is your own work. The wise actor has a clear picture of what is under their control and what is not. Keep your attention on that, and you will find your way into the land of confidence. Keep loving the plateau; keep the beginner's mind, the growth mind-set; keep repeating; keep redirecting; keep moving out of comfort zones; keep your attention off yourself and on the character, how they are moving their life forward. Remember Michael Chekhov's wise words: "Repetition is the growing power."[15] Put in your 10,000 hours with the right attitude, and confidence will suddenly arrive without you having to call it, just like a cat at feeding time.

Oddly enough, the more you ignore confidence, the greater chance you have of gaining it because you have freed yourself of the need for it. It's like going on a date. No one wants to date that person who's desperate. A certain aloofness (lack of desperation) is necessary to date with confidence. And remember most of all: Confidence is not the work itself. Confidence is a *by-product* of a healthy artistic practice exercised over time. This bears repetition: *Confidence is not the work itself; it is a by-product of the work.*

Confidence is ultimately attached to your ego. The desire to feel confident is the desire to feel good about yourself in the work. And by now you know what I am going to say here: Ego is fear; fear is ego. The desire for confidence is actually a roundabout manifestation of fear. Fear is a tricky bugger. It likes to disguise itself, dressing up in lots of different costumes. Yes, it is true that when you feel confident, and you will after some time, when you move into stages 3 and 4 of acquisition, the work feels satisfying, perhaps even fantastic. But working to feel satisfied is not the same as working because you love the work itself and then feeling satisfied *after* the fact. They are two completely different beasts.

Don't confuse trust in your ability for confidence. Trust in your ability is always deeply rooted in you, in your body, in your corporeal experiences. It is always there, deep down, literally in your body; it is what makes you antifragile. Fear, the opposite of confidence, can't magically unravel all the experience and technique you have built up over time. Fear doesn't have that power over you. What fear does know is that it *can attack your relationship with confidence*, which is fragile and vulnerable. Knowing the difference between the two is the difference between acting from a citadel or a house of cards. So, the question becomes, What is the mechanism or mechanisms by which I can directly and consistently tap into my rooted ability? The answer is faith.

As mentioned earlier in this book, *confidence* in Latin is *confides* (*confides*), which translates as "with faith" or "with trust." Confidence is born from faith—not religious faith, although that may help you, too, but faith in self. True confidence is having faith in your human, God-given ability to accomplish the acting task at hand. This means you need a lot of trust: trust in your process, in your technique, in your experience, in your imagination, in your humanity, in your director, and in your fellow actors.

Paradoxically, it is only through faith, intimacy, vulnerability, and surrender that you will discover confidence, strength, and power in your acting. True confidence arises from faith: faith in yourself, your abilities, your imagination, your experience, and your scene partner. The greater your ability to let your guard down, let go of the desire for control, and surrender to what is happening in the moment, the greater levels of confidence you will experience in performance. Faith is the path to freedom and liberation in performance.

But suffice it to say, if you want to be able to play action fully, if you want to electrify the space between, you need to surrender, trust, have faith, and work with courage and the beginner's mind. If you practice this over time, your relationship with confidence will strengthen, stabilize, and become more reliable.

Trust and Faith Strategies

What do you do if you don't feel confident and are about to perform? First of all, immediately redirect the target of attention off the thing creating interference and back onto your breath. Breathe slowly and deeply, and say to yourself that the feeling will pass. "This too will pass" is something I say to myself on such occasions or "I can get through this" or "I know what to do, so just do what I know." Then, find a new target for your attention, one that is outside yourself (i.e., not about you), and allow your curiosity about this target (your scene partner, imagery, your physical surroundings, sounds, other sensory stimuli) to distract you from the stimulus causing interference.

Now, it's easier said than done when one is in the moment and about to perform, but be persistent. Keep redirecting your attention off yourself, onto your breath, and then back out onto the world around you. If this becomes part of your regular practice, if this becomes your new habit, then when the shit hits the fan, you will be well primed to do it under high-pressure situations.

Be kind to yourself and others around you. Practicing positive self-talk sets the stage for your performance. The most confident people I have met (at least my anecdotal observation of them) are also the kindest, most patient, and most giving. Leading with kindness goes a long way and strengthens your relationship with confidence. "How you talk about your work is how your work will happen" doesn't just apply to technique. It also applies to you, your performance ego, and the other human being with whom you are working. Practice positive talk filled with kindness, compassion, and understanding. A helpful by-product of this is you will make more friends on set, and professional colleagues will want to hire you again. Working with kindness literally begets work by first allowing you to do your best work while, secondly, making others around you want to work with you again.

Importantly, if you are feeling inadequate about your ability to perform in any way, shape, or form, redirect the target of your attention outside yourself. The feeling of doubt (opposite of confidence) is a form of self-consciousness. Let the neural pathways in your brain, those natural helpers that have been grooved by years of practice, take over and work from the subconscious state of your brain. Fear, unless you are being chased by a lion, usually resides in the prefrontal cortex and is a manifestation of the story you are telling yourself. Chances are, you actually aren't in real danger.

Source an image of yourself possessing all the qualities you know you possess in your acting: "Imagine it; see it; be it." Visualize an image yourself free of doubt, worry, fear, and anxiety. Focus on an image of yourself possessing freedom, ease, joy, potential, imagination, spontaneity, and any other qualities you wish to work with in your acting. Then, imagine this image floating into your body, or step into an imaginary image of yourself possessing positive performance qualities that release your potential and quiet interference, what Michael Chekhov calls "incorporating the image." Remember that the way to speak to your intuitive side is through imagery. Images are the lingua franca of intuition.

Oddly enough, doubt is the one necessary ingredient for faith. You can't have faith without doubt, so a healthy practice is to make friends with your doubt. In fact, your doubt is telling you something. It's telling you that you care about what you are about to do. That is a good thing. Accept it. Doubt is an opportunity to access your faith. Embrace it. When doubt is born, so is your faith. Instead of freaking out, which may be your habit, thank your body for reminding you to have faith in yourself. Remind yourself that faith lives hand in hand with doubt (or any of its close cousins: anxiety, worry, fear); remind yourself that you have put in the work, you have prepared (assuming you have), and then target your attention back outside yourself. Note to cynics: This is not some woo-woo bullshit. This works. Try it. Repeat it. Develop it into your practice.

Another piece of helpful advice is to ask yourself, "Does my character feel confident at this moment?" Chances are, they do *not*. Chances are, they are in deep trouble (which is why the playwright wrote the story) and need to extract themselves from it. They don't feel confident, so you don't need to feel confident, either. And your job is to act *as if* you are them, so this state of being is helpful. Remember: Your job isn't to feel but to do. Acting is action. Your job is to react to the given circumstances. And you know how to do that. You have practiced it over time, and you are prepared. Feeling and doing are not the same thing. Remember that feelings arise from doing, so start doing what the character is doing to move their life forward, focus all your attention and energy on that, and the appropriate feelings will arise, whether you like them or not.

If, however, you are beset by a significant drop in trust in your own ability and none of the above, you can always play the "as if" trick. If you are nervous before an audition or performance, remind yourself that you are an actor and simply act *as if* you are confident. This practice invites confidence. It is more likely when you speak to your subconscious this way that confidence will appear.

Another more physical technique is to add the quality of movement of confidence to what you are doing. A quality of movement is how you physically move. As a human being, you are always in movement, so you can always add any quality to that movement. Even if you are sitting still, your body remains in some form of movement. You can sit still with the quality of movement of confidence. You are not trying to *be* confident or *act* confident when you do this. You are simply asking your body to move with the quality of confidence and see what happens. It is the "how" to what you are doing. You simply adjust the "how."

You can do it now, while reading this. Begin to read with the quality of movement of confidence. Move your hand, tap, lift your arm with the quality of movement of confidence. Now, breathe with the quality of movement of confidence. Stand up and sit down with the quality of movement of confidence. Walk around the room with the quality of movement of confidence. Notice your experience of this as you do. It will come along in the doing. Play with other synonyms for *confidence*, like *ease*, *power*, *calm*, or even *joy*.

Using one of these techniques, the feelings of insecurity, fear, or fragility will most likely pass. If it for some reason doesn't and often appears when you perform, then I would seek out a performance therapist who specializes in the mental game or a sports psychologist. They can provide more detailed help through psychological strategies for success. Chances are, however, it is just a bundle of nerves and will subside on its own. One of the ancillary by-products of these strategies is that they distract you from thinking about your desire to feel confident, which has the side effect of helping you feel more confident without chasing that particular rainbow.

Fail Better

Have you ever tried? Ever failed? Try again. Fail again. Fail better.

—Samuel Beckett[16]

An interesting irony about confidence is that people who have a positive relationship with confidence also have a positive relationship with failure. This may seem paradoxical, but as I have explained, the landscape of actor training is littered with paradoxes. These performers may not like to lose or experience failure, but they accept and understand that failure is not only an integral part of the growth process, but it is also essential. Accepting failure as a part of your process helps build your own antifragility as a performer. And believing in your own antifragility has the mirror effect of lessening the pain that comes from failure.

Here's a key point: You don't need to like failing. Who does? You simply need to accept in your heart that if you are going to have any experiences in the art form, then you are going to experience failure. In fact, experiencing failure means you are in the game. You want to be in the game, right? You can't fail if you're not in the game.

You miss 100 percent of the shots you never take.

—Wayne Gretzky

I recall my high school soccer coach, Marty Ryczek, once asked me, "If you knew you were going to lose every game, would you still play?" Immediately, I understood what he was saying. If my answer to this was yes, then I would truly love the game. If it was no, then I didn't. That's not to say that one doesn't love winning. It just means that the joy of playing the game itself, of doing the thing, not the result, is where the true win lives. The numerical match outcome is a secondary win.

The scientific method is a process of elimination: elimination of possibilities via experimentation and objective observation of the results. If an experiment fails, it does so only in the sense that the thesis at hand wasn't the answer or didn't provide the expected or hoped-for outcomes. It is, however, simultaneously a success in that it has eliminated one possibility. In other words, it has narrowed the field of possibilities. This is a positive outcome. Although scientists are emotionally invested in their work, they are also able to sit outside the experiment and observe its process objectively. You, too, need to develop a way of working that inculcates objective observation into your own performance process.

Objective Observation

In the seminal sports psychology tome *The Inner Game of Tennis*, author W. Timothy Gallwey argues that for "natural learning" to occur, one must move to a place of objective observation of one's own work through "nonjudgmental awareness."[17] Negative results (increased interference) are generated by after-the-fact valuations of a performance due to what Gallwey calls the "Two Selves." The first skill to learn, according to Gallwey, is the art of letting go of the human inclination to judge your acting as either good or bad. You must let go of the judging process in order to increase the release of your potential in performance. *You must learn to unlearn the judgmental*; this will lead to spontaneous, attentive play.[18]

As discussed in part I of this book, the stories we tell ourselves about what we are doing determine how we do it. How you talk to yourself is a primary shaper of how you will perform. If there is a story being told, then there must be a dialogue of some sort. By definition, a dialogue involves two parties, even if the dialogue is solely within the mind of one person. Therefore, if you are talking to yourself, there must be two selves. When "I talk to myself," it is the "I" that talks to the "myself." Gallwey called the "I" the "Self-1" and the "myself" the "Self-2." Self-1 is the teller, and Self-2 is the doer. Obviously, the "I" and the "myself" must be separate entities, or there would be no conversation, so one can conclude that within each actor, there are two selves. Self-1, the "I," gives instructions; the other, Self-2, the "myself," performs the action. Self-1 adds value or judgment to something after the fact (it went well or poorly), while Self-2 represents your body's own natural ability to do whatever is being asked of it; Self-1 is, therefore, the analytical self, and Self-2 is the intuitive self. Self-2 does the job at hand, and then Self-1 returns after the action is completed with an evaluation of the performance: "That went *well*" or "That went *poorly*."

One of the major postulates of *The Inner Game of Tennis* is that within each performer, the relationship between Self-1 and Self-2 is a prime factor in determining one's ability to translate knowledge of technique into effective action. In other words, the key to better acting lies in improving the relationship between the conscious teller, Self-1, and the natural capabilities of the unconscious doer, Self-2.

As discussed in chapter 5, we now know from discoveries in neuroscience that imagery is the lingua franca, the mother tongue, of intuition. Therefore, the way to decrease the voice of Self-1 is through the incorporation of positive images, which speaks to the intuition directly, awakens Self-2, and releases the power of the performer's potential. This way of learning stimulates your own desire to play freely without observed judgment and frees you to take risks and tap into the subconscious release of your own creative individuality. Without loss of rigor, this liberates you from the chains of praise as well as the fear of criticism. This frees you from your own ego. It bears repeating here: *For the actor, fear is ego; ego is fear.*

As mentioned earlier, one of the greatest forms of performance interference is *self-consciousness*; that is, when the *target of the actor's attention is themselves*. Performance fear is simply ego; any performance practice, such as the repeated use of either praise or criticism (i.e., judgment) increases self-consciousness, which increases the ego and results in the adverse effect of increased fear. This is true even when everyone has the best of intentions and feeds the actor nothing but praise. Even positive feedback stimulates the ego and creates a ripe Petri dish for fear to grow. The resulting outcome is that you need more and more praise to keep effective. It is a vicious circle.

What is important to understand here is that neither goodness nor badness is an attribute of the act itself. It is not the work. Your work is always just your work. It is never good or bad. It simply is, until judgment enters the picture, after the fact. Judgment is an ex post facto evaluation, either good or bad, of any effort. It is the act of assigning a negative or positive value to an event—after the fact. Thus, judgments are personal, ego reactions to the sights, sounds, feelings, and thoughts within our experience. The goal in training is to let go of judgment and move observation over to a nonjudgmental point of view, one where you experience harmony between Self-1 and Self-2 and play "out of your mind."[19]

This new perspective is called objective observation. You need to train yourself to develop a practice of objective observation in order to decrease interference (Self-1) and increase potential (Self-2), which is your natural self, thereby maximizing your ability to perform freely and fully. When asked to give up judging one's own performance, the judgmental mind usually protests. Judgment thrives on judgment. In fact, the more judgmental you are of others and the world around you, the more judgmental you are likely to be of yourself. It will be that much harder for you to quiet your own inner critic.

Letting go of judgments does not mean ignoring errors. It simply means seeing events as they truly are—just the facts—and not adding anything to them. It doesn't ignore the facts. It just sees them for what they are: *facts*—neither good nor bad.[20] This healthy way of working develops a practice in the actor, which leads to the increased release of their full potential in performance. A performance practice that works from a place of objective observation is one that frees the performer to reach their highest potential with the least amount of interference.

Luck

Luck = Preparation + Opportunity

Luck is when preparation meets opportunity. You need to be prepared and create opportunities for yourself to be lucky. If you only work on one of these two components, luck won't appear. For luck to manifest in your career, you need to be in a constant process of preparation and always working to move your craft forward. I mean *always*. And you need to be constantly working to create active and dynamic opportunities for yourself to exercise your ability, constantly. Luck appears serendipitously. You can't plan it, but you can create ripe conditions for it to grow. I don't know for sure that as an actor you will be lucky. I just know for sure you will need to be lucky. So prepare and create opportunities for yourself, then pray Lady Luck blesses you with her presence.

Role versus Character

There is, in my experience, an important difference in an actor's performance between using the words *character* and *role*. More specifically, it is a difference in believability, especially on camera. I'll share with you my two cents here after thirty years in the business, and then you will, of course, ultimately make up your own mind as to what works and feels best for you.

I endorse using the word *role* in your work instead of *character*. "I am playing the role of _________" ends up with a more believable performance than "I am playing the character of _________." Now, this may seem like splitting hairs, but at the professional level, that may be the difference between you getting the job or someone else. I don't want to see you working your work, and neither does your director or the audience. Often, when actors speak of their work using the word *character*, I can see them acting. I don't want to see you acting. I want to witness a human being navigating imaginary circumstances.

Trust me: You will end up with much more believable performances when you play a role because you will feel, paradoxically perhaps (there's that word again), that even though the character lives a life completely different from your own daily self, it is somehow closer to you when it's a role you are playing instead of a character. *Role* feels personal; *character* feels distant. The difference may seem semantic, but it has been both my personal experience and observation of others that there is a significant difference between the two, and it is the all-important difference of *believability*. And you don't want to mess that one up. More than anything, you want to be believable. From that, all else follows in your performance. *Role* feels intimate, infinitely closer to the chest, to humanity, to personal experience. You can really inhabit a role because that's exactly what you do all day long, every day. Remember: You want your acting to be alive with intimate harmony. It must feel *as if* it is actually happening to you.

We play many roles in our everyday lives, and they all feel part of who we already are. I believe all the characters we play must feel like they are somehow a part of us. They should feel that way, for we are all human. So whether we want to admit it or not, we all have the possibility within us to do any act a human being is capable of. Actors accept that. We understand that. Actors must grasp that because we are professional human beings. We are professional empathizers. It is my professional job to empathize with what the fictional character goes through. I may never choose to act the way my character does in my daily life, but I possess the possibility deep within to do so.

Longtime Los Angeles–based acting teacher and author of the seminal book *Acting for the Camera* Tony Barr addresses the character-versus-role debate quite elegantly: "I have abandoned the word 'character' as much as possible in the classroom and use in its place the word 'role.' And for a good reason. When an actor thinks of playing a character, he places himself inside another person, an imagined one. He shoehorns himself into that other being in his mind and loses sight of himself; he distances himself from the role."[21]

We don't play characters in life. We inhabit roles. Characters are removed from our human experience. They live on the page as ink, in the land of literature and the invisible work. Roles are what we live in all the time in our human experience, and we play many roles throughout one single day: parent, friend, coworker, lover, boss, son, daughter, helper, enemy, and so on. Characters are somehow not us, whereas roles are us. "The role I'm playing" feels much more human than "the character I'm playing" and, I believe, at the end of the day, from the audience's perspective, much more truthful. When I watch you perform, I don't want to feel like I'm watching an actor creating a character. I want to feel I am witnessing an authentic human being, albeit a fictional one. The word *role* is a believability booster for your visible work.

Character versus Characterization

Many actors confuse *character* with *characterization*. There are very important differences between these two words. *Character* is defined by your actions or what you do. *Characterization* is how the part on the page is different from you in your everyday life. This is addressed in part D of question 1 in the "Five Questions" section of chapter 7.

> How is the character different from you in your thoughts, feelings, desires, and actions?

Aristotle's *Poetics* defines *character* by what someone does. The old quote "Tell me what someone does, and I'll tell you who they are" bears repeating here. We are what we do. If someone goes to church to pray every morning before work, that tells you who they are. If someone drinks a bottle of wine at lunch every day, that tells you who they are. If someone steals when they think no one is looking, that tells you who they are. If someone treats all others with kindness and puts the interests of others before their own, even at their own expense, that tells you who they are. As human beings, who we are is the sum of our actions. The entire premise of this book can be summed up by saying "Character is action." Therefore, it can be said that if you play your action in each moment of every scene, you are delivering the character. You are living a role.

The *fashion* in which or *how* you play those actions determines the characterization. Chances are, you won't be doing it in the manner you normally do in your own life, so any physical, vocal, tempo, rhythm, or other imaginative behavioral adjustments you make in how you play the role is characterization. Tony Barr in *Acting for the Camera* calls this "reshaping" yourself.[22] I love that. How you reshape yourself is your characterization. Your actions are the character.

Competition

Whether you believe acting is competitive or not, if you choose to play in the A game of acting and you audition for roles on Broadway, Off-Broadway, at major regional theaters, and in Hollywood films and primetime television shows, you will be in competition with other actors for those roles. That's a fact. How you think about this fact determines how you will do in these arenas. That much is certain. How you think about competition is how you will perform under pressure. Everyone acts well in the shower, but how about in the limelight? How do you perform under real-world pressure, under intense, professional, showtime pressure?

Many people choose to believe that there is no such thing as competition in the arts. Personally, I think this sort of thinking is misleading. It is selling rainbows. If they are told that competition is a bad thing and that acting is not in fact competitive, then what do they do when they enter an audition and feel like it is? They have been sold a false promise. And one thing I know for sure: It certainly will feel that way one day. All the "Woo-woo, there's no such thing as competition, let's just hold hands and skip through the tulip garden together" thinking will fly out the window the day you sign your contract for that meaty, series-regular television part. You will see how much you will be making per episode (and already start to spend it in your head), show up for your final network screen test, and run into the other actor who is up for the same part.

But okay, fine, I get it. This sort of wishful-thinking mind game allows you to remain hopefully (perhaps naïvely) impervious from the assumed negative qualities of competition. The thinking goes, "Competition is a bad thing because it involves someone winning and someone else losing, and really, there is no such thing as winners and losers in art or acting, so if I don't think that way, this won't really exist." If this works for you, great. Keep thinking this way. Call me after your network screen test, and let me know how it went. I believe the exact opposite.

Implicit in this thinking is that competition has a negative effect on performance. I couldn't disagree more and believe competition is the key ingredient to releasing our excellence. In fact, I believe the only way to truly tap into our excellence (not mediocrity, not comfort, not safety, not averageness, not homeostasis) is through subjecting ourselves to high-pressure situations where we must perform to the best of our own ability. Competition provides this elemental cauldron of concentrated pressure necessary to perform with excellence. It is, in fact, the only true path to excellence.

In ancient Greece, competitions were sacred endeavors, religious festivals, in fact, where competitors offered their performances as tributes to the gods. The competitive struggle was considered not only noble but also virtuous. To the Greeks, the word *competition* means "the act of striving together toward greater human achievement." The English word *competition* has its etymological roots in the late Latin word *competere*; the root *com* means "together," and *petere* means "to seek, to strive, or to aim at." Striving together. Seeking together. Aiming together. Competition, therefore, is the act of striving together toward greater human achievement. I love this. It is from this understanding of competition that the Olympic Games were born. This is exactly what I believe competition is: *striving together toward greater human achievement.*

Competition implies that only through the feat of each of us bringing the best of our ability to the performance at hand (sports, acting, business, or otherwise) do we all move forward and grow as humanity. I say yes to this definition of *competition* and the subsequent relationship with it. This is a healthy and positive understanding of the word *competition*, one that allows each of us to flourish under pressure and reach levels of ability that we never thought possible. Yes, competition implies and involves discomfort, but we need this outside pressure to push us out of our comfort zones.

Competition is not about beating someone else. Quite the contrary, the true understanding of competition, as the ancient Greeks knew all too well, is about seeing how much excellence we can release when it counts the most. But we all need outside pressures from others to achieve the level of the extraordinary. I believe those who hold *competition* as a negative word are actually operating from a place of fear and will never know their fullest potential. The Greeks understood that winning meant performing to the fullest of our abilities and that "true competition," as Gallwey writes, "is identical with true cooperation."[23]

When I was a young actor beginning my career in New York City, I taped an index card to the refrigerator in the kitchen of our small apartment on 123rd Street. Scribbled on it in blue ballpoint ink were the words "Outwork everybody." Now, truth be told, I didn't know what that meant and still don't. Neither did my roommate, Stephen, who used to chuckle and mumble, "Outwork everybody," under his breath as he grabbed stale milk from our fridge and injected his daily dose of Fruit Loops each morning. What does it actually mean to outwork everybody? This is ultimately unknowable in the literal sense. That said, I also simultaneously knew, deep down in my heart, exactly what it meant. I had to face that damn card the very first thing every morning when I went to make my breakfast before my coffee was even brewed. It hung there on our shitty yellow fridge in our tiny, dark kitchen like some omnipresent power staring me down, looking me in the eye as if to say, "So, whatcha got today, big boy?"

I knew what it meant because I had been a competitive soccer player for most of my life. It meant that my career, my work, my art, my acting is my own responsibility. If I am serious about being a professional actor, then I must do everything in my power to develop my own ability, and then do more and more and more again. No one else can do that for me. It means sacrifice. It means dedication. It means discipline and denial of a certain lifestyle; it means working way beyond my comfort zones. It means doing everything in my own control to release my fullest, God-given potential. It means my career is up to me.

And here is where competition comes in: I would think about all the other faceless actors in New York City doing the same thing, and this thought, these images, would fuel my fire to work even harder. These images would get my ass out of bed in the morning. If there was no competition, if there were no other actors, then I wouldn't need to work as hard. I would ask myself, "How many acting classes are they going to this week? How many plays are they reading? How many shows did they see? How much time did they put in at the gym? How many yoga classes? How many hours did they prepare for their auditions?" This all fueled me; it motivated me. These images and thoughts fired me up and kept my nose to the grindstone and kept me from the human tendencies of homeostasis, procrastination, complacency, and laziness. Competition brought out the best in me. It brings out the best in all of us when we have a healthy and positive relationship with it.

After about five years of auditioning in New York, I began to know my competition personally. I would see the same twenty or so guys at virtually every audition. In particular, I would often get called back with one actor in particular, a very successful New York Broadway actor. For a two- or three-year spell, I would see him at virtually every other audition. One year, he beat me out for a lead in a Broadway show; I understudied him in that show. After the show closed, it came down to me and him again, out of the whole city, for a series regular role for a new television show; this time I won the role. But here's the important part of this, and in fact, there are two parts: The first part is that every time I had an audition, I would imagine seeing him in the waiting room at the audition. And even though I had already put in hours of preparation for that audition, the image of him would make me go back and put in two more hours of preparation. He not only helped me prepare, but he also made me better. Let me repeat: *He made me better.*

The second part is that he and I are friends. He is a lovely human being, and we have nothing but kind words for each other. If I were to see him today, I would walk up to him and give him a hug and ask if he was free for lunch or a beer. In fact, when I came home to my apartment after the screen test for that television show, he had already left a message on my answering machine, congratulating me on winning the part. Now that's class. The competition between us was never about me putting him down, about beating him, or him beating me or putting me down; quite the contrary, it was about both of us releasing our best under high-pressure situations. We made each other better through our competition. This is the true sense of the word *competition*. It is absent of jealousy and the desire to put someone else down. It is solely about the release of self-excellence.

Victory, then, is not putting someone else down or beating someone else or you winning the role instead of them; it is being able to say to yourself at the end of the day, "I did everything in my power to do my very best—everything." Releasing your fullest potential is winning itself. If someone else gets the part, so be it. But if you showed up with your best, you can look yourself in the mirror and say, "Bravo." You can live with that and yourself. Then you get to try it all again another day. That's a life of purpose and meaning, one worth offering to the gods. Competition applies the necessary pressure to release excellence, no matter the outcome. You don't get diamonds or pearls without pressure.

Frustration (the First Sign of Creativity)

The old dad joke goes something like this: A guy walks into a doctor's office, complaining that he's frustrated, as he wakes up every morning with a headache. The doctor asks him what he thinks might be causing these headaches? The guy says, "Well, I bang my head against the wall every night before I go to sleep, and then I wake up in the morning with these headaches."

The doctor says, "I see. Well, stop doing that."

You have a relationship with frustration, and it is a part of your acting process whether you know it or not. It is either helping you in your work or causing you artistic headaches. Frustration is actually neither good nor bad; it is simply a part of your human experience. In essence, it is a part of you. Mostly it lies dormant until the moment you become blocked by what you are doing. Most people don't like the feeling of frustration and have a negative relationship with it. One definition of *insanity* is doing the same thing over and over again, expecting a different outcome.

However, the smart actor understands that not only is frustration the first sign of creativity; it is also an essential part of their artistic process. Frustration is a feeling to be cherished. Of course, there is no problem solving without the necessary problem. Every creative person understands this fact and embraces it, even reluctantly. Each role you play and job you take will present itself with unique or habitual artistic challenges. How you handle these problems determines how successful your performance will be. It is the perceptive actor who welcomes this and channels the energy of frustration toward positive ends.

Actors become frustrated for a variety of reasons. Frustration seems to appear out of nowhere and most often when we least desire it. What all forms of frustration have in common is that we have the perception that things are not going the way we wish. Never mind acting, welcome to life. What you do in this moment of recognition, however, determines the outcome of your subsequent work. Many actors allow frustration to build within them, becoming frustrated with the fact that they are frustrated, hence compounding the problem. Sound familiar? This is the opposite of working smart. This only increases interference while decreasing potential and is not a recipe for successful performance. Your acting will suffer if you work this way.

Our bodies interpret blockage as the feeling of frustration. If you have a negative relationship with frustration, then things are not going to go well for your process from that point onward. If, however, you have a positive relationship with frustration, then your acting holds the possibility of moving to new heights. Although it may not feel that way, frustration is actually your artistic friend.

The first thing you must do is examine your relationship to it. If you are like most people, you will come to the quick conclusion that you have a negative relationship with frustration. So, the second thing you must do is change that relationship. Luckily, this is easier than it may seem.

Strategies for Dealing with Frustration
When frustration appears, you have two choices:

1. You can continue doing what you're doing the way you are doing it and, consequently, continue to be frustrated. This allows frustration to build exponentially on itself and rarely ends well. "Well, stop doing that."
2. You can apply the "Notice, Stop, Redirect" process to what you are doing—notice you are becoming frustrated; realize your body is telling you that creativity is needed at this moment; stop what you are doing;

breathe deeply for a minute or two; make a new choice; redirect. If you don't have immediate alternative solutions, then simply put your work down, go for a walk, clear your mind, exercise, make some tea, play with your dog, or simply take a break. Get some emotional, mental, and physical distance from the choice that was causing the frustration.

The next new choice you make may or may not solve the problem at hand, but at least you recognize that continuing to drive a round peg into a square hole is not going to bring you artistic joy or satisfaction, nor will it solve the problem at hand. Keep fluid, playful, humble, and curious in your approach to problem solving. The more frustration becomes your friend, the more excited you will be to tackle more challenging roles.

The Power of Yes

Frustration comes from wanting things to go a different way than they are. A simple exercise to do when you become frustrated is to point at the problem at hand, no matter what it is, and say "Yes" out loud as you point. Literally say "Yes" to the origin of your frustration. Don't worry if it feels silly because it works. What you will most likely notice is that the power that frustration has over you will diminish almost immediately. Simply by saying yes to the cause of your resistance, you begin to accept it and redefine your relationship to it. It won't make the problem go away, but it will help put you in a more productive state of mind to solve it. Say yes to it.

Attention versus Concentration

As mentioned in part I of this book, there is a big difference between using the words *attention* and *concentration* in your acting process. This may seem like splitting hairs, but in practice, the difference is significant. Concentration is about you, and attention is about the world outside you. You will recognize this from your own experiences. Concentration, which pulls focus back onto yourself, makes you more self-conscious, while attention, requiring an outside target, liberates you.

If I ask you to concentrate on this book right now, you oddly become the target of your own focus as you try to read this page. There is a thick, almost dense effort involved in concentrating, one that is far from the feeling of ease. The brow furrows, and often the breath becomes restricted. The work feels heavy when concentrating.

> It is the lightness of touch which more than anything else makes the artist.
>
> —Michael Chekhov[24]

If I now ask you to pay attention to what you are reading, there is a lightness to the effort, almost a freeing of sorts. The breath remains fluid, and the brow releases. There is a palpable enjoyment in the task at hand. Concentration is about you; attention is about what's outside you. By this point, it should be clear to you that to play action, the target of your focus needs to be outside yourself. Therefore, it behooves you to pay attention to your target while playing action instead of trying to concentrate.

You know this from your own relationship with orange juice. Yes, orange juice. Crappy orange juice comes in concentrate, shoved down a flimsy tube, and stored in the frozen foods section covered with old, dirty freezer frost. You want your acting to be like the good, freshly squeezed stuff. Paying attention is freshly squeezed.

Creative Individuality and Interpretation

> In short, the creative individuality of every artist always expresses itself in a dominant idea which, like a leitmotif, pervades all his creations. The same must be said for the creative individuality of the actor-artist.
>
> —Michael Chekhov[25]

At the end of the day, everything you do in your training and all the technique you acquire is in service of what Michael Chekhov calls your "creative individuality."[26] Each role you play is an opportunity to share how you perceive and receive the human experience, filtered through your imagination. We want to see what *you* are going to do with the role, how you *interpret* it. What do you have to say with your work? What about the role inspires you? How do you wish to express this inspiration?

Growing up, I would often observe my mother, a classically trained opera singer, coaching younger singers in our home. Time and time again, she would say, "You've got to feel the music in your soul. I can teach you technique, but I can't teach you interpretation. That you must develop on your own, for your interpretation is yours alone. It's got to come from you." Similarly, the technique of playing action is in service of your own artistic voice. It is a means to an end, not the end itself. No one wants to see what you think is the correct way to perform a particular role or watch you try to get a technique right. We want to see what you have to *say* with the role. Like technique, the role is a means for your self-expression. But it is not the selfish ego-expression of the daily self. Interpretation arises from a creative state of being, when you are working from your artistic self and have channeled your quotidian energy through the filter of your imagination in service of the play.

Michael Chekhov says, "In moments of inspiration the I of an artist undergoes a kind of metamorphosis."[27] This transformation of self requires your compassion for the role you are playing and what the character is going through. It is your artistic self that must interpret the part and imbue the role with creative feelings.

Birds and Frogs

Something to keep in mind as you continue your actor training is that you will need to constantly toggle between two perspectives, that of a bird soaring high in the sky and that of a frog hidden deep in the mud. Occasionally, you will need a bird's-eye view of the actor's craft, surveying the landscape far and wide; exploring; seeking out new approaches, challenges, and experiences. Conversely, there will be times when you need the singular-minded perspective of a frog hugging the ground that sees the details and do a deep dive on one aspect of the craft at a time. Birds see wider; frogs see deeper. However, one is not better than the other.

As mathematician Dyson Freeman wrote in 2009, "It is stupid to claim that birds are better than frogs because they see farther, or that frogs are better than birds because they see deeper." The world, he wrote, is both broad and deep: "We need birds and frogs working together to explore it."[28] Keep this in mind as you continue down the path to mastery as an eternal student of acting; see both widely and deeply, always.

On Being Sexy

Let me tell you what I think sexy is. Sexy is someone who is comfortable in their skin and doesn't give a rat's ass what anyone else thinks about them. Sexy is when someone is so involved in what they are doing that their whole being is lit up from within by the joy of engagement because they've forgotten about themselves. Sexy is someone paying attention to that thing or person they love that is outside themselves. Sexy is when your attention is off yourself.

If when you perform, you are thinking about how sexy you are or how sexy you want to be or about being right or about how good you are or how put-together you want the world to think you are or how smart you want people to think you are or how great your life is or how talented you are, then you aren't sexy. Sexy is when you pay attention to the world outside yourself. It's much more fun; it's easier; it's also a huge relief, so do that.

The Label Libel

> Writing anything is a treason of sorts. Even the cold recitation of facts is never the thing itself. The events described are somehow diminished in the telling. A perfect bowl of bouillabaisse, that first all-important oyster plucked from the basin d'Archachon, both are made cheaper, less distinct in my memory once I've written about them.
>
> —Anthony Bourdain[29]

In the introduction to this book, I write that one can learn *about* acting from a book, but one cannot learn *how* to act from a book. Nothing could be truer. As is reiterated throughout, all questions about acting are answered in the doing—all of them. Let me now take this one step further. At this point in our journey, I want to not only intentionally bookend (pardon the pun) this work by reminding you of this truism but also make you aware of an unfortunate phenomenon called the "label libel."[30]

The label libel is the negative effect naming a process has on learning the process itself. As soon as any process, in our case acting, is given a name or a label, the student of this process thinks they know it. They conflate the name of the process for the process itself. Consequently, the name has the immediate debilitating effect of reducing curiosity about the actual process. The student actor becomes less interested in acting when they learn names for acting. Paradoxically, the label dangerously misleads students into believing that they know what the process is, even though the process of acting is in fact just that: a process. It has no terminus point. Acting is not a thing; it is an activity.

As Postman and Weingartner so eloquently write in *Teaching as a Subversive Activity*, as soon as a process is given a label, "What's its name?" becomes a substitute for "How does it work?"[31] We mistake cerebral, intellectual knowledge of the name itself for the experiential workings of the actual process. The more complex and intricate the process, the more dangerous the name for said process becomes.

You may be able to identify a bike by name but still not be able to ride the bike. So, too, with acting. You may be able to talk about playing action (and this book does a lot of that), but talking about it or reading about it is not doing it. The value of this book, seemingly paradoxically, is not the book itself nor the names for things herein but in the actual on-your-feel execution of the process, which might be called playing action here and radiating and receiving elsewhere or not have a name at all.

> What's in a name? That which we call a rose by any other name would smell as sweet.
>
> —Juliet[32]

Acting by any name is a continuous and ongoing active investigation that can *only happen on your feet, in the doing, in real-time relationship with another human being or imagery*. Remember: The process and the names given for different aspects of the process are not the same thing. This book is simply an orientation tool and reference point, a way to organize for yourself a highly complex series of human activities, called acting. It provides context, process, and guideposts.

The point here is not to confuse the method of inquiry in written form with that of the work we do as actors on our feet, in the doing. The labels are only a map to help orient you, the actor, in your own experiences. As acting is a happening, learning how to act must be a happening, too. The process of acting and learning how to act are both processes of inquiry. Inquiry is always alive and active. So, now is the time to put the book down and do. Acting is doing.

Finding the Right Teacher

> If you meet the Buddha on the road, kill him.
>
> —Lin Chi

The implication of this quote, advice by the ninth-century sage Lin Chi to one of his monks, is that those who think they've found all the answers need to start questioning. Even though the original context for this quote is religious or, more precisely, philosophical, I believe it holds for the pursuit of any knowledge, including actor training. Beware the day you believe you have met the Buddha, the day you have "arrived," the time when you believe you have mastered acting. In the context of actor training, beware the acting teacher who tells you they have all the answers or that their particular technique is the only way, for there are as many ways as there are actors and teachers.

Yet, finding the right teacher or teachers for you is of utmost importance. If you take your work and your career seriously, then you need an artistic home in which to train and grow. Like in any professional discipline, you need not only a place to work out regularly—ideally, daily—to stay in game shape but also a trusted coach, a guide, an experienced and skilled facilitator to provide you with the objective outside eye necessary to stay in a relationship of inquiry with your craft.

Any learning environment must be organized around a certain set of beliefs, methodologies, and desired outcomes. An acting studio is no different. Those beliefs and tools when articulated by the teacher will eventually graft themselves to names and labels, which will then be called a certain technique. This technique will be articulated and conveyed through a means of instruction. It is not merely the technique per se that is the criteria by which you should examine and choose a training studio but, perhaps more importantly, *how* that methodology is conveyed and transmitted to the students by the teacher.

Put another way, who you are in the room with is of utmost importance. The first thing you should ask yourself when shopping around for a teacher is, "Do I want to be in the room regularly with this particular person to work on my craft?" You are going to spend a lot of professionally intimate time with this person, and to get to the place of vulnerability, surrender, and your unprotected self, necessary conditions for inspired acting, you need to be able to not only trust the person guiding the room but also desire to be in the work with them.

The word *sensei* means "one who has gone before." As someone who occupies many acting studios, I consider myself simply another actor in the room, one who has gone before. Accordingly, I operate from this core principle. Similarly, teachers in Montessori schools are strategically called facilitators, not teachers. This is not just linguistic judo, as there is a concrete and discernable difference between the meaning of the two words—*teacher* and *facilitator*. A classroom occupied by a teacher is, by definition, teacher-centric. A classroom occupied by a facilitator is student-centric. A teacher delivers knowledge to their students from outside the student experience. A facilitator helps release the intrinsic knowledge the students already have within them through a process of continuous, active inquiry. A teacher has a set pedagogical agenda that must be imparted to the students in a certain way—learning is, in this manner, prescriptive.

A facilitator, however, acts merely as a guide in a thoughtfully designed exploratory environment of collective inquiry, where the students have as much to teach the class as the facilitator, and they are allowed to discover not only what they need to learn but also, perhaps most importantly, how they actually learn. The most important thing, first and foremost, for you as an actor in training is to learn how you learn, not how somebody else learns or how the teacher wants you to learn, but how you learn. You need to get yourself in a studio with someone who gets that and understands you, helps you learn how you learn. Like the old parable goes:

> Give a man a fish, and you feed him for a day. Teach a man to fish, and you feed him for a lifetime.

The fish in this scenario is you learning how you learn. Therein lies your true artistic power and longevity. This is the key to an artistic and professional career grounded in perpetual inquiry and the beginner's mind—learning how you learn. Once you've learned that, you can learn virtually anything. We human beings were born to learn.

Personally, I prefer to think of myself as a facilitator. I believe my job when working with my acting students is to simply facilitate learning. I *facilitate* the release of their intrinsic knowledge via the careful design of pedagogical experiences. I myself operate in my own acting studio from the belief that all my student actors already have all the knowledge they need deep inside of them. It is one of my credos. My job, therefore, as the "teacher" in the room, is to help facilitate the release of this organic knowledge. This produces the most profound and sustained release of potential in student actors, for they gain ownership over their own work this way. I humbly suggest you seek out an acting studio occupied by a sensei (one who has gone before) who works from this philosophical and practical belief.

Beware the teacher-centric classroom. There is an important reason for this: The objective of your training is not to acquire any technique for the purposes of getting it right, to please the teacher, or to get their approval but *to gain ownership over your own acting.* Any learned technique should ultimately release your potential, not satisfy someone else's teaching agenda. I believe if I have done my job well, my students shouldn't need me anymore.

> Love the Buddha; become the Buddha; kill the Buddha.

I have learned from dozens of wonderfully talented and generous acting teachers over the course of my career. They taught a myriad of different techniques in a variety of ways, and yet I learned an enormous amount from each of them. That said, they all had a few qualities in common. So after you have answered the first question, "Do I want to spend time in the room with this person?" then there are some other criteria by which I suggest you evaluate your potential facilitator.

Technique

Effective facilitators have a rigorous grasp on the particular technique they teach. In other words, and pardon my French, they "know their shit inside and out"; they have walked the walk and live the work. The technique is alive in their bodies. Look for a facilitator who models their technique in their teaching and effortlessly embodies the technique. Gifted facilitators don't need to be the best actors in the business, but they do need to be able to solve the problem of acting from the inside out, using the particular technique they profess. They do need to be able to actually articulate the technique in the doing.

You wouldn't pay money to be in a math class with a teacher who couldn't actually solve the equation on the board. The same holds true for acting technique. You want to be in the room with someone who not only understands how to solve the problems themselves (for all acting is problem solving) but also can help you discover how you will go about solving the problems of acting for yourself. They are not simply trying to get you to do what they do. Perhaps more important than their own mastery of their technique is *how* they share that technique with you. Consider the following:

- Who were this facilitator's teachers?
- How long have they been teaching?
- What do their former and current students have to say about the class?
- Are the students in that class actually learning the technique?
- Are their students gaining ownership over the technique or just parroting the teacher?
- Is their acting actually improving? By what metrics?
- Does the technique appear to be helping the students grow? Do you see tangible, repeatable growth in their work?
- Are the students in the class having breakthroughs?
- Do you like the students' acting? Do you find it compelling and imaginative?
- Are the students working on their feet or sitting around? Actors learn by doing. If the acting teacher talks too much (one of the most ubiquitous crimes in our industry) or, even worse, talks a lot about *themselves*, get out immediately!

Diagnostic Eye

Effective facilitators have sharp diagnostic eyes for what to look for in the work and how to provide constructive feedback to their students in a helpful and positive manner. You should look for a facilitator who is able to expertly assess and diagnose a scene or exercise to the end of providing their students with specific and helpful feedback that moves their work forward. If the scene is five minutes long, what does the teacher choose to work on when the scene is done? Why? What is the effect of this feedback on the student working? How is it tied to the technique? Consider the following:

- Is the facilitator giving specific, individually tailored feedback? Or are they giving more or less the same note to all the students?
- Is the feedback helpful?
- Are the students able to process the note? Or do they seem confused and frustrated with the feedback?
- Does the feedback lead to breakthroughs, greater awareness, or growth?

Atmosphere

Effective facilitators create dynamic atmospheres in their acting studios, where students feel free to risk failure. They give permission to their students and encourage them to dare to fuck it up rather than try to get it right. Although the atmosphere should always be playful and filled with joy, a professional pressure must also be present in the room, where everyone understands they are there to do something significant and important. Actor training is a discipline in service of an artform. Students are there to work on a craft, not screw around. Likewise, you will want a facilitator who creates an environment in their studio of permission, trust, respect, playfulness, humor, generosity, and kindness, as well as a seriousness of purpose with an appropriate level of professional pressure.

You should feel that you can access your artistic self, take risks, step out of your comfort zone, and fail better. There is no learning without failure. The facilitator should ideally create an atmosphere of objective observation with a minimal amount of personal judgment. The room should be as egalitarian as possible. Again, beware the teacher-centric acting studio; the days of the egomaniacal acting teacher are long gone. Consider the following:

- What's the overall vibe in the class?
- Do the students seem engaged and happy to be there? Or do they seem scared and tentative?
- Are the students free to explore their process?
- Are the students encouraged to take risks? Or do they seem afraid?
- Are students eager to get up and work? Or are they hesitant and unprepared?
- Is there an ethos of training for adversity?

- Do you sense a pursuit of excellence in the room? Or is mediocre work accepted? Or is the atmosphere one of "work quickly so we get through everyone"? "Getting through everyone" is not sufficient or desirable. You want to be in an atmosphere that strives for excellence.

Reaching the Individual

Effective facilitators are able to reach the individual student in front of them, each time, every time. They don't just spray the room with general knowledge like a cat in heat but tailor their own work to match the idiosyncratic needs of the unique human being in front of them. They respond to the particular person before them and adjust their facilitation accordingly. Consider the following:

- Does the facilitator respond deftly and with nuance to the different human beings who cycle through the class? Or does the facilitator respond to all the students with the same prescriptive answers?
- Does the facilitator appear to be making an effort to truly "see" the individual in front of them who is working and then reach them with technique that best suits their way of working? Or do they give the same rote prescription for all the ailments in the room?
- Does the facilitator lead their actors to breakthroughs before letting them sit back down?

Idiosyncratic Teaching Voice

Effective facilitators have their own personal voice and style. They are masters at expressing who they are as human beings and conveying their passion for the art of acting through their own teaching. They should love facilitating, and you should feel it in your bones. Beware the teacher who is over it. Consider the following:

- Does this facilitator seem to both love their work and the art of acting?
- Does this facilitator seem comfortable in their own skin as they navigate the room?
- Is the facilitator's energy positive, and does it radiate to all the students in the class?
- Does this facilitator model the work in the room?

In my humble opinion, you will want to find the facilitator who most helps you release the fullest and most potent version of your artistic self and who creates the least amount of interference in you as they do so. It may take some shopping around to find this person or these people, but you will eventually find them. They are out there. There may even be many of them. You will learn a myriad of different techniques from all of them and gratefully place the tools they helped you discover, or rediscover, in your actor toolbox. Like falling in love or buying a home, you will ultimately feel in your gut who is the right facilitator for you, for you will come alive in the space between while working in their presence.

Gratitude

> Let us rise up and be thankful, for if we didn't learn a lot today, at least we learned a little, and if we didn't learn a little, at least we didn't get sick, and if we got sick, at least we didn't die, so let us all be thankful.
>
> —Buddha

Arguably, the most important lesson I've learned in my thirty-plus years of acting is perhaps the simplest and most profound, and that is always work from a place of gratitude. The essence of inspired acting is the practice of presence. The greatest present we can give ourselves as actors is presence itself. Nothing keeps us present like gratefulness. It not only keeps us from taking things for granted, but it also adds value to all we do and roots us in the moment, improving our performance. Think about it: How truly blessed are we to do what we do? This is not to be taken lightly or for granted. For this gift, we should always give thanks. Many people go through life searching for their purpose. If you are an actor, you have already found it. What a monumental blessing that is. This is a huge gift to be appreciated and for which to be grateful.

Your acting will be more alive, powerful, and dynamic if you continuously add active gratitude to your process. Across all the arenas of your career, be grateful for every audition, every job, every script, every role, every scene, every scene partner, every rehearsal, every class, every opportunity you have to act—and see what happens. I am certain you will discover another level in your acting if you work from a place of gratitude and receive many gifts. Playing action with gratitude will not only add new dimensions to your acting, but it will also exponentially increase your enjoyment of it. Gratitude is the elixir of the space between.

I am grateful you took the time to read this book. I hope it helps you. Good luck!

Yours in acting,
Hugh

Epilogue

By ourselves is evil done
By ourselves we pain endure
By ourselves we cease from wrong
By ourselves we become pure.
No one saves us but ourselves
No one can and no one may
We ourselves must tread the path
Teachers only show the way.

—Dhammapada

Thank you, Mark. Love you, brother.

~

Notes

Preface

1. Earle Gister, Teacher Development Program, Actors Center (New York City, 2003–2005).
2. Gister, Teacher Development Program.

Part I

1. Alan Watts, *The Way of Zen*, 55.

Introduction

1. Earle Gister, Teacher Development Program for the Actors Center (New York City, 2003–2005).
2. Gister, Teacher Development Program.
3. Michael Chekhov, *Lessons for the Professional Actor* (Baltimore, MD: Performing Arts Journal Publications, Johns Hopkins University Press, 1985), 65.
4. Chekhov, *Lessons*, 65.
5. Michael Chekhov, *To the Actor: On the Technique of Acting*, rev. ed. (New York: Routledge, 2002), 85.

Chapter One

1. Translated from *Saikontan* (Vegetable Roots Talks), Yuhodo, Tokyo, 1926.
2. Alan Watts, *The Way of Zen*, illustrated ed. (New York: Vintage, 1999), 44.

3. Earle Gister, Teacher Development Program, Actors Center (New York City, 2003–2005).

4. James Baldwin, *The Fire Next Time* (New York: Knopf Doubleday, Vintage International, 1992).

5. W. Timothy Gallwey, *The Inner Game of Tennis*, rev. ed. (New York: Random House Trade Paperbacks, 1997), 5.

6. Gister, Teacher Development Program.

7. Alan Watts, "Do You Do It or Does It Do You?" audio recording.

8. George Leonard, *Mastery: The Keys to Success and Long-Term Fulfillment* (New York: Plume, 1992), 39.

9. Peter Rader, *Playing to the Gods: Sarah Bernhardt, Eleonora Duse, and the Rivalry That Changed Acting Forever* (New York: Simon and Schuster, 2018), 7.

10. Michael Chekhov, *To the Actor: On the Technique of Acting*, rev. ed. (New York: Routledge, 2002), 90.

11. Chekhov, *To the Actor*, 87.

12. Abraham H. Maslow, *Religions, Values, and Peak-Experiences* (London: Penguin Books, 1964).

13. Maslow, *Religions*.

14. Michael Gelb, *Body Learning: An Introduction to the Alexander Technique*, 2nd ed. (New York: Henry Holt, 1992).

15. In Anton Chekhov, *The Three Sisters* (1901), act 4.

16. Chekhov, *To the Actor*, 90.

Chapter Two

1. Earle Gister, Teacher Development Program, Actors Center (New York City, 2003–2005).

2. Declan Donnellan, *The Actor and the Target* (St. Paul, MN: Theatre Communications Group, 2002), 84.

3. Gister, Teacher Development Program.

4. Lloyd Richards, Teacher Development Program, Actors Center (New York City, 2005).

5. William Shakespeare, *Hamlet* (1609; 1865–1866), 3.2.

6. Sanford Meisner and Dennis Longwell, *Sanford Meisner on Acting* (New York: Vintage Books, 1987), 16.

7. Uta Hagen, *Respect for Acting* (New York: Macmillan, 1973), 139.

8. Gister, Teacher Development Program.

9. Isaac Newton, *Sir Isaac Newton's Mathematical Principles of Natural Philosophy and His System of the World*, translated by Andrew Motte (1729), revised by Florian Cajori (Berkeley: University of California Press, 1934), 13.

10. Richard Feynman, "Conservation of Energy" (lecture), 1970, in *Feynman Lectures on Physics*, https://www.feynmanlectures.caltech.edu/I_04.html.

11. Shakespeare, *Hamlet*, 3.2.

12. Gister, Teacher Development Program.

13. Gister, Teacher Development Program.

14. Richards, Teacher Development Program.

15. Konstantin Stanislavski, *An Actor Prepares* (New York: Theatre Arts Books, 1936), 38.

16. David Zinder, *Body, Voice, Imagination*, 2nd ed. (New York: Routledge, 2009), 32.

Chapter Three

1. Sanford Meisner and Dennis Longwell, *Sanford Meisner on Acting* (New York: Vintage Books, 1987), 10.

2. Konstantin Stanislavski, *An Actor Prepares* (New York: Theatre Arts Books, 1936), 122.

3. Stanislavski, *Actor Prepares*, 51.

4. Meisner and Longwell, *Sanford Meisner*, 26.

5. Richard Feynman, "Conservation of Energy" (lecture), 1970, in *Feynman Lectures on Physics*, https://www.feynmanlectures.caltech.edu/I_04.html.

6. Declan Donnellan, *The Actor and the Target* (St. Paul, MN: Theatre Communications Group, 2002), 33.

7. Lloyd Richards, Teacher Development Program, Actors Center (New York City, 2005).

8. Earle Gister, Teacher Development Program, Actors Center (New York City, 2003–2005).

9. Michael Chekhov, *To the Actor: On the Technique of Acting*, rev. ed. (New York: Routledge, 2002), 77.

10. David Zinder, *Body, Voice, Imagination*, 2nd ed. (New York: Routledge, 2009), 138.

11. Dante.

12. Chekhov, *To the Actor*, 158.

13. Jim Fannin, "The Power of Thought," *Life in the Zone* (S.C.O.R.E. Performance Systems, 2007), CD.

Chapter Four

1. Sanford Meisner and Dennis Longwell, *Sanford Meisner on Acting* (New York: Vintage Books, 1987), 16.

2. Meisner and Longwell, *Sanford Meisner*, 16.

3. Konstantin Stanislavski, *An Actor Prepares* (New York: Theatre Arts Books, 1936), 34.

4. Stanislavski, *Actor Prepares*, 37.

5. Stanislavski, *Actor Prepares*, 116.

6. Michael Chekhov, *Lessons for the Professional Actor* (Baltimore, MD: Performing Arts Journal Publications, Johns Hopkins University Press, 1985), 39.

7. Maria Osipovna Knebel, *A Director's Guide to Stanislavsky's Active Analysis*, trans. James Thomas (London: Methuen Drama, 2016), 100.

8. Viaslav Dolgachev, Teacher Development Program, Actors Center and the National Alliance of Acting Teachers (New York City and Los Angeles, 2003–2006, 2008, 2017–2018, 2020).

9. Lloyd Richards, Teacher Development Program, Actors Center (New York City, 2005).

10. Richards, Teacher Development Program.

11. Knebel, *Director's Guide*, 101.

12. Stanislavski, *Actor Prepares*, 256.

13. Masao Yokota, "Intuition as Mental Image Processing: Some Psycholinguistic Considerations on Intuitive Sensory Data Structuring and Processing Based on Mental Image Directed Semantic Theory," International Joint Conference on Awareness Science and Technology and Ubi-Media Computing, 2013.

14. Alan Watts.

Chapter Five

1. Alan Watts.

2. Matthew A. Killingsworth and Daniel T. Gilbert, "A Wandering Mind Is an Unhappy Mind," *Science* 330, no. 6006 (November 12, 2010): 932.

3. Killingsworth and Gilbert, "Wandering Mind," 932.

4. *The Adventures of Buckaroo Banzai across the 8th Dimension*, directed by W. D. Richter (Los Angeles: Twentieth-Century Fox, 1984). This is arguably the best science fiction film ever made and one of the finest examples of Jeff Goldblum's subtle artistry.

5. Robert Barton, *Acting Reframes Using NLP to Make Better Decisions in and out of the Theatre* (New York: Routledge, 2011), 8.

6. W. Timothy Gallwey, *The Inner Game of Tennis*, rev. ed. (New York: Random House, 1997).

7. Jim Fannin, *"The Power of Thought," Life in the Zone* (S.C.O.R.E. Performance Systems, 2007), CD.

8. David Rock, *Your Brain at Work: Strategies for Overcoming Distraction, Regaining Focus, and Working Smarter All Day Long* (New York: Harper Business, 2009).

9. Gregoire Borst and Stephen M. Kosslyn, "Visual Mental Imagery and Visual Perception: Structural Equivalence Revealed by Scanning Processes," *Memory and Cognition* 36, no. 4 (2008): 849–62.

10. Fannin, *"Power of Thought."*

11. Alan Watts.

12. Watts, chap. 3.

13. Robert Leahy, *The Worry Cure: Seven Steps to Stop Worry from Stopping You* (New York: Harmony, 2006).

14. Leahy, *Worry Cure*, chap. 3.

15. Earle Gister, Teacher Development Program, Actors Center (New York City, 2003–2005).

16. Jack Feldman, Christopher Del Negro, and Paul Gray, "Understanding the Rhythm of Breathing: So Near, Yet So Far," *Annual Review of Physiology* 75, no. 1 (2013): 423–52.

Chapter 6

1. Alan Watts.

2. Earle Gister, Teacher Development Program, Actors Center (New York City, 2003–2005).

3. Brené Brown, "The Power of Vulnerability," June 2010, TEDxHouston talk, 20:04, https://www.ted.com/talks/brene_brown_the_power_of_vulnerability?language=en.

4. Gister, Teacher Development Program.

5. Alan Watts.

6. Earle Gister, Teacher Development Program.

7. Earle Gister, Teacher Development Program.

Chapter Seven

1. Quoted in Maria Osipovna Knebel, *A Director's Guide to Stanislavsky's Active Analysis*, trans. James Thomas (London: Methuen Drama, 2016), 105.

2. Knebel, *Director's Guide*, 97.

3. Lloyd Richards, Teacher Development Program, Actors Center (New York City, 2005).

4. Knebel, *Director's Guide*.

5. Richards, Teacher Development Program.

6. Knebel, *Director's Guide*, 128.

7. Knebel, *Director's Guide*, 99.

8. Earle Gister, Teacher Development Program, Actors Center (New York City, 2003–2005).

9. Gister, Teacher Development Program.

10. Gister, Teacher Development Program.

11. Gister, Teacher Development Program.

12. Gister, Teacher Development Program.

13. Viaslav Dolgachev, Teacher Development Program, Actors Center and the National Alliance of Acting Teachers (New York City and Los Angeles, 2003–2006, 2008, 2017–2018, 2020).

14. Gister, Teacher Development Program.

15. Gister, Teacher Development Program.

16. Gister, Teacher Development Program.

17. Gister, Teacher Development Program.

18. Gister, Teacher Development Program.

19. Gister, Teacher Development Program.

20. Gister, Teacher Development Program.

21. Gister, Teacher Development Program.

22. Richards, Teacher Development Program.

23. Gister, Teacher Development Program.

24. Gister, Teacher Development Program.

25. Michael Chekhov, *To the Actor: On the Technique of Acting*, rev. ed. (New York: Routledge, 2002), 71.

26. Chekhov.

27. Michael Chekhov, *Lessons for the Professional Actor* (Baltimore, MD: Performing Arts Journal Publications, Johns Hopkins University Press, 1985), 62.

28. Chekhov, *To the Actor*, 64.

29. Chekhov.

30. Chekhov, 69.

31. Warren Robertson, *Free to Act: How to Star in Your Own Life* (New York: Putnam, 1978), 87–90.

Chapter Eight

1. Maria Osipovna Knebel, *A Director's Guide to Stanislavsky's Active Analysis*, trans. James Thomas (London: Methuen Drama, 2016), 99.

2. Knebel, *Director's Guide*, 95.

3. Knebel, *Director's Guide*, 119.

4. Lloyd Richards, Teacher Development Program, Actors Center (New York City, 2005).

5. Jim Fannin, *Life in the Zone* (S.C.O.R.E. Performance Systems, 2007), CD.

6. Eric Maisel, *Performance Anxiety* (New York: Back Stage Books, 2005), 42.

7. Knebel, *Director's Guide*, 97.

8. Earle Gister, Teacher Development Program, Actors Center (New York City, 2003–2005).

9. Sharon Marie Carnicke, Teacher Development Program, National Alliance of Acting Teachers (Los Angeles, 2017).

10. Carnicke, Teacher Development Program.

11. Konstantin Stanislavski, *An Actor Prepares* (New York: Theatre Arts Books, 1936), 263.

12. Gister, Teacher Development Program.

13. Knebel, *Director's Guide*, 96.

14. Declan Donnellan, *The Actor and the Target* (St. Paul, MN: Theatre Communications Group, 2002).

Chapter Nine

1. Alan Watts, "The Centipede's Dilemma," in *The Way of Zen*, illustrated ed. (New York: Vintage, 1999), 44.

2. Michael Chekhov, *Michael Chekhov's Lessons for Teachers*, expanded ed. (New York: MICHA, 2018), 12.

3. Michael Chekhov, *Lessons for the Professional Actor* (Baltimore, MD: Performing Arts Journal Publications, Johns Hopkins University Press, 1985), 65.

4. David Rock, *Your Brain at Work: Strategies for Overcoming Distraction, Regaining Focus, and Working Smarter All Day Long* (New York: Harper Business, 2009).

5. Konstantin Stanislavski, *An Actor Prepares* (New York: Theatre Arts Books, 1936), 266.

6. Robert Barton, *Acting Reframes Using NLP to Make Better Decisions in and out of the Theatre* (New York: Routledge, 2011), 10.

7. K. Anders Ericsson, Ralf Th. Krampe, and Clemens Tesch-Romer, "The Role of Deliberate Practice in the Acquisition of Expert Performance," *Psychology Review* 100, no. 3 (1993): 363–406.

8. Quoted in *In Search of Greatness*, directed by Gabe Polsky, Hulu, 2019.

9. George Leonard, *Mastery: The Keys to Success and Long-Term Fulfillment* (New York: Plume, 1992), 39.

10. Leonard, *Mastery*, 19.

11. Carol Dweck, *Mindset: The New Psychology of Success* (New York: Ballantine Books, 2007).

12. Quoted in *Charlie Rose*, aired April 27, 2009, on PBS.

13. Nassim Nicholas Taleb, *Antifragile: Things That Gain from Disorder* (New York: Random House Trade Paperbacks, 2014).

14. Adapted from the unofficial motto of the US Postal Service.

15. Chekhov, *Lessons*, 65.

16. Samuel Beckett, *Worstward Ho* (New York: Grove Press, 1983).

17. W. Timothy Gallwey, *The Inner Game of Tennis*, rev. ed. (New York: Random House, 1997), 17.

18. Gallwey, *Inner Game*, 11.

19. Gallwey, *Inner Game*, 19.

20. Gallwey, *Inner Game*, 21.

21. Anthony Barr, *Acting for the Camera*, rev. ed. (New York: William Morrow Paperbacks, 1997), 27.

22. Barr, *Acting for the Camera*, 65.

23. Gallwey, *Inner Game*, 109.

24. Michael Chekhov, *To the Actor: On the Technique of Acting*, rev. ed. (New York: Routledge, 2002), 13.

25. Chekhov, *To the Actor*, 86.

26. Chekhov, *To the Actor*, 85.

27. Chekhov, *To the Actor*, 86.

28. Quoted in David Epstein, *Range: Why Generalists Triumph in a Specialized World* (London: Pan MacMillan, 2019), 200.

29. Anthony Bourdain, *Kitchen Confidential: Adventures in the Culinary Underbelly* (New York: Bloomsbury USA, 2000).

30. Marshall McLuhan, "We Need a New Picture of Knowledge," in *New Insights and the Curriculum*, ed. Alexander Frazier (Washington, DC: Association for Supervision and Curriculum Development, 1963).

31. Neil Postman and Charles Weingartner, *Teaching as a Subversive Activity* (New York: Dell, 1969), 25.

32. William Shakespeare, *Romeo and Juliet*, 1957, 2.2.43–44.

References

Aaron, Stephen. *Stage Fright: Its Role in Acting*. Chicago: University of Chicago Press, 1986.

Baldwin, James. *The Fire Next Time*. New York: Knopf Doubleday, Vintage International, 1992.

Barr, Anthony. *Acting for the Camera*. Rev. ed. New York: William Morrow Paperbacks, 1997.

Barton, Robert. *Acting Reframes Using NLP to Make Better Decisions in and out of the Theatre*. New York: Routledge, 2011.

Beckett, Samuel. *Worstward Ho*. New York: Grove Press, 1983.

Blair, Rhonda. *The Actor, Image, and Action: Acting and Cognitive Neuroscience*. New York: Routledge, 2008.

Borst, Gregoire, and Stephen M. Kosslyn. "Visual Mental Imagery and Visual Perception: Structural Equivalence Revealed by Scanning Processes." *Memory and Cognition* 36, no. 4 (2008): 849–62.

Bourdain, Anthony. *Kitchen Confidential: Adventures in the Culinary Underbelly*. New York: Bloomsbury USA, 2000.

Brown, Brené. "The Power of Vulnerability." June 2010. TEDxHouston Talk. 20:04. https://www.ted.com/talks/brene_brown_the_power_of_vulnerability?language=en.

Carnicke, Sharon Marie. *Stanislavsky in Focus: An Acting Master for the Twenty-First Century*. 2nd ed. New York: Routledge, 2008.

———. Teacher Development Program for the National Alliance of Acting Teachers. Los Angeles, 2017.

Charlie Rose. Aired April 27, 2009, on PBS.

Chekhov, Anton. *The Three Sisters*. 1901.

Chekhov, Michael. *Lessons for the Professional Actor*. Baltimore, MD: Performing Arts Journal Publications, Johns Hopkins University Press, 1985.

———. *Michael Chekhov's Lessons for Teachers*. Expanded ed. New York: MICHA, 2018.

———. *To the Actor: On the Technique of Acting*. Rev. ed. New York: Routledge, 2002.

Colvin, Geoff. *Talent Is Overrated: What Really Separates World-Class Performers from Everybody Else*. New York: Penguin, 2008.

Csikszentmihalyi, Mihaly. *Flow: The Psychology of Optimal Experience*. New York: Harper Perennial, 1990.

Dolgachev, Viaslav. Teacher Development Program, Actors Center and the National Alliance of Acting Teachers. New York City and Los Angeles, 2003–2006, 2008, 2017–2018, 2020.

Donnellan, Declan. *The Actor and the Target*. St. Paul, MN: Theatre Communications Group, 2002.

Duhigg, Charles. *The Power of Habit: Why We Do What We Do in Life and Business*. New York: Random House, 2012.

Dweck, Carol. *Mindset: The New Psychology of Success*. New York: Ballantine Books, 2007.

Epstein, David. *Range: Why Generalists Triumph in a Specialized World*. London: Pan MacMillan, 2019.

Ericsson, K. Anders, Ralf Th. Krampe, and Clemens Tesch-Romer. "The Role of Deliberate Practice in the Acquisition of Expert Performance." *Psychology Review* 100, no. 3 (1993): 363–406.

Esper, William, and Damon DiMarco. *The Actor's Art and Craft: William Esper Teaches the Meisner Technique*. New York: Anchor Books, 2008.

Fannin, Jim. *Life in the Zone*. S.C.O.R.E. Performance Systems, 2007. CD.

Feldman, Jack, Christopher Del Negro, and Paul Gray. "Understanding the Rhythm of Breathing: So Near, yet So Far." *Annual Review of Physiology* 75, no. 1 (2013): 423–52.

Feynman, Richard. "Conservation of Energy" (lecture). 1970. *Feynman Lectures on Physics*, https://www.feynmanlectures.caltech.edu/I_04.html.

Gallwey, W. Timothy. *The Inner Game of Tennis*. Rev. ed. New York: Random House Trade Paperbacks, 1997.

Gelb, Michael. *Body Learning: An Introduction to the Alexander Technique*. 2nd ed. New York: Henry Holt, 1992.

Gister, Earle. Teacher Development Program, Actors Center. New York City, 2003–2005.

Hagen, Uta. *Respect for Acting*. New York: Macmillan, 1973.

Isenman, Lois D. "Toward an Understanding of Intuition and Its Importance in Scientific Endeavor." *Perspectives in Biology and Medicine* 40, no. 3 (Spring 1997): 395–403.

Karageorghis, Costas I., and Peter C. Terry. *Inside Sport Psychology*. Champaign, IL: Human Kinetics, 2011.

Killingsworth, Matthew A., and Daniel T. Gilbert. "A Wandering Mind Is an Unhappy Mind." *Science* 330, no. 6006 (November 12, 2010): 932.

Knebel, Maria Osipovna. *A Director's Guide to Stanislavsky's Active Analysis.* Translated by James Thomas. London: Methuen Drama, 2016.

Kogan, Sam. *The Science of Acting.* London: Routledge, 2010.

Leahy, Robert. *The Worry Cure: Seven Steps to Stop Worry from Stopping You.* New York: Harmony, 2006.

Le Gallienne, Eva. *The Mystic in the Theatre: Eleanora Duse.* Carbondale: Southern Illinois University Press, 1973.

Leonard, George. *Mastery: The Keys to Success and Long-Term Fulfillment.* New York: Plume, 1992.

Maisel, Eric. *Performance Anxiety.* New York: Back Stage Books, 2005.

Maslow, Abraham H. *Religions, Values, and Peak Experiences.* London: Penguin Books, 1964.

McLuhan, Marshall. "We Need a New Picture of Knowledge." In *New Insights and the Curriculum*, edited by Alexander Frazier. Washington, DC: Association for Supervision and Curriculum Development, 1963.

Meisner, Sanford, and Dennis Longwell. *Sanford Meisner on Acting.* New York: Vintage Books, 1987.

Nachmanovitch, Stephen. *Free Play: Improvisation in Life and Art.* New York: G. P. Putnam's Sons, 1991.

Newton, Isaac. *Sir Isaac Newton's Mathematical Principles of Natural Philosophy and His System of the World.* Translated by Andrew Motte (1729). Revised by Florian Cajori. Berkeley: University of California Press, 1934.

Orlick, Terry. *In Pursuit of Excellence: How to Win in Sport and Life through Mental Training.* 3rd ed. Champaign, IL: Human Kinetics, 2000.

Polsky, Gabe, dir. *In Search of Greatness.* Hulu, 2019.

Postman, Neil, and Charles Weingartner. *Teaching as a Subversive Activity.* New York: Dell, 1969.

Rader, Peter. *Playing to the Gods: Sarah Bernhardt, Eleonora Duse, and the Rivalry That Changed Acting Forever.* New York: Simon and Schuster, 2018.

Richards, Lloyd. The Teacher Development Program, Actors Center. New York City, 2005.

Richter, W. D., dir. *The Adventures of Buckaroo Banzai across the 8th Dimension.* Los Angeles: Twentieth-Century Fox, 1984.

Robertson, Warren. *Free to Act: How to Star in Your Own Life.* New York: Putnam, 1978.

Rock, David. *Your Brain at Work: Strategies for Overcoming Distraction, Regaining Focus, and Working Smarter All Day Long.* New York: Harper Business, 2009.

Saikontan (Vegetable Roots Talks). Yuhodo, Tokyo, 1926.

Shakespeare, William. *Hamlet.* 1609; 1865–1866.

———. *Romeo and Juliet.* 1597.

Stanislavski, Konstantin. *An Actor Prepares.* New York: Theatre Arts Books, 1936.

———. *An Actor's Work.* New York: Routledge, 2008.

———. *My Life in Art.* New York: Routledge, 1924.

Taleb, Nassim Nicholas. *Antifragile: Things That Gain from Disorder.* New York: Random House, 2014.

Watts, Alan. *Do You Do It or Does It Do You?* Audio recording.

———. *The Way of Zen.* Illustrated ed. New York: Vintage Books, 1999.

Yokota, Masao. "Intuition as Mental Image Processing: Some Psycholinguistic Considerations on Intuitive Sensory Data Structuring and Processing Based on Mental Image Directed Semantic Theory." International Joint Conference on Awareness Science and Technology and Ubi-Media Computing, 2013.

Zinder, David. *Body, Voice, Imagination.* 2nd ed. New York: Routledge, 2009.

Index

~

About the Author

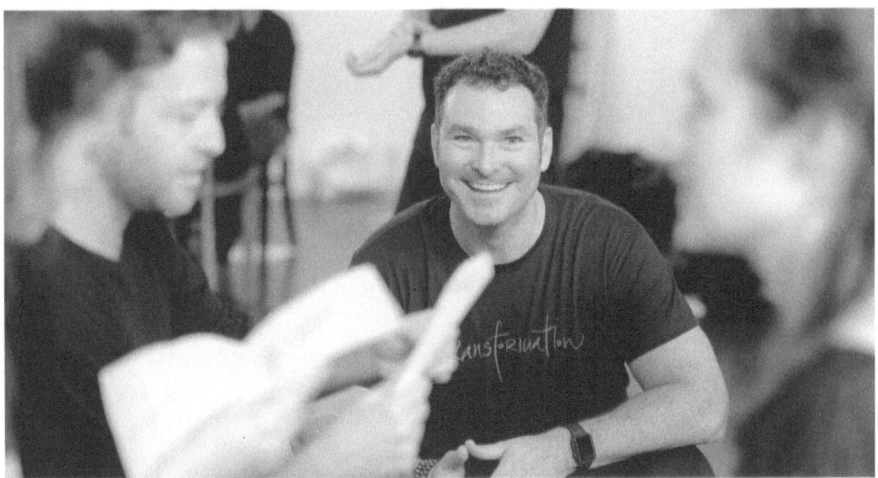

Author photo by Maurice Bender

Hugh O'Gorman is the author of *The Keys to Acting*. He is an actor, director, teaching artist, and co-executive director of the National Alliance of Acting Teachers. Since 2002, he has been the head of acting at California State University, Long Beach. His acting credits include Broadway, Off-Broadway, and more than a dozen of the nation's most respected regional theaters. His many television credits include AMC's Emmy Award–winning show *Remember WENN* (SAG Award nomination) and HBO's *John Adams*. Hugh teaches acting in Los Angeles.

9 781538 139295